Harry Langdon

HARRY LANGDON

KING OF
SILENT COMEDY

GABRIELLA OLDHAM
and
MABEL LANGDON

UNIVERSITY PRESS OF KENTUCKY

Copyright © 2017 by The University Press of Kentucky

Scholarly publisher for the Commonwealth,
serving Bellarmine University, Berea College, Centre College of Kentucky,
Eastern Kentucky University, The Filson Historical Society, Georgetown College,
Kentucky Historical Society, Kentucky State University, Morehead State
University, Murray State University, Northern Kentucky University, Transylvania
University, University of Kentucky, University of Louisville, and Western
Kentucky University.

Editorial and Sales Offices: The University Press of Kentucky
663 South Limestone Street, Lexington, Kentucky 40508-4008
www.kentuckypress.com

Photographs are from the collection of Harry Langdon Jr.

Cataloging-in-Publication data is available from the Library of Congress.

ISBN 978-0-8131-6965-1 (hardcover : alk. paper)
ISBN 978-0-8131-6967-5 (epub)
ISBN 978-0-8131-6966-8 (pdf)

This book is printed on acid-free paper meeting the requirements of the American
National Standard for Permanence in Paper for Printed Library Materials.

Manufactured in the United States of America.

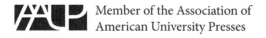 Member of the Association of
American University Presses

Contents

Foreword

My father came into this world with a unique desire to entertain, which he did through his uncanny ability to use body language to communicate human emotions—happiness, sadness, anger, and love—in the theatrical art of pantomime. The theater was his calling, and he eventually transitioned from the stage to the medium of silent films. This book contains the intimate details of the life of Harry Langdon and his lifelong dedication to making people laugh.

Fate intervened when my father met my mother, Mabel. They married at a very auspicious time, having just survived the stock market crash and the advent of talking movies, which relegated my father's forte—pantomime—to a secondary role as verbal humor took center stage. Some believe that my mother's encouragement to put the past behind him, surmount these new challenges, adopt a fresh outlook, and begin the next phase of his career allowed my father to finally enjoy the success he deserved.

My father shared his best moments, as well as his most challenging ones, with my mother over their twelve years of courtship and marriage. He had always wanted a child, and although he was approaching his fifties when I came along, he seemed to have boundless energy for me. And my mother was equally devoted and caring, building a wonderful home for her busy husband and young son.

Over the years, my mother carefully gathered and stored articles about my father and hundreds of still photographs, along with the memories of their intimate talks about what motivated him as a comedian and his philosophy of life during a career that spanned vaudeville to talkies. Long after my father's passing, my mother met with Gabriella Oldham to collaborate on the manuscript that eventually became this book. Although she did not live to see it published, it is thanks to my mother that this wonderful legacy has been preserved.

Harry Langdon Jr.

Introduction

On May 3, 1927, Miss Lillian L. Doria of Chicago wrote a fan letter to Harry Langdon, requesting an autographed picture. She also mentioned her disappointment in his latest film, *Long Pants,* compared with his previous triumph, *The Strong Man.* Responding with a personally signed letter, Langdon apologized that *Long Pants* had failed to meet her expectations and invited her to write again so that he could tell her more about his new, as-yet-untitled film. He also encouraged her to keep offering her "criticism and comments" and assured her of his ongoing friendship.[1]

Whether a personally crafted note or a standard template for responding to the hundreds of fan letters Langdon received at the height of his stardom, this remnant of his correspondence is a poignant reminder of his character. It gives us an inkling of Langdon's gentle demeanor: courteous, reserved, soft-spoken even in print, yearning to be liked and apologetic if he fell short of that goal. His phrasing reveals the dual nature of one of the most popular silent comedians of the 1920s—on a par with Charlie Chaplin (with whom he was often paralleled), Buster Keaton, and Harold Lloyd. By the end of that decade, however, Langdon was no longer included in this group of master comedians. A series of disastrous professional and personal circumstances had nearly ensured his place in oblivion. Only in the 1970s, three decades after his death, did audiences become reacquainted with Langdon's films and recognize that his meteoric rise in silent films was neither an illusion nor a fluke. His unique comedy style was a natural gift, molded by a gentle nature that resonated both self-assurance and self-doubt; he was both celebrity and homebody. The story of Langdon's life is one of success measured not in fame and fortune but in perseverance.

To understand what made Langdon the fourth king of silent comedy, we must look at a surprisingly large body of work completed in a short amount of time, but one with a checkered pattern of strengths and weaknesses. We must also examine the three distinct phases of his life that influenced one another to cumulatively create his unique persona. Often overlooked is the first phase of Langdon's work on the stage, which included many forms of popular American entertainment at the turn of the twentieth century. Mesmerized by the theater as a child, a teenaged Harry joined amateur shows, circuses, medicine shows, and minstrel shows until he settled into the vaudeville circuit, playing both small towns and big cities, dinky theaters and the Palace. In every venue he honed his comedic and artistic skills, discovering the essence of the persona that ultimately became fulfilled in film.

Langdon's vaudeville act was in fact the impetus for his start in motion pictures, where he became a fast-rising star under Mack Sennett. There, he found the creative team, including aspiring director Frank Capra, that would catalyze his eminence as a comedian, as well as lead to his rapid descent from stardom. This second phase of his career in silent films has been the focus of any discussions of Langdon's greatness, and rightly so. During this time he created his iconic routines and finessed a persona that rivaled Chaplin's. However, it is important to link this phase to his prior stage experience, not only to identify the genesis of his character but also to make sense of the weaknesses that surfaced as Langdon assumed independent control of his filmmaking. Attaining a celebrity that quickly superseded the star level he had reached in vaudeville, Langdon regrettably found that his aspirations did not always match his abilities. His own tragic flaw and a bitter clash with Capra set in motion a reversal of fortune that was almost breathtaking in its speed and intensity.

The third phase of his career is usually considered the reason Langdon was forgotten or, worse, demoted from the pantheon of greatness. His films from the sound era, many of which were produced by Hal Roach, were made with a variety of directors and reflected an assortment of scenarios that alternately constricted Langdon's special style and showcased it. But a deeper examination of these shorts also reveals certain aspects of Langdon's professional life that are rarely considered: that he enhanced the best of his comedy with a new element—his voice; that he worked continuously on the stage, in radio, and in film, countering the long-held impression that he died broke, alone, and unemployed; and that the endearing qualities of his innocent persona continued to surface in his sound films and won him renewed respect and compassion from contemporary critics.

For the personal story of the man behind the work, perhaps the most important result of Langdon's fall from greatness was that it gave him an intense awareness of the real meaning of success.

In presenting these phases of Langdon's personal and professional lives, this biography has had a most curious evolution. In 1983 I met film distributor Raymond Rohauer to discuss the possibility of completing a biography of Harry Langdon that he was working on with Mabel Langdon, Harry's widow. Rohauer had been in a decades-long partnership with Mabel to reestablish the Harry Langdon Corporation as well as to restore Langdon's silent films and reintroduce them at worldwide revivals. The biography was a dream for both of them, as no serious work had yet been published that examined Langdon's films and established his position among the great silent comedians, much less told his story with any narrative continuity and accuracy. Rohauer shared with me a very rough draft of the manuscript, assembled by one or more long-gone researchers in his office. It outlined Langdon's life story and detailed the plots of each film, but it lacked critical perspectives and had not integrated valuable excerpts from contemporary film reviews and new interviews conducted by Rohauer and Mabel. After I screened all the available films at his New York office and reworked the manuscript, Rohauer arranged for me to take a trip to Los Angeles, where I spent an enjoyable week at Mabel's home reviewing her files, touching the famous hat and jacket, and listening to her reminisce about life with Harry. I also met Ed Bernds and Jules White, interviewed Priscilla Bonner, and visited Harry Jr. at his photography studio, where he shared memories of a father he had known for only ten years. As work on updated versions continued, Mabel provided her input and gave her approval for each new draft.

Coincidentally, by 1982, William Schelly had published his book *Harry Langdon,* and in 1983 Professor Joyce Rheuban wrote a critical study entitled *Harry Langdon, the Comedian as Metteur-en-Scène,* both of which reconsidered this misunderstood and neglected comedian by examining the structure and composition of his films, his comedy style, and his persona.[2] In the second edition of his book, published in 2008, Schelly specifically mentioned that in the 1980s he had been "rebuffed" by Mrs. Langdon, whom he had approached for an interview: "She stated that work on her book about her husband was in its final stages, so she preferred not to be interviewed for mine. When I learned through other sources that Mrs. Langdon's book had been 'imminent' since 1966, I concluded that perhaps it would be a long time before it saw print, if ever. (As it has turned out, that book was never published.)"[3]

Meanwhile, after finalizing the manuscript, a series of challenging circumstances caused me to leave the project in 1985. The biography continued to change hands but never found a publisher. Unfortunately, both Rohauer and Mabel passed away (in 1987 and 2001, respectively), never having achieved their goal of publication. But life pleasantly rolls full circle sometimes, and I had the chance to revisit the biography for the University Press of Kentucky in 2014. I reached out to Harry Langdon Jr. to get a sense of his interest in resurrecting this work. He was most supportive and immediately retrieved the many iterations of the manuscript from storage so that we could give it one more go-round. The great advantage of a thirty-year interval between then and now—which also included my experience publishing four books—allowed me to reread this dormant manuscript with new eyes. Harry Jr. also shared precious scrapbooks his father had compiled and his mother had updated that helped me feel like I was entering Langdon's world in a way I had not experienced earlier.

From the outset, I wanted to avoid the usual treatment of Langdon as a helpless and sad elfin character whose only claims to fame were a couple of silent masterworks by an up-and-coming director. Langdon's struggles to assert and channel his many talents and recognize his untapped potential were frequently overlooked in the more familiar narrative of a talented comedian who got lost in mediocrity. One way to break this image was to remove his perennial association with his "weakling" persona (the "little elf," the "helpless baby," the "tragic clown") and bestow on him the deserved rank of "king." One photograph, which I envisioned as the book's cover as soon as I saw it, especially spoke to this stature, with his enigmatic smile capturing a sense of both untouchable celebrity and vulnerable humanity.

In revising the biography, I felt it was important to acknowledge the four key references of the last thirty years, each tackling the life and work of Harry Langdon from different angles. In addition to the Schelly and Rheuban books, James L. Neibaur published *The Silent Films of Harry Langdon (1923–1928)* in 2012, exploring the significance of each silent film.[4] That same year, Chuck Harter and Michael J. Hayde published the mammoth *Little Elf: A Celebration of Harry Langdon*, which is essentially two books in one: a biographical narrative and an encyclopedic compendium of plot summaries and critical reviews. These works should be applauded for their reappreciation of Langdon's comedy and their attempts to set straight(er) the story of egoism and failure that haunted the comedian while he was alive and lingered for decades after.

Film historian and author Edward Watz recorded in his glowing introduction to *Little Elf* his own involvement with the biography undertaken by Raymond Rohauer and Mabel Langdon. Not mincing words over Rohauer's ego and his other negative traits that have, not unreasonably, permeated his reputation, Watz indicated that he disengaged from the project partly because of a clash over Frank Capra's version of what happened: "After a while it became impossible to work with either Rohauer *or* Mabel on a Harry Langdon book. Rohauer was determined to include the Capra interpretation of events; and Mabel was equally determined that nothing of the kind would be included that might place Harry in a less than saintly light."[5] It is my hope that during the thirty-plus years this manuscript has changed hands, slept in storage, and been revived—and with the intervening publication of other research that has attempted to balance the Langdon myth and truth—this biography meshes the best of both worlds: the hard work of Langdon scholars as well as the memories of Mabel and Harry Jr. of a man who was a comic genius and a beloved husband and father.

I

Vaudeville Roots

By the time his second son was born, William Wiley Langdon from Clinton, Missouri, had nearly given up his wanderlust. William had roamed the American Midwest, working as a sign painter, until he met and married Illinois girl Lavinia Lookingbill.[1] William and Lavinia resided in Illinois and Wisconsin before eventually settling among the 30,000 inhabitants of Council Bluffs, Iowa, sometime in the early 1880s. They had already started their family: first came John, and then a year later, on June 15, 1884, Harry Philmore Langdon was born.

Council Bluffs might have appealed to William for its business potential. On the east bank of the Missouri River and directly across from Omaha, Nebraska, Council Bluffs had become a thriving hub with the expansion of the railroads in the late 1860s and early 1870s. It was said that Abraham Lincoln had selected a spot on Lafayette Avenue in Council Bluffs as the eastern terminus of the transcontinental railroad.[2]

Even though he settled in Council Bluffs, William never lost the urge to keep moving. He and Lavinia and their brood of five boys (John, Harry, James, Charles, and Claude) and one girl (Gertrude) replanted themselves in several different neighborhoods within the town.[3] They bought a small house on East Pierce Street in 1885, moved not far away to Vine Street for about a year in 1889, and then relocated again to Harrison Street in 1891. Harry attended elementary school—the extent of his education—when the Langdons resided in the Avenue B school district. In 1894 the family lived in a more centrally located apartment on West Broadway, from which little Harry could more easily ride the streetcar across the bridge into Omaha. There, big-city life and the theater were far more captivating to Harry than working in the family business as a painter.

William had established a painting business with his brothers. The Council Bluffs directories from 1882 to 1922 listed W. W. Langdon as a house and sign painter. He was joined throughout the years by sons Charles in 1893, John four years later, and Claude in 1910. Girls were clearly not part of the family business and settled for more feminine occupations: the name of baby sister Gertrude first appeared in the records in 1914 as a music teacher. James, whose lifelong nickname was Tully, was variously listed as a painter for his father and as a clerk, a cutter, and a butcher at the local Keeline and Pace stores. In 1912 Tully was finally listed as an "actor"— a startling divergence from the family occupation. This was no doubt thanks to his older brother's burgeoning influence; while nearly every other Langdon male was painting or paperhanging, Harry was escaping to the theatrical world whenever he could. Harry's name appeared in the records only once—in 1901 as a painter, a temporary and likely reluctant hiatus while in between theatrical jobs on the road. The next time Harry's name appeared in the directory was in 1913 as an "actor," and so it remained for all subsequent entries—and for the rest of his life after leaving Council Bluffs.

As William built his family business, Lavinia—typically listed as a "housekeeper" in census records—tried to keep her children in line, and Harry seemed to be the only outlier in the group. William was reputedly not very religious, but Lavinia was a devoted member of the Salvation Army, a Christian group dedicated to following the Scriptures and serving humanity to bring them closer to God's salvation.[4] In 1865 William Booth and his wife had founded the Salvation Army in London, basing it on a military model with ranking officials, uniforms, and flags and with a mission of serving as "soldiers" in God's army.[5] Their mission of providing "soup, soap, and salvation" to those in need spread to the United States in 1880, initially in Philadelphia and then outward across the country. A Council Bluffs corps of the Salvation Army opened in October 1886, closed in November 1911, and later reopened in April 1920. Although none of the Langdons served as officers, Lavinia—and as many of her children as she could persuade—must have regularly congregated at various locations along East Broadway for Sunday services, which were often held both morning and night. They likely participated in midweek prayer meetings and the open-air meetings or marches for which the Salvation Army was noted. Especially at Christmas, family dinners were offered, along with activities for children. In 1893 one meeting site was Dohany's Opera House at 15 Bryant Street, an amazing coincidence for Harry, who had discovered the theater as a refuge from his mundane life. Built on the site of

Most of the Langdon family in Council Bluffs, Iowa. Clockwise from left: baby Gertrude, Lavinia, Charles, John, William, and James, with Harry in the center.

Palmer's Concert Hall, which had been destroyed by fire, the Dohany was dedicated in 1882 and had a seating capacity of 1,400, which must have made it an inspiring venue for Salvation Army meetings. When it was not hosting weekly prayer ensembles, the Dohany offered lively vaudeville programs with ventriloquists, singers, dancers, comedians, dancing animals, and novelty acts. The audiences were often both appreciative and rambunctious in their criticism.[6]

Harry found the theater far more fascinating than either the classroom or business. For him, nothing could compare to the music and makeup, the flickering stage lights, and the applause. All of it touched Harry's artistic sensibilities at a tender age. He was already exploring his musical talent, a gift that Lavinia claimed came from his uncle Isaac, who would have made a great church musician if he had not wasted his talent playing the piano in saloons and being shot to death in a drunken brawl. Harry tinkered with the banjo, piano, trumpet, and other wind instruments and was sneaking into the Dohany to see the shows—and just as quickly being ousted as a pest. It is touching to imagine that, at least briefly, the Dohany would be both inspiration and aspiration for young Harry. There, he witnessed his deeply religious mother's model of spiritual strength, even if the extent of his own participation was rattling a tambourine to accompany the robust singing of hymns. But he was also absorbed in the theater's colorful representations of entertainment and the thrill of public recognition. These possibilities fed his young spirit, which refused to be boxed into a traditional job. Both aspects of Harry's life at the Dohany would continue to influence his childhood years and direct his future.

As a remarkably sensible eight-year-old, however, Harry realized he could not achieve the spotlight right away. He resigned himself to delivering the *Omaha Bee* in a residential neighborhood, sometimes selling newspapers all day and sleeping in the press room at night. Still, this was monotony for a boy whose fantasies were activated simply by passing the theater. His large family could not afford to indulge in the social extravagance of actually attending a performance (nor would his religious mother have approved of a show-business life, which upstanding citizens generally regarded as scandalous and immoral). To help at home, Harry dutifully rode across the river to Omaha, peddled his papers, and contributed his earnings to the household. To amuse himself between filial obligations, Harry discovered a talent for drawing caricatures. Staff at the newspaper's editorial offices praised his work, and Harry even sold an occasional cartoon to the *Bee*.

Two years later, when his delivery route was switched to include the downtown section where the Dohany stood tall and proud, ten-year-old Harry would dart into the showplace at the end of his workday and study the vaudeville programs. He attended so frequently that he memorized some of the skits and performed them, to the delight of his neighborhood pals. In an interview for the French weekly *Mon Ciné* in 1925, Harry (a new movie star at the time) reminisced that he had built an impromptu theater out of old planks, crates, and curtains in his father's backyard and provided entertainment to the local kids, initially for free and then for "money"—meaning beads and candy sticks. His production, entitled "The Grand Theatre of the World, and Omaha," was lavishly designed, at least from a child's-eye view. Harry had assembled fruit boxes to create a suit of medieval armor and charmed his way through multiple long mono- logues—primarily because he was the only actor available. He began to sense the power that came from being his own director, producer, and writer. The adoring accolades of his young, naïve audience only fueled his desire for more.[7]

Harry also recruited his brother Tully and taught him the choreogra- phy he had learned through observation, including a song culminating in a fancy split. To raise more "funds" for his home productions, Harry brought Tully to a local restaurant, stood in the doorway, and asked whether the diners wanted to see some live entertainment. Given the evi- dent determination of the two boys, the diners usually agreed to the per- formance. Harry then accompanied Tully on the mouth harp to a song-and-dance routine capped off by the well-rehearsed split. The coins Harry collected from the diners formed the basis of what he called the "company treasury."[8]

While Lavinia wondered what had possessed her wayward son, Wil- liam was often less than pleased with Harry's homespun theatrical pur- suits. One day, in an effort to construct a vehicle intended to be a train, Harry used a barrel for the wheels, affixed a coal oil bucket to serve as the funnel, and then deposited William's celluloid collars into the bucket and set them on fire to supply the necessary smoke. Then, hiding "offstage" in the "wings" of his performance space, Harry pulled the barrel along by a rope to create a rolling locomotive effect. While the neighborhood kids marveled at the illusion, William was furious that his personal possessions had become disposable props for this foolhardy spectacle. Harry found he could not sit for quite a while after his father expressed his disapproval of the act.

Despite their concern over the behavior of their precocious offspring, William and Lavinia considered Harry special. According to family lore, they had almost lost him when, at a very young age, Harry suffered a terrible disease (likely diphtheria) that closed his throat, leading the doctor to tell them there was no hope of survival. A grief-stricken William sat on the front porch just as the local veterinarian rode by and asked what was wrong. The veterinarian advised William not to give up and directed him to fill a tub with water and lye in the barn. Over Lavinia's objections, the two men carried the ailing Harry in a sheet and rocked him over the tub so that he could inhale the dreadful fumes rising from the brew. Miraculously, Harry's throat opened and he could breathe freely again, but the fumes also damaged his vocal cords, leaving him with a voice that was higher than normal. Whatever the cause of this vocal quality, Langdon's voice later had both positive and negative effects on his stage and film work.[9]

Harry's parents knew they would eventually lose their son—if not to illness, then to the theater. So they resigned themselves to the likelihood that Harry would not carry on the family business with his brothers. Harry, however, never doubted his "calling." Passionately stagestruck, he found personal fulfillment at the theater that nothing else offered. He had no personal friendships that bound him to home or school (which he barely attended). The neighborhood kids were useful primarily as an enthusiastic audience, and they no doubt looked forward to Harry's exciting stories. He was a one-man show, re-creating the world on his miniature stage. He was always on the hunt for the next adventure that would take him beyond his boundaries. Others around him may have had fantastic aspirations, but Harry was the only one among his family and friends who made them real. It was neither bravery nor daring: for Harry, it was a natural instinct and an impulse he had to follow.

Not even his pet duck, which followed him everywhere, could hold Harry back when the theater beckoned. William knew Harry had fled to some theatrical daydream when he spotted the duck wandering through the streets searching for his companion. William would then set off to drag Harry away from the Dohany and back home. This occurred frequently because, when left to his own devices, Harry would even forget to come home for dinner. When mealtime passed and Harry's seat at the dinner table remained vacant, his parents knew they would find him in the backstage corner of the Dohany. In 1896 tickets cost ten to thirty cents, and whenever Harry could afford the price of admission, every cent was worth the sacrifice.

Harry wasted no time finding jobs in the theater and was amenable to being a ticket taker, usher, prop boy, cashier, call boy, sign painter, or even painter of footprints on the sidewalk, used to entice patrons to walk into the "opry house." At such times, Harry no doubt thanked his father, at least mentally, for exposing him to the painting business. At night, Harry steadfastly memorized the parts of both lead actors and bit players.

Like many theaters of the day, the Dohany featured amateur nights, which allowed the management to save money by not having to pay for professional entertainment. Proud relatives welcomed the opportunity to cheer their gifted offspring and boo the competition. One Friday, on his first amateur night, Harry was introduced to the actual experience of stage acting—and stage fright—in front of a paying audience.

Obviously impressed with his flair for imitation, the manager of the Dohany asked Harry to be the house entry at next Friday's amateur show. Although Harry's act was not polished, the manager felt assured of getting a halfway decent performance. Harry practiced his song-and-dance number in front of a mirror at home, and his performance onstage—a combination of innate talent and unintentional comic mistakes caused by nervousness—won him enthusiastic applause and laughter. In later years, Langdon spoke of feeling like a "successful flop" as he stumbled through his song-and-dance set. The stage director and the manager, however, convinced Harry that he had been the hit of the show. They may have thought Harry's "stardom" would never go beyond the amateur stage, but he was perfect for their purposes, and they encouraged him to continue performing. He persevered, motivated perhaps by the dream of being a star one day. Harry eventually won an assortment of prizes, including canaries, cut-glass bowls, and goldfish. His family once boasted that, thanks to Harry, they had six large clocks for their parlor.

Harry, now twelve years old, no doubt believed that show business was his destiny. So when the Kickapoo Indian Medicine Show visited Council Bluffs, it left with a new member. The spectacle of "Natives" in full regalia and quick-talking salesmen peddling miraculous nostrums convinced Harry to join without delay. The Kickapoo show was the brainchild of John E. Healy and his partner Charles F. Bigelow in the late 1880s. They devised the idea of touring with a show that exhibited Indian life and "authentic" members of the Kickapoo tribe (their winter residence was a "wigwam" in New Haven, Connecticut). In bottles, tins, and boxes depicting Wild West–style Indians in feathered and beaded garb, the company sold "all-natural medicines"—oils, tonics, pills, salves, and soaps that cured everything from coughs, chills, fevers, piles, ulcers, worms, and cancers to digestive and kidney irregularities. The roster of natural ingredients, meant to impress ailing clients and persuade them to part with their dollars, included licorice, dandelion, burdock root, aloe, horehound, cloves, camphor, myrrh, and sassafras. Mother Nature was sometimes assisted by a 60 percent alcohol content.[10]

Trouper that he was, Harry hawked the medicine, engaged in rigged fights, sang and danced, and did whatever his boss—a tough type by the name of "Dutch" Schultz—told him to do. He pitched tents, slept in a trunk, and filled medicine bottles in secluded spots or hotel rooms, out of sight of the gullible small-town residents. Ignoring the obvious huckstering that was a big component of the medicine show, Harry enjoyed providing comedy entertainment to the spectators before they were slowly separated from their cash.

Besides bed and board, the medicine show paid Harry $7 a week. Not surprisingly, the enterprising boy left the Kickapoo show behind in Foley, Alabama, when he was offered a better job with a minstrel show in nearby Mobile. Years later, Langdon claimed he had been offered—but was never paid—$35 a week. Despite this financial instability, Harry relished being part of a genuine theatrical troupe. Although it was only a small minstrel show (twelve members), Harry was no longer merely one-third of an entire quack-show operation (Dutch, his wife Matilda, and Harry). The minstrel troupe offered higher-class entertainment, with a full program of song, dance, banjo strumming, and harmony. Harry honed his comedic pacing during bits interspersed throughout the program in the guise of joke exchanges between "end man" and "interlocutor" or master of ceremonies, the key performers in the usual lineup of blackface minstrels.[11] Langdon continued to use blackface as part of his acrobatic acts over the next few years.

These were auspicious beginnings for a boy who was barely a teenager and yearning to be on the stage. Harry witnessed multiple forms of popular entertainment; then he performed and improvised. Although he was sometimes stranded and stuck with hotel bills, he accumulated experience, adventure, and enough money to eke by until the next gig. Perhaps Harry's most valuable education was learning how performers were able to "double," "triple," and "quadruple"—that is, switch their skills as the need arose. During Harry's itinerant circus days, for instance, clowns were also

Harry as part of a minstrel show, expertly balanced on his bottles.

acrobats and musicians. Harry had already played multiple staff roles at the Dohany, so it was no stretch for him to be versatile on the road.[12] For an elementary school dropout, this was certainly a version of continuing education.

One of the show-stopping feats that Harry developed and performed for years was a balancing act with beer bottles. According to a 1931 article, Harry recalled that at the tender age of ten he had been "mentored" by one Charles W. Nichols, who engaged him to distribute bills and carry posters for his shows. Nichols also bought him an elephant outfit, which Harry wore as he walked on "all-fours" and balanced on bottles. Not surprisingly, the act was a "wow" and good "enough to win a kiss" from impressed female spectators.[13] In a later version of this stunt, Harry (sans elephant outfit) balanced a table on four bottles, then set another four bottles and a second table on top of the first, and then set a chair on top of *that,* which he sat in and rocked. He eventually whittled the act down to one chair balanced on the slim necks of two bottles, which was even more dangerous. Harry met his enthusiastic audience after the show and amazed them by caricaturing their likenesses. Soon after, he packed up and moved on to the next audience in the next city. He was, without perhaps even realizing it, uncannily perpetuating William Langdon's wandering-feet syndrome. But instead of fixing his goal on one job, Harry eagerly experimented with whatever options fortuitously appeared at each juncture of his travels.

Even if he had never succeeded as a performer, Harry could have returned to Council Bluffs with sage advice on survival. No doubt grateful to the memory of his musical uncle Isaac, Harry once used his improvisational musicality to save his job. He had boasted to one of his many road-show bosses that he could double on the organ if the need arose, but unfortunately, that was one instrument he could not play. So one day, when Harry was asked to accompany an entertainer on a portable organ, he created some music by playing only the black keys because, he said, they were easier to hit than the white keys. The singer and the manager were outraged, but they believed Harry's explanation that he was just rusty. Harry stayed up all night practicing on the organ, keeping the manager awake as well. Through sheer determination, he kept his job.

Harry also learned how to survive fierce weather on his travels. While in the circus, Harry and his performing pig Swamproot lived through a month of heavy rain in Missouri—more rain, he reminisced, than might fill a whole circus season. He and Swamproot could hardly circle the ring in the mud, much less execute their comical tricks. In a typically humorous reinterpretation of his adventures years later, Langdon said he had "discussed" the situation with his pig, and they mutually agreed to quit the show to avoid being "permanently mildewed" by the end of the season.

Other survival stories, however fabulous and randomly assigned to Harry's adolescent years, retell episodes that could well have happened, or they could be stories he invented to illustrate a typical experience. Langdon did not refrain from describing the unscrupulous side of show business, with its quacks, outlaws, and con artists. Once, sixteen-year-old Harry was intrigued by a man named Chester, who had no difficulty talking Harry into taking a freight train to Chicago. They soon observed a man suspiciously flicking a substantial amount of money in full view, in stark contrast to his less fortunate appearance. Inspired by a vision of Robin Hood, Chester urged Harry to help him retrieve the money that this person clearly must have stolen from its rightful owner. A dubious Harry joined Chester and this other fellow by the riverside after the train had berthed. Between these two men, Harry later said he felt "like a piece of cream cheese on a pneumatic drill." The man with the money eventually pulled out a gun, and Chester wielded a sand-filled lead pipe. At the sounds of a gunshot and a thud, Harry dove into the river for cover, only to be fished out by Chester, who was now flashing the money with glee. Surmising that Chester had no intention of ever returning the money to its rightful owner, Harry fled on the first freight train home. He never saw Chester again, he said, until much later when he recognized the same face in the papers—arrested and serving a life sentence for a bank job.

Another story depicts eighteen-year-old Langdon as a carnival member, participating in Government Land Gift Deal festivities. Harry was hardly off the train before a gunfight erupted and he saw the sheriff carting away a limp assailant. Several days later, or so the story goes, a cyclone nearly blew the town away, which was fitting justice in Harry's opinion—although the cyclone also blew away his employment. Another time, Harry was working at the St. Louis World's Fair and subsisting on a dime a day, which he frugally split between one nickel hot dog sandwich in the afternoon and another in the evening. He was eventually hired by the sympathetic stand operator as performer, ballyhoo, and behind-the-scenes manager. He was now earning up to $30 a day, an amount far surpassing the value of his amateur night prizes.

Whenever Harry returned home, his worried mother knew, with creeping resignation, that he would soon be leaving again. Once she had tried to hide his clothes to prevent him from joining a minstrel show. But now, when the inevitable day dawned, Lavinia simply replenished Harry's small wooden travel box filled with his essentials. The box was easy to carry and served as a sturdy pillow. On one momentous return visit, Lavinia sent Harry up to his room, where he found a brand new trunk and a small Bible ready to accompany him on his next journey. The trunk could not be tucked under his arm or used to rest his head, but it symbol-

Turn-of-the-century Langdon characters.

The Langdon family, still together years later. *Back row:* Claude, Tully, John, Charles, and Harry. *Front row:* Gertrude, Lavinia, and William.

ized what Harry wanted more than anything (except for performing onstage): his parents' acceptance. Many years later, Langdon reflected that this was the moment he knew his mother had stopped hoping to change his mind about his peripatetic life and accepted his choice. It was a day and a gesture that Langdon would never forget.

In 1899, after two full seasons on the road, Harry actually did feel homesick and was glad to "jump ship" when the troupe neared Council Bluffs. To his younger siblings, he was a seasoned performer; to his parents, he was a small source of income, and sometimes they were glad to have one less mouth to feed when he was away. Still, they thought if they let him vent his wild aspirations on the road, he would eventually tire out and settle into a practical occupation. During one of his rare homesick moments, Harry even became a barber, and his boss acknowledged that he could be an asset to the tonsorial profession. Within a short time, however, Harry disappeared again, only to return a few months later with more fantastic tales. On one such homecoming in 1901, William Langdon (who had apparently had enough) promptly installed Harry in his sign-painting shop—the one time his name appeared in the local directory as a member of the family business. Harry listlessly stabbed away at his work, exercising his drawing abilities but knowing full well where his heart belonged.

Harry's next employment was at a strange hybrid venue called Mickey Mullins' Boxing and Variety Saloon in downtown Omaha. Located at Sixteenth and Capitol, it was a "theatre saloon" that offered weekly prizefights and, alternately, vaudeville acts. In this roughhouse, a performer might be assaulted by the patrons for telling the wrong joke. Harry learned to gear his material to his audience's mentality and won a lucky break at Mickey Mullins' Saloon. One patron who caught his act was Eddie Grego, stage manager at the Boyd, the most prestigious vaudeville house in Omaha. Grego introduced Harry to Jerome Seybrinski, the manager, and asked him to demonstrate his better routines, including one about golf that Harry had developed in his spare time. Seybrinski then offered him the attractive sum of $25 a week, and Harry joined the Boyd's bill as a local addition to the program supplied by the Spedden and Paige booking office in Chicago. After a successful week, Jack Zimmer, the stage manager for Spedden and Paige's traveling company, asked Harry to join the troupe and finish the tour with them. Once the company returned to Chicago, Harry could audition for B. J. Spedden himself, who might book him with the organization's main company that was led by Spedden and toured all the major cities, including New York.

Harry's imagination somersaulted after hearing the offer that promised to establish him comfortably in a legitimate vaudeville niche. He was impressed by the reviews of his performance, printed in the *Omaha Bee* and other newspapers, which called him a "bright new find." Harry naturally envisioned all roads leading to the Palace Theatre in New York, the epitome of vaudeville success. The wistful boy who had sneaked his way into theaters in Council Bluffs had finally been "discovered" doing what he did best and what he knew he would do for the rest of his life.

Harry Langdon accepted the offer.

Harry's siblings were not so enthusiastic about show business from the performing perspective, but they were a rapt audience for his private rehearsals. The youngest members of the Langdon clan—Charles, Claude, and Gertrude—were usually present with ready applause. Harry knew his act needed a special touch to distinguish it from the other stage fare on the bill. Claude, who was only seven in the spring of 1899 when Harry joined the Spedden and Paige circuit, may have been the unwitting catalyst who helped his older brother define his emerging comedic character.

Harry was eager to polish a golf routine for the tour. He had developed it in the mold of the standard vaudeville comedy acts of the period, with a few coarse jokes, a soft-shoe turn, and a song to leave the audience cheering. As a special twist, Harry wanted the routine to parody the postures, mannerisms, and language of real golfers, whom he had observed with much fascination. He had come to enjoy golf and recognized it as a growing national interest. All this was beyond little Claude, who had never seen a golf game and could not appreciate a verbal or visual parody of it. Harry was disappointed at Claude's blasé reaction, given that the same lines and gags had succeeded with some audiences at the Boyd. Claude's fading attention did not bode well, since Harry knew that if audience members were as intellectually naïve as his little brother, he would lose them too. He recalled directing his jokes to the mentality of the spectators at Mickey Mullins' as a strategy to avoid their disapproval (and possible physical assaults). What strategy would work to overcome boredom? Pantomime was a possibility: Harry decided to *move* in frustration instead of talk about it; he would convey meaning without words through physical expression, much as a child would. Maybe with simple, clear facial expressions and gestures that were universally human and innate from an early age, anyone could be entertained by a purely visual scenario.

Harry improvised on the routine from a child's perspective and found that Claude was suddenly entranced. But Harry also observed another phenomenon: Tully was doubled over in laughter at the novel interpretation. He had seen the golf routine repeatedly and had become inured to even the funniest gags, yet this time, he was reacting differently. Harry had not considered using childlike clowning on anyone but a child, but if it had this effect on Tully, adult audiences might also respond enthusiastically.

Harry tried out this new approach onstage, hesitantly at first. Originally, if he missed hitting the golf ball, he looked disgusted and uttered an expletive ("Shucks!" or "Drat!"). Now, upon missing the ball, Harry simply stared at it in disbelief, put his fingers to his mouth in a child's gesture of embarrassment, and offered the shade of an apologetic smile. This twist won audience approval. If he added moves expressing helpless confusion, Harry was rewarded with strong laughter and prolonged applause. He later claimed that the first time he tried this refined routine onstage, even the musicians and the stage manager laughed—the highest accolade a performer could achieve.

In the spring of 1899 Harry performed his golf routine, aptly called "After the Ball," on the Small circuit, which covered minor towns in Illinois, Michigan, and Iowa. When he demonstrated it for B. J. Spedden at Chicago's Blackstone Theater, he received praiseworthy reviews, but Spedden told Harry that, good as it was, the routine was not suited for the "big time." Still, Spedden liked Harry's talent and potential and informed him that Jack Zimmer would be in Omaha in August to audition some acts for the winter season. If Harry could devise a solid routine, he might stand a chance.

And so "Johnny's New Car" was born.[14] Harry tinkered with the idea and enlisted the help of Tully and oldest brother John. Using his carpentry and artistic skills, Harry concocted a little breakaway car made out of wood. The entire act centered around the car stalling and spiritedly resisting all efforts of the three boys to restart it. Eventually the engine exploded and the wheels and fenders dropped off with perfect timing. Everything that was movable, hissable, or flyable launched surprise attacks on the bumbling trio.

It was a timely act. Cars were a novelty in 1899, especially in small towns, and they were the subject of both derision and curiosity. The vehicles familiar to audiences were predominantly homemade contraptions that had been precariously assembled by their owners. They were ill-tempered and tended to sputter or explode at the slightest move. Automobiles had not yet become a form of daily transportation; they were either an adventurous sport or a life-threatening challenge. Shapes, sizes, and modes of propulsion varied. The most efficient engine was still under debate: steam-powered, gasoline-powered, and even electric conveyances rattled down the roads. Licensing was hardly enforced, and there were few rules of driving. The average conservative American probably regarded the progressive horseless carriage with apprehension or even hostility.

This attitude proved fortunate for the Langdon brothers' parody of these mechanical monsters. The breakaway car became one of the most ingenious stage devices used in vaudeville. The boys lovingly put the vehicle together during the summer of 1899 with the assistance of Charlie Daley, a trained mechanic who worked for the Council Bluffs police department. Hidden in the car were numerous controls, buttons, and release levers that activated springs and explosive charges throughout its

"Johnny's New Car" onstage, against Harry's painted scenery. Harry is on the running board, and brother Tully and soon-to-be-girlfriend Rose are at left.

body. As the three Langdons milled around the car in seemingly spontaneous confusion, giving it ineffectual kicks and shoves, the audience never suspected that intense rehearsals preceded every performance. The boys maximized each incident with backward flips, pratfalls, and other exhibitions of mock terror—all fairly standard slapstick fare. But, thanks to the clever props and innovative staging, such as a transparent drop that created the illusion of depth with special lighting, the act usually succeeded in bringing down the house—along with the car.

When Jack Zimmer saw the audition of "Johnny's New Car" in August, he heartily approved, as did the other auditioning acts. He offered the boys a tour starting in Omaha and moving through Kansas City, St. Louis, Springfield, and Bloomington. The last stop would be Chicago, where it was well known that only successful acts that had survived all types of audiences ever arrived. John, Harry, and Tully would be earning $100 a week. William and Lavinia no longer had any objections to sending their three eldest sons to the stage; the $50 the boys promised to mail home would more than double the family's income from sign painting. "Johnny's New Car" was a hit for two seasons. John, however, began to suffer from acute homesickness, and when his father found it difficult to carry on the family business by himself, John did not hesitate to return to sign painting. Tully loved show business, however, and was content to be the straight man or second lead to Harry.

After two seasons, Spedden and Paige decided to retire the car routine, thinking it had been exhausted by now, and Zimmer asked Harry to work solo in the 1901–1902 season. He would have the summer to refine old routines, invent new ones, and freshen the act. But Harry was not ready to send "Johnny's New Car" to the scrap heap. In 1903, as he began touring the West and Midwest with a road company of the musical *The Show Girl,* a Broadway hit from the previous year, Harry found that audiences remembered him from "Johnny's New Car." Soon he reinstated the car routine in his vaudeville appearances. Without realizing it, Harry was committing himself to a role that might cause him to lose his identity. This had happened to some of his more distinguished peers in dramatic theater. For example, James O'Neill (father of playwright Eugene) had long been branded as the Count of Monte Cristo, despite his other important roles; William Gillette was likewise identified as Sherlock Holmes for decades. Langdon might have to drive his breakaway car for the rest of his vaudeville career. In 1903, however, Harry could only envision being on the threshold of success. He had found a comfortable niche in vaudeville and did not mind parking himself there for a while.

Harry also found the idea of dwelling in that niche more appealing when he thought he could share it with an attractive, high-spirited girl. Back in the summer of 1901 he had stayed in Milwaukee, where Jack Zimmer managed a downtown vaudeville theater. Harry was preparing for the new season by dusting off his golf routine and spinning out a takeoff of the strongman acts that were popular in circuses and vaudeville. Zimmer placed Harry on the bill once or twice a week so he could test his gags and incorporate his colorful road-life experiences into new routines. The Milwaukee theater also encouraged local talent to participate in amateur nights. One young entry that summer was a dark-haired beauty named Frances Rose Musolf who sang the popular tune "My Sweetheart's the Man in the Moon." Rose, as she was known, won first prize that night, probably because her German Polish relatives showed up and gave her the loudest cheers.

Harry, who was in the habit of watching acts from the wings, particularly liked the girl he saw onstage that night. He approached Rose shyly

Frances Rose Musolf.

afterward and engaged her in conversation. Rose was eighteen, a few months older than Harry. He noticed an outgoing, almost aggressive streak in her—the makings of a tomboy if her strict Catholic family would have let her behave like one. She was, of necessity, a perfect lady, but behind her eyes Harry saw mischief and determination.

Harry was impressed. He now recognized that his own comedy, based on helplessness and confusion, was an offshoot of his own personality. He was timid with girls, and his accomplishments in the romantic department were meager indeed. Rose seemed capable of taking the lead in social matters. Harry maneuvered an invitation to her house to meet her parents, her five sisters, and her brother. As staunch Catholics, they balked when they learned he was Protestant, but his reputation as a veteran of two seasons in the legitimate theater counted in his favor, and Harry continued to see Rose that summer.

Harry was not surprised when Rose told him that she had been offered a contract to sing with a trio on the Alton circuit for the 1901–1902 season (her assertiveness seemed to work as well on talent agents as it did on Harry). He wished she could have asserted her way onto the Spedden and Paige circuit, because the only time they spent together that season was the few weeks they both played St. Louis. Harry was convinced that Rose was the girl for him, and he found a way to end their separation: revive the old car act that audiences still clamored for, but have a girl as his foil instead of his two brothers. Rose was immediately convinced, but not so her parents, who bristled at the idea of their daughter touring with a man to whom she was not married. Nor would they consent to a mixed-faith marriage, if the issue arose.

Reluctantly, the couple postponed their plans to work together until Rose was old enough to make her own decisions. In the meantime, Harry hunted for another female partner for the act, certain that the idea of including a woman's touch would invigorate the jalopy routine. He and Tully succeeded in locating a petite blonde from Omaha named Cecile Keliher, who clearly had no objection to touring with men to whom she was not married. The car act evolved into a skit in which Harry invited Cecile for a ride in his new car just as Tully, her other beau, arrived to visit her, so all three went for a spin. When the car stalled, Tully used every opportunity to sabotage Harry's attempts to fix it and thus diminish his place in Cecile's heart. Tully ultimately won Cecile, while Harry was left with a junk heap. Tully enjoyed his dapper new role of stealing the girl from the hapless Harry because it allowed him another season on the stage—and it also afforded him the chance to court Cecile, with whom he had become infatuated.

Zimmer accepted the new act, Spedden approved it, and Harry, Tully, and Cecile toured the midwestern circuit in 1902–1903. Harry had proved that the presence of a lovely girl brightened the act. He had only to prove to the Musolfs that letting Rose join it would be equally successful. Mr. and Mrs. Musolf relented when they learned that Rose and Cecile could room together—or, rather, chaperone each other—and that no fate worse than death awaited her. So the act was adapted once more to become a foursome. In the 1903–1904 season the new version toured the eastern states, including Ohio, Indiana, Kentucky, and Pennsylvania. Rose convincingly played Harry's nagging wife in the front seat, while Cecile and Tully played a couple in the backseat and fed straight lines to the leads.

Harry had fallen under the spell of Rose's alluring yet dominating personality. He accepted her leadership willingly and may have even welcomed it, because it relieved him of the chore of making decisions. He meekly deferred to her in nearly all matters offstage. When it came to theatrical decisions, however, Harry always asserted himself. He knew show business intimately, and he was unquestionably the star. Harry Langdon carried the show, which even Rose had to concede.

Still, Rose felt the need to settle problems that affected her personal status with Harry—namely, eliminating Cecile. As the act scored solidly in the East and worked a second year in the Midwest, touring in Illinois, Wisconsin, and Missouri, Rose found fault with everything Cecile did. Upon seeing Harry enter Cecile's room one day, Rose launched a jealous tirade, reducing Cecile to tears and causing her to quit. Harry, not out to steal Tully's girl by any means, had only been returning a borrowed magazine. But whether Rose knew that or not, she had managed to reestablish herself as the sole female in the skit and in Harry's life. The act was reduced to a love triangle once again.

Having lost her chaperone, Rose hastened to quell her parents' objections to her traveling the country with two unmarried men. Her next priority was to expedite Harry's marriage proposal. At the age of twenty, he was experiencing a bout of uncertainty, and he wanted to avoid any family rancor over religious differences. Rose abandoned the idea of a formal ceremony and evaded all conversations about churches and clergymen. She succeeded in obtaining a simple proposal and a wedding. Family annals do not disclose the exact strategy involved, but on November 23, 1904, Harry and Rose were married by a Milwaukee justice of the peace, with Tully and the justice's wife in attendance.[15]

The Musolfs reconciled themselves to the irrevocable, and at Christmas they held a celebration party for their headstrong daughter and her new husband when their schedule brought them back to Milwaukee. There was no honeymoon. The newlyweds traveled the Spedden and Paige circuit for the rest of the season. Harry could at least relax in the assurance of steady employment with his successful routine. Booking agents actually considered married acts reliable because the actors were not likely to quit suddenly. A husband-and-wife team could watch over each other, minimizing discord over time spent apart or suspected infidelity. Even the possible redundancy of working and living with the same partner day after day was superseded by the couple's devotion to performing for new audiences and improvising routines.

Harry freshened the act by adding new jokes and allusions to current

Harry and Rose in "Johnny's New Car."

topics and updating his breakaway car to keep abreast of automotive developments in Detroit. Cars were becoming more responsive to the driver's touch, and convenience was key. The audience's focus was now turning from the novelty of the car to the reactions and interplay of the passengers. They watched as the car's breakdown incensed the nagging wife and magnified her spouse's clumsiness. In short, the act paralleled the institution of marriage itself. By this time, the popularity of the Langdon act relied on audience members projecting themselves into the roles of the performers: men understood the husband, women identified with the wife, and, above all, everyone wanted to comfort Harry. His character was not only comically bumbling; it was childlike and defenseless against both marriage and machine, producing a funny yet sympathetic brand of humor. Without realizing it, Harry Langdon was primed to drive a long road—twenty years' worth of driving, to be exact—remodeling "Johnny's New Car" and building his own character. He left Spedden and Paige for other, more

Harry with one of the many vaudeville troupes he joined in his career. Rose is at the lower left.

prestigious vaudeville circuits, eventually working for every major booking office in the country.

One interesting item from the *Waterloo (Iowa) Times-Tribune* in February 1906 praised the Langdon act for creating "roars of laughter with their quips and funny expressions" and featuring a pretty song and dance. The act also spotlighted Harry's bottle trick, where he sat in a chair balanced on two beer bottles and "assumed an attitude of repose." The reviewer particularly noted Harry's comical expression, which belied the breathtaking peril of the feat. Finally, the "automobile feature" that closed the routine was "always the occasion for vigorous applause and encores," according to the enthusiastic reviewer. In this version of the performance, Rose sang a song with "one of the most catchy choruses imaginable," at which cue Harry drove onstage in a red automobile to pick her up and roll away, sharing "one of the prettiest duets ever heard on this stage." Only a few days later, however, the newspaper alerted its readers to a freak accident involving Harry: during his chair-balancing routine, the neck of one of the bottles snapped and he fell on its jagged edge, suffering a three-inch-long, one-inch-deep leg wound. He was forced to recuperate in the local boardinghouse but was back to work within a few days.[16]

The act had grown in terms of its length, presentation, and personnel. During some seasons, only Harry and Rose performed; at other times, Tully accompanied them. Occasionally, Rose's sister Cecil joined the act.[17] There were years when Harry worked solo or with Tully, while Rose, who was booked on the same bill, appeared as part of a female singing group or as a single. Regardless of the configuration, however, *Billboard* announced on September 15, 1906, that the Langdons "are booked solid for the season by the Western Vaudeville Managers' association. The auto is proving a novelty in the continuous and the act is making a hit everywhere." It would garner the same unvarying success into the early 1920s. In 1907–1908 Rose was a singing cowgirl, an unusual attraction at the time. The Langdons were working for Kohl and Castle that year, and it was probably the bookers, not Rose, who insisted on Harry performing alone.

During some runs, "Johnny's New Car" was pure comedy and slapstick; at other times, it included some nostalgic musical harmonizing before the mayhem exploded. Gus Edwards's "In My Merry Oldsmobile" was one of 1905's hit songs and became a long-lasting favorite. It seemed like a natural fit and would be a staple in Langdon's act for many years. Although Rose's claim that she introduced the tune is not wholly true, she may have sung it more often than any other performer. The durability of "Johnny's New Car" assured a permanent place for the song.

Harry also wove golf references into "Johnny's New Car." He already had a golf skit in his repertoire, and golf had become a fervent recreational interest for him. He integrated the sport into the act by having the car pick him up at the golf links, allowing him to indulge in a few golf jokes before turning to the ornery jalopy. Part of the routine's evolution also involved making the backdrop more physically impressive. Harry himself painted a street scene for a 1906 variation of the routine that he called "A Night on the Boulevard." Using the principle of perspective, he drew a real street scene with buildings receding into the horizon. The streetlights were electrically illuminated from behind, casting a soft glow to the set. Apparently, audiences were moved to applaud the scenery even before the ensemble appeared.[18] In addition, through the use of special lighting effects, Harry created the illusion of the car driving along the road and disappearing, with its glowing taillights diminishing in intensity and leaving the stage in darkness.[19]

Framed by the stage proscenium, which distanced him from the audience while still allowing him to feel their emotional responses, Harry was building his sense of the contrast between broad acting and subtlety. To a great degree, this awareness was rooted in Harry's observation of brother Claude's earlier fascination with "small reactions." Onstage, Harry executed broad moves to reach the furthest tiers of the theater, but he also used the stillness of his body to create more intimate expressions, free of slapstick or exaggeration. This caused the audience to pay more attention to the unexpected, and it startled them into stunned and genuine releases of laughter.[20]

In 1911 the Langdons presented "A Night on the Boulevard" at the Fifth Avenue Theatre in New York City and received the *New York Telegraph*'s approval on November 11: "the skit has been a riotous laugh from its first presentation and bids fair to obtain for itself a special niche in the hall of vaudeville comedy fame." The Langdons were steadily employed around the country, performing variations of their act, for the next decade. A survey of random reviews over these years shows a remarkable record of positive responses and appreciative audiences, regardless of time or place. Harry had a knack for adapting the show to new innovations and refreshing his material just enough to maintain its appeal. He had, in fact, developed a strong, durable, and iconic image on the stage that would endure until vaudeville yielded to motion pictures and Langdon emerged as a silent screen star with a new identity. But that transition was still several years away.

While the Langdons were spinning in their private microcosm onstage, World War I was raging in Europe. It is not clear why Harry never enlisted in the military, and he never addressed the reason except to say that he was performing in New York at the time. Tully joined the army in 1917 and

Rose, Harry, and Tully.

was sent overseas. Rose hastily introduced her young brother Oscar to take Tully's place. That winter, the act played on the West Coast—Los Angeles, San Francisco, Portland, Seattle—with three Musolfs and only one Langdon. Meanwhile, Tully went missing, and the army erroneously reported that he was dead. Fortunately, he was found alive in a hospital, although the details of his wartime experiences were never revealed. After recovering, Tully returned home in 1919 and declared his desire to return to the stage with Harry.[21]

In 1920 the entire Langdon family decided to revive their wanderlust one last time and move from Council Bluffs to Los Angeles, which had impressed Harry with its refreshing scenery, welcoming weather, and employment prospects. It seemed like an ideal location for his family to settle down. Harry watched Los Angeles grow under the vibrant influence of the burgeoning film industry, although he was not yet considering it as a viable alternative for his creative expression. He was thinking more that the luxuriant landscape and climate would benefit his ailing father. Claude would carry on the family sign-painting business in Iowa before moving with his wife to California. Meanwhile, Charles and John, both unmarried, would establish a sign-painting firm in Los Angeles. As for Tully, the trauma of the war seemed to haunt him. He began to drink heavily and often disappeared while on a bender. According to family memories, Harry and Claude were obliged to scour Los Angeles looking for Tully, pay for any property damage he had caused, and return him to their mother's house to "dry out."[22]

William—the original and most avid traveler of the family—never got to make his last journey. The day before the family was scheduled to board the train to Los Angeles, he died at the age of seventy of a cerebral hemorrhage. An item in the August 21, 1920, edition of the *Council Bluffs Daily Nonpareil* captured the irony of his death in the headline—"Dies on Eve of Leaving the City"—and reported that "their furniture [was] all packed ready for shipping." A follow-up item on August 25 noted that Harry and brothers "Tulley" and Claude, along with brother-in-law Thomas Melroy, were among the pallbearers. William was buried in Council Bluffs.

As the Langdons settled in their new home, the film industry was rousing the sleepy West Coast community into a resonating hub of glamour and experimentation, talent and promise. In the meantime, Harry remained content to drive through vaudeville in his makeshift jalopy, never suspecting that his stage days were numbered because of a revolutionary new medium that had already propelled many unknown entertainers into unimaginable fame and fortune. Little did Harry Langdon realize that in a short time, he too would be standing in the cinematic spotlight.

A quote from the February 14, 1920, issue of the *Dramatic Mirror* testifies to the longevity of the Langdons' car act: "Harry Langdon, assisted by two very winsome lassies billed as Rose and Cecil, appears in 'Johnny's New Car.' It is not by any means a new act, but it is screamingly funny to anyone who ever even saw an automobile. Langdon, in appearance, is a joke, and the pretty girls in the act help to bring out his ridiculous characteristics."

By the fall of 1920, Harry's irrepressible routine had gained the distinction of working on Broadway—New York City's Great White Way. A two-act musical comedy revue named *Jim Jam Jems* opened at the Cort

Theatre on October 4. Most of the presentations at the Cort were family affairs, with John Cort acting as producer and brother Harry Cort as playwright. *Jim Jam Jems* stepped into the Cort after the successful *Abraham Lincoln,* which could have continued into the winter season except that, as *Weekly Variety* observed, "the new Cort piece could hardly be buffeted about on the road waiting for a Broadway berth." Nearly $14,000 was taken in during its first week, showing that, according to the trade paper, it had the "makings."

The name of the show was derived from a small in-vogue magazine known for its risqué humor. Very little in *Jim Jam Jems,* however, lived up to its spicy name. It had a conventional "double-standard" plot: a rich, middle-aged divorced man thinks nothing of his frequent romantic flings but is horrified that his niece attends dances. The girl retaliates by advertising for a gentleman, and the respondent is a reporter for the little humor magazine—hence the title and the extent of the plot. The play, staged by Edward J. McGregor, also spanned some elegant New York locations: the Plaza Hotel, the Astoria Hotel, and the Astorbilt. Trusty stereotypes such as the "dancing niece," the "scandal-sheet reporter," and the "comedy detective" and characters labeled "Miss Pad," "Miss Pencil," "Miss High," and "Miss Low" sang and danced merrily through the scenes.

The Corts knew enough to pad the meatless plot with music and fun, and they engaged vaudevillians to sparkle up the proceedings. Frank Fay, as popular in legitimate theater as in the less esteemed "two-a-day," won enthusiastic laughs, particularly for his burlesque dramatics. He was the biggest name in the show, having been a vaudeville headliner since 1913. He had arrived on Broadway in 1917, and by 1933 he was producing his own show, *Frank Fay's Fables,* for which the equally alliterative *Jim Jam Jems* was an important stepping-stone. Skilled in every phase of show business, Fay could provide an inexhaustible supply of gags and was an unsurpassed master of ceremonies.

The surprise of *Jim Jam Jems* was Joe E. Brown. This vehicle rescued him from deepening oblivion in burlesque and propelled him into legitimate theater and, later, movies. He had been half of the vaudeville team Provost and Brown for years. After Provost retired, Brown landed lowly comedy roles in burlesque before John Cort spotted him for *Jim Jam Jems.* *Weekly Variety* acknowledged that Brown had one of the "funniest looking 'pan[s]' ever hung on a comic. As a butler he was the real life of the party, using a sort of delayed pass system of talking—opening his mouth widely, then uttering the sounds." A homely face and big mouth would become Joe E. Brown's trademarks in more than fifty films.

Langdon delivered his breakaway auto in the first act of *Jim Jam Jems*, with Rose ("Miss Taken") and her sister Cecil in their roles as helpers and hecklers. For the remainder of the show, Harry performed without his partners. *Weekly Variety* called him "a comic joy in the first act with his auto scene. . . . It looked like a new version of the act as seen in vaudeville. For the rest of the evening, Langdon had to be content with bits, but he rarely came on without delivering a laugh." The *New York Times*, however, coolly remarked that *Jim Jam Jems* was simply a "setting of a soubrette [Ada Mae Weeks] in a leading role." The review found the lyrics "commonplace" and observed that the piece suffered from a "superabundance of comedians and a lack of wit." Jazz and fox-trot permeated the show, and the Langdons were "another 'team'" that made *Jim Jam Jems* "a very full if not particularly inspiring evening."

Unlike his 1902 stint in *The Show Girl* as part of the road company, Langdon was now appearing in an original, legitimate theater production. This Broadway credit boosted his position among vaudeville booking managers in subsequent seasons. As he continued to tour with his act, Langdon's chances of being discovered by the film industry were increasing. But vaudeville was dying out, and soon even the history of a solid Langdon act would no longer assure permanence on the stage. It was inevitable: Harry was going to lose his niche and would have to find a new one.

The next three years were a continuous replay of Harry's car and golf routines. The short skit was divided into three scenes: "In the Ruff," introducing the characters and situation; "Treated Ruff," presenting shenanigans at the clubhouse; and "Ruff Riding," culminating in the car catastrophe. The advertisements for Langdon's shows were often specifically addressed to "autoists," "automobilists," and golfers, and they promised an act that was sure to entertain as well as instruct. One ad from a Philadelphia newspaper exclaimed:

> Do You Drive Your Own Car? Do You Play Golf?
> See Harry Langdon at B. F. Keith's Theatre.
> Learn What Not to Do!
> You Never Saw the Kind of Golf He Plays!
> He Tells You What to Say to the Motor Cop!
> Greatest Comedy of the Year![23]

Harry (*second from left*)—a serious golfer—on the links with his buddies.

Harry also became a bit of a spokesman for his favorite sport, sharing his views of golf in articles such as "All Nation Taking to Golf" from 1921. He observed that the game had become so popular that he could hardly get into the links to play. Lest anyone consider it a child's game, though, Harry defended it as having the great benefit of "strenuous exercise." He announced, "If golf has one blessing to confer on the nation, it is this—red corpuscles." Sharing his humorous and quaintly phrased philosophy of life and work with the public would become a mainstay throughout Langdon's career.

Langdon usually had high billing on programs featuring a panoply of acts that ranged from the classy to the corny, offering something for everyone. Advertisements often listed the roster of performers so audiences knew what to expect. There was Vincent O'Donnell, billed as the "miniature McCormack," who was a knickerbocker-clad boy with a sublime vocal range. The Four Casting Mellos provided aerial surprises, while the Eight Blue Devils juggled umbrellas, balls, and saucers and balanced all the members of their troupe on one bicycle. The renowned Olsen and Johnson

Top: Langdon's caricatures of "After the Ball." His fellow performers on the bill included the Eight Blue Devils (*Houston Evening Post,* October 31, 1922). *Bottom:* A sketch of Langdon's car skit at the Majestic (*Houston Evening Post,* November 8, 1922).

sometimes appeared on programs with their snappy wit and songs, while Ruth Roye, the "queen of syncopation," rendered the day's popular "coon songs" and jazz numbers and Eddie Leonard burst out with his famous song "Ida, Sweet as Apple Cider" while performing in blackface as America's greatest minstrel.[24] Short skits often included original scripts set in exotic locations depicted by evocative backdrops and props, and even short films made their way onto the programs, including one mentioned on Harry's bill for "Aesop's Film Fables." There was such a diverse menu that audience members often chose which acts they wanted to see and departed soon thereafter, leaving the last acts on the bill to play to a near-empty house.

The Langdons were also part of the festivities celebrating B. F. Keith's "Third of a Century Anniversary." An elegant blue-linen program proudly chronicled the timeline of one of the country's most famous vaudeville circuits since its founding in 1887: beginning as a "store show" with only six performers, it built a small theater with 382 seats for $32,000; by 1921–1922, the seating capacity in all of B. F. Keith's theaters totaled 1,406,262, and it had invested $3.8 million to build its newest theater in Cleveland. Langdon was one of a steady group of performers in this golden age of vaudeville—a reality that was often forgotten once his film career eclipsed his stage work.

In retrospect, Harry's refinement as a stage performer led to the character that would become his film persona. At the time, however, his golfer-driver-comic character was busy adapting to both his daily routines and his live audiences. There was no denying that, in the process, Harry had devised a unique persona, and certain theatrical reviews of the early 1920s were prescient in highlighting some of the traits that would become the foundation for his screen character. For instance, on October 5, 1920, a reviewer for the *Herald Tribune* remarked, "Harry Langdon, with this trick automobile and his 'vacant stare,' brings a bit of vaudeville's very best into a new realm." A reviewer in Memphis noted that Langdon could stand onstage without uttering a word and cause an uproar in the audience. The *Boston Herald* praised Langdon for blazing "his own trail as to method. He knows the value of repose; he speaks without talking and in the art of pantomime he excels." To these astute reviewers, it seemed that even from the stage, Langdon's facial expressions and subtle mime—which would become his most valuable trademarks—stood out as key elements of his comedy. Harry's "discovery" of what made his kid brothers laugh back in his Council Bluffs "home theater" stayed with him, and he used it to his advantage. According to one newspaper article, Langdon even worked a miracle with an elderly resident of Council Bluffs and, coincidentally, a longtime neighbor of the Langdons. Mrs. Eliza Fields had never been to the theater because her mother had warned her it was evil. But as she told the reporter, she had decided to see a show for the first time at age seventy-nine because there must be some good in the theater if Harry Langdon was in it. She had no reaction to any of the acts on the Orpheum bill that day, but when Langdon and "his nut auto" appeared onstage, Mrs. Fields finally smiled.

Langdon's face must have been an extraordinary vision onstage without the benefit of a camera to magnify its expression: deadpan stare, pursed lips, wide, childlike eyes darting to and fro, and makeup that filled his countenance with otherworldly radiance. Harry's ill-fitting hats and oversized clothes directed the audience to study his face as the only anchor in this odd swirling mix. Even to those in the most remote balcony seats, the blanched face bobbing about in a mess of clothes, pieces of car, and shrewish passengers evoked humor and sympathy simultaneously. Harry's was an unusual scenario, but even more so, he had created a fantasy character that felt human to the core.

After a quarter century of honing his act, Harry's alter ego was on the brink of achieving the refinement and delicacy that the camera lens would demand. In 1923 Harry's car would make its final detour to a destination that was the unexpected culmination of his childhood dreams.

2

Golden Silence

Motion pictures were about a year old when Harry first ran off with a medicine show. The "flickers" were shown by enterprising carnival showmen in tents or by traveling exhibitors in rented halls. These curious optical illusions were initially less than a minute long and depicted segments of real life—people walking to stores or leaving factories, ocean waves crashing on the beach, parades. These visions cast on an impromptu screen, often just a suspended bedsheet, were a novelty that would have worn off in time had not undaunted experimenters and luck collaborated on the idea of motion pictures as entertainment.

By the end of the nineteenth century, a stage magician in France, Georges Méliès, was using film to create effects beyond reality. He not only launched a rocket to the moon in his short film *La Voyage dans la Lune* (*A Trip to the Moon*, 1902) but also gave the adventure a story line. In America, as Harry was steering his way through "Johnny's New Car" for the fourth season, *The Great Train Robbery* (1903) contributed one of film's first fictional plots, mixing suspense, humor, and excitement through rudimentary crosscutting. Soon, the primitive illusions incorporated continuity as an ingredient in narration, and audiences began to take notice. Movies were no longer curious *réalités* but outlets of fantasy, drama, adventure, comedy, and romance.

As the Langdons toured with their act, filmed entertainment prospered. Inevitably, this had consequences for vaudeville, which until that point had been the most popular form of entertainment. A few wary vaudeville houses included ten-minute films as part of their programs, initially only on special occasions and then on a regular basis. Story-framed movies became vehicles for even mediocre theatrical or vaudeville personalities. As both the decade and the new industry progressed, these once anonymous actors began to publicize their names, either onscreen or behind the scenes. The first was the "Biograph Girl"—Florence Lawrence—who paved the way for movie stars to be fully credited by name. From 1908 on, small-time actor D. W. Griffith was recognized as the day's most respected, albeit controversial, director, with an impressive roster of short films and longer features that used daring techniques and covered bold topics. By 1912, a Canadian boilermaker, Mack Sennett, was known as the creator of the Keystone Kops and their feminine counterparts, the Bathing Beauties; he had organized his own comedy studio by 1917. By the mid-1910s, Dorothy and Lillian Gish, Mary Pickford, and Mabel Normand had all achieved more fame and money in motion pictures than vaudeville headliners dreamed possible. A virtually unknown Charlie Chaplin came to American vaudeville from British music halls in 1914 and was earning a million tax-free dollars a year by 1916.

Vaudeville became an endangered species in large part because of motion pictures. Numerous vaudeville houses were closed down and refurbished as movie theaters or eventually palaces. Other showcases were built especially to screen films. At a fraction of the cost for live actors and orchestras, a film exhibitor could book thrills that were re-created onscreen much more realistically than they could be onstage. By charging a nickel or a dime per patron for multiple daily showings, he could earn more than he would in a vaudeville house charging a dollar a seat.

Perhaps film's most dramatic and dynamic impact on audiences was how the camera positioned the spectators within the action. One of the earliest accounts of an audience's visceral response to film followed the premiere of *A Rough Sea at Dover,* a thirty-nine-second British film by Birt Acres and Robert W. Paul that was included in the program at New York City's Koster and Bial's Music Hall on April 23, 1896. A reviewer for the *Dramatic Mirror* observed, "Wave after wave came tumbling on the sand, and as they struck, broke into tiny floods just like the real thing. Some of the people in the front rows seemed to be afraid they were going to get wet, and looked about to see where they could run to, in case the waves came too close."[1]

Vaudevillians, including the Langdons, gradually felt the impact of film. Some chose to ignore it and believed there would always be an audience for live vaudeville. Some vehemently opposed the "flickers" as an affront to their theatrical artistry (pratfalls and dancing dogs notwithstanding). Legitimate actors derided film's flat, artificial representation of life as a passing fad. Joe Keaton, patriarch of the celebrated roughhouse vaudeville act the Three Keatons (starring son Buster), declared the new medium an insult to an act perfected on the stage. He spurned William Randolph Hearst's offer to have the Three Keatons portray the *Bringing up Father* comic strip on film, claiming that their work was too good to be shown for a nickel on a dirty bedsheet.[2] Many steadfast holdouts against the new medium were reduced to burlesque—not the razzle-dazzle revue of theater parody it was in its heyday but a dreary succession of strippers and raunchy comedians. More often, however, the temptation to appear before the camera—and the generous offers from prospering film studios—proved too alluring for both theater luminaries such as Sarah Bernhardt and Enrico Caruso and relative unknowns such as Chaplin and Roscoe "Fatty" Arbuckle of American burlesque. Regardless of whether their work translated successfully from stage to celluloid, the movies' tantalizing appeal and lucrative promise were overreaching the attraction of vaudeville.

In addition to achieving wealth and fame was the possibility of settling down in a real home with high-class accessories—no more wandering from one small town to another and living out of trunks. After more than twenty years on the road, Rose Langdon considered these to be attractive incentives to turn to the movies. With Tully acting as agent, she arranged for influential producers to see "Johnny's New Car," hoping that Harry could sell the act as potential movie material. As for Rose, she would have settled for the role of housewife, maybe even mother. At the age of forty, she knew the opportunity to play young leading ladies would dissolve before the relentless eye of the camera. As Rose was not amenable to playing character roles (that is, older women), she voluntarily resigned from show business. As long as Harry could still benefit from its rewards, Rose was content.

Harry also toyed with the prospects of film work. He knew the formula for success in comedy but recognized the vast distinction between a theater audience, which a wise performer could mold to his routine by picking up their cues, and a movie audience, which was watching the actor "after the fact." Langdon once reflected that vaudeville allowed the performer to feel an audience's reaction and spontaneously adjust his act accordingly, whereas film was a done deed, made without any clear sense of the audience's response to clue the actor into the real impact of a gag. Langdon would later find, to his surprise, that even audience previews, intended to provide helpful feedback on what worked and what did not, were hardly foolproof.

Hillstreet Theatre, where Langdon was "discovered."

In truth, buoyed by the sturdiness and longevity of his routines, two-plus decades of live performing were exhausting, especially as Langdon was carrying the whole act on his own, absent a more balanced split among his teammates. Moreover, he was tired of the repetitive monotony and arduous traveling. If he ever felt the urge to rein in his wanderlust, this was the moment. He even contemplated opening a scenic studio, but dabbling in art would have been merely a respite that recharged his battery for performing—as it had when Harry was a boy—and eventually he would have sought another audience to entertain.

The scenario that officially moved Langdon from stage to film is somewhat confused and incomplete. Certainly a number of important people in the film industry saw his vaudeville routine before his final performances in March 1923 at the Hillstreet Theatre at the corner of Hill and Eighth Streets in Los Angeles. Comedy star Harold Lloyd claimed that he "discovered" Harry Langdon in 1923 for producer Mack Sennett. Lloyd may have seen Langdon onstage at some point, for all comedians attended vaudeville shows to gauge audience reactions. According to one report, Hal Roach was with Lloyd when he saw Langdon.[3] However, the likeliest scenario is that theater owner and producer Sol Lesser caught Langdon's act at someone else's suggestion or on his own at the Hillstreet Theatre and recognized Harry's potential.

Lesser found that Harry was willing to talk business and offered him $250 a week to appear in short films for Principal Pictures. Harry accepted in the last week of March 1923. A press release titled "Vaudeville Star Enters Movies" revealed the deal:

> Harry Langdon, one of Vaudeville's most popular comedy head-liners, has closed his footlight career and begun his picture work at Principal Pictures Corporation's studios in Hollywood.
>
> His contract covers several years and calls for six feature comedies a year, two-reel length. Principal Pictures has gathered together the cream of the silent comedy field to support Langdon, and one of the best comedy directors in the business will be engaged.
>
> Work on Langdon's initial story is being rushed while the comedian is studying the mysteries of movie make-up.[4]

In a slightly different version, the *Exhibitor's Herald* announced on July 7, 1923, that Principal had contracted Langdon for twelve two-reel feature comedies and that the first would be "an aeroplane story written by Langdon."

Lesser assigned the job of directing Langdon to Alf Goulding, a journeyman with a long but undistinguished career in short comedy films. As the first test project at Principal, Harry's car routine was filmed. Unfortunately, when Lesser saw the finished product in the projection room, he found the act lacked the audience appeal he had detected in the theater. Ironically, after keeping Harry afloat for so long and introducing him to motion pictures, the legendary breakaway car routine never saw the light of the big screen.

Typical of many conversions from stage to screen, the vaudeville routine had fallen flat. No one connected with the project—not even Harry—understood why the act worked onstage but failed onscreen. Clearly, the dimensionality of the stage and live action was missing, and Harry himself may have lost something in the translation. As Langdon later articulated in his "philosophy" of comedy, without the barometer of a live audience, his pacing may have become stilted and aimless.

Test shots for Sol Lesser.

Lesser was alarmed that his new investment was proving to be unfunny. Primarily a businessman who was unfamiliar with the nuances of comedy, Lesser sought to cut his losses. He thought of Mack Sennett, with whom he had concluded a successful deal: Lesser had rented Sennett's Bathing Beauties to travel with his 1919 wartime exploitation picture *Yankee Doodle in Berlin* in order to attract paying customers. Lesser showed *Harry's New Car* to Sennett and, anxious to unload what he thought was a lemon in more ways than one, informed Sennett that he was willing to sell Langdon's contract at a low price.[5] Sennett could never resist a bargain; moreover, he had an instinct, unlike the practical and nervous Lesser, that the little guy in the breakaway car could add something to his comedy films. The Principal Pictures contract, which ultimately stipulated ten two-reel shorts at $250 a week and provided for raises up to $1,000 plus 10 percent of the profits, was never completed. Only the filmed version of the car routine and two other shorts, *Horace Greeley Jr.* and *The White Wing's Bride,* were shot in the spring and early summer before Langdon's contract was sold to the Sennett studio.[6] One film, which underwent several title changes during the course of production, was announced in the *Exhibitor's Herald* as *The Skyscraper.*[7]

A curious article in the September 15, 1923, edition of the periodical

Camera, entitled "Langdon Brings Famous Coat to Screen," was one of the first to focus on Harry's use of props to accessorize his persona. The item in question was in fact a carryover from his vaudeville days: a triangular-shaped overcoat that he had worn in his stage routine. For the reporter, this coat had the potential to become an iconic symbol of Langdon's blossoming character, similar to Charlie Chaplin's cane, Harold Lloyd's glasses, and the checkered cap of another popular comedian of the time, Lloyd Hamilton. The reporter noted Harry's "slight advantage over his brother stage comedians"—namely, his work as a cartoonist, which had equipped him to recognize what was visually funny. Because a cartoonist is limited to drawing lines to convey the essence of humor, Harry understood that small details onstage can evoke and support laughs. For his stage work, he had used the overcoat, with just the right pleats, folds, and girth, to tap the audience's urge to laugh beyond any reasoning. The seeds had been planted for Harry to consider—if not explain—the nuances that would add depth to his comedy.

Despite the publicity, these initial film experiments were never released to the public because Sennett wanted his own films to be Langdon's first. The deal was closed in the fall of 1923, and Harry Langdon became a member of Sennett's troupe. According to his original contract with Mack Sennett Comedies, witnessed and notated by Sennett's general manager J. A. Waldron, Langdon was to start on November 5, 1923. Waldron's handwritten notes stipulated that Langdon was to be billed individually and in large type on the screen as "Principal Comedian in each picture" and that "no other Comic [would] play [a] principal part." According to these notes, Sennett offered Langdon $750 a week for two pictures, with periodic options and salary increases up to $2,000. These incredible terms were arranged before Langdon had even stepped onto the Sennett lot.[8]

About a month after the Sennett-Langdon contract was signed, the *Los Angeles Morning Telegraph* announced on December 20, 1923, that Sennett had found a new comedian with the "potentialities of a Chaplin." This was a clear statement—even a subtle jab—that Sennett was profiting indirectly from Chaplin's "Tramp" character and his increasing fame. The parallel between Chaplin and Langdon was both accurate and a rueful reminder that Sennett had lost Chaplin as his star and could now only watch him move on to greater accomplishments without him. By this time, Chaplin had made a long string of successful short films, and his first feature with First National, *The Kid*—for which he was director, producer, writer, editor, and star—was the second-highest-grossing film in 1921. Perhaps "discovering" Langdon was Sennett's opportunity to mold a new star to replace the one that got away.

In his 1960 autobiography *King of Comedy*, Sennett drew blatant comparisons between the two comedians: "Like Charlie Chaplin, you had to let [Langdon] take his time and go through the motions," he wrote. "I thought for a while Langdon was as good as Chaplin. In some of his pathetic scenes he was certainly as good." Sennett observed, "On screen he resembled Chaplin in one kind of appeal. He was always the small figure of frustrated good will beset and bewildered by a cruel world of hard rules and economics." Sennett even acknowledged the need to milk Langdon's unique charisma by calling him, ironically, "as bland as milk, a forgiving small cuss, an obedient puppy, always in the way, exasperating, but offering the baby mannerisms with hopeful apology."[9] Despite the many parallels, there was one key difference between the two comedians, as noted by Sennett and many others: Chaplin was ultimately an adult, while Langdon remained childlike in both his demeanor and his thinking. Nevertheless, Sennett's analysis of Langdon's persona was articulated in hindsight. It would take time for Sennett and his creative team to even understand what Langdon's onscreen character would be, as his enigmatic qualities as a stage performer were not easily translated to the new medium.

Interestingly, Langdon himself attributed his "discovery" to Mack Sennett. Although the details differed, the truth was that their association propelled Langdon to film stardom. In his memory of the story (which aligned with Harold Lloyd's later version[10]), Langdon suggested that he had not even considered film work, although it held some appeal to him. Apparently, Sennett had been in the audience at the Orpheum one night and visited Langdon in his dressing room afterward to talk terms: $150 a week to make two-reel film comedies. Langdon agreed to consider the proposal, even though he was earning much more in vaudeville. But for Sennett, it was a take-it-or-leave-it offer. Despite feeling that the move might be a mistake financially, Langdon took the risk, left vaudeville, and signed up with Sennett. As Langdon saw it, he was taking a step backward to run forward to greater success. Langdon vowed to himself that if he had not made a "dent in Hollywood's surface" within one year, he would move out. By the end of that time, however, Harry Langdon's "step back" had put him on a beeline to a lucrative contract that launched a new career as one of the most esoteric comedians to come out of the Sennett laugh factory.

Langdon's first starring film vehicle for Sennett was *Picking Peaches*. Production started in the fall of 1923 under the working titles *Trifling* and *A Ribbon Clerk's Romance,* and the short was released in February 1924. It was an encouraging start to a new year and a new career, for the Sennett organization spared little to make the film a hit. The twenty-minute short is packed with fast action, several changes of locale, thrill gags, a bedroom mix-up, and Sennett trademarks—a climactic madcap chase and the Bathing Beauties. For this first role, Harry plays an incorrigible flirt who has an eye for every walking skirt, including his wife's best friend.

As much as Harry's character, the roaming husband, is meant to align with the film's typical slapstick, he adds glimpses of unusual sophistication and subtlety to an otherwise frenzied comedy. Harry's expressive eyes become the center of attention in the midst of chaos and disaster, shifting slowly to reveal a range of emotions that, up to that point, other Sennett protagonists had stressed only by exaggeration. Thanks to the camera, for the first time the focus can be on Harry's subtleties. The camera brings him close to his audience, and the view is revealing. Distance between audience and star is bridged, and Harry's broad pantomime, which was necessary for the stage, is pared down to underacting for the camera. Harry's eyes remain the barometer for the film's comedic climate, acting as subtle commentators on each situation. Perceptive newspaper reviewers had discerned this trait during Harry's stage performances, and it was a feature Harry knew how to exploit. It would become a routine: once his eyes spoke, his body reacted accordingly to orchestrate the uncanny number of meanings behind the look. His eye "acting" was so valuable to his work that an item in the *Post Enquirer* reported that the comedian had insured his "eloquent orbs" for $50,000 in case "Langdon's eyes lose their 'voice.'"

Picking Peaches documents the genesis of an iconic film character. During one scene, a strong contrast is established between a typical Sennett character and Harry's hero. The bathing-suit contest emcee, a Sennett stereotype, leers at the models and gawkily pinches one girl until he is stopped by a strategically placed umbrella. He emotes and smooths his mustache—a blatant villain. By contrast, Harry conveys the same wishful thinking as the emcee when eying the models, yet without wild gesticula-

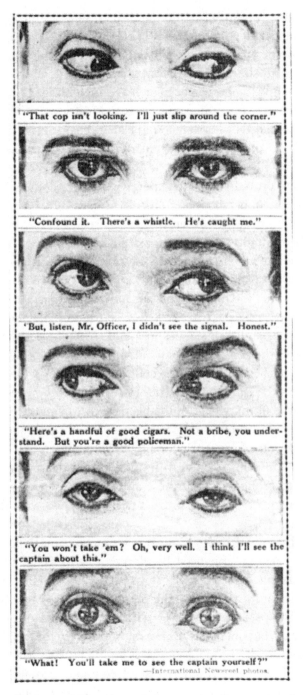

Clipping of Harry's ocular repertoire (International
Newsreel photo).

tions; he registers both infatuation and the disappointment of rejection with looks and slight gestures. Harry injects an unexpected layer of feeling that a stereotype cannot evoke. *Picking Peaches* is thus decorated with nuances of surprising expressiveness. Harry's pace is unhurried but not languorous; it adds a new perspective to a Sennett film populated by character types who are fluent in comic spills and histrionics. The "Old Man," as Sennett was called by his staff, found Harry's characteristics fascinating, even though he knew his own formula for success depended on stereotypes bounding through space.

Perhaps to prove that Sennett knew what he was doing when he hired Langdon—even if he did not fully realize why—*Picking Peaches* was launched with a variety of expensive process sequences involving animation, which the tightfisted Sennett did not normally use. In one scene, Harry feels an attack of jealousy upon thinking that his wife (played by Alberta Vaughn) is unfaithful, and his sympathetic face transforms into one of outrage; to prod him along, a cartoon devil with a pitchfork appears on his shoulder. As Harry runs offscreen spurred by the devil, the figure falls to the floor and disintegrates in a puff of smoke. In another scene, Harry hides in the bed of a woman he thinks is his wife (but is not), and the woman's husband lies down and puts his arm around the person next to him, whom he thinks is his wife. Harry's incredulous eyes peer out from above the framing edge of the blanket, conveying sheer dread. The husband not only conjures up a cartoon question mark above his head but also confronts Harry with a look that could kill: on cue, a procession of small cartoon daggers flows from his eyes into Harry's. Subtlety was not a Sennett strongpoint, but these animated sequences prove that he thought enough of Langdon to celebrate his arrival with these costly embellishments.

Even substandard Sennett gags that were mechanical in the hands of lesser comedians are enhanced by Harry's treatment. In the breakfast scene, for example, he accidentally stuffs his mouth with his wife's powder puff, mistaking it for a flapjack. The mistake is reduced to a typical slapstick gag with special effects as Harry emits a stream of powder from mouth *and* ears, but not before his eyes subtly react to the fact that what he is eating is not food. Without gagging or rolling his eyes, Harry displays a naïve face baffled by a situation that is indeed tough to swallow.

To make the plot a proper Sennett brew, the department store where Harry works is holding a swimsuit competition on the beach, starring

Langdon surrounded by Bathing Beauties.

none other than the Bathing Beauties—the Old Man's excuse to fill his films with pretty girls cavorting in 1920s beachwear. Via film editing, Harry does a quick change at the seashore: he walks into the water and emerges a few seconds later in a bathing suit and a little cloth hat. Next, an ice cream gag turns from typical slapstick to a special Langdon episode. Having dropped his ice cream on a girl's back, he scoops it into the cone again and then shares it with her; they exchange mischievous slaps before Harry wipes the ice cream almost tenderly from their mouths and contentedly hugs her. His lingering action is far from romantic poetry, but it is an unexpected innovation to standard slapstick fare.

Cutaways introduce a series of comic coincidences between Harry, his wife, the other woman, and her husband. The confusion is neatly capped with a standard Sennett car chase sequence. However, Harry always remains the star and contributes surprising scenes that are respites from the usual slapstick panic. For example, Harry arrives at the store manager's apartment, where he sees telling silhouettes on the shade and hears a woman scream—the landlady has accidentally locked herself in the bathroom with a mouse. Harry bursts in, desensitizes the manager with a table, and breaks into the bathroom, where the mania is briefly laid to rest with a curious Langdon touch. The woman aims a few slaps at Harry: the first slap is well targeted; with the second slap, Harry ducks and sits on the tub, hand to mouth and wide eyes looking woebegone; when he stands, the woman attempts a third slap and spins herself directly into the tub. The variation on the second slap is a glimpse into Harry's calm, little-boy approach to perplexity. This gesture is later balanced by the sequence in which Harry suffers the menacing daggers from the husband; to cap off the sequence, Harry escapes, but not before giving the enraged husband's giant hand a "naughty-boy" slap.

For all his meanderings, Harry winds up in a hospital, bruised and bandaged, accompanied by his faithful spouse. Harry's eyes, though, spot a pretty nurse, and through a clever film transition, he imagines her uniform dissolving into a bathing suit. There is no further need for titles or even action, for Harry in a medium shot encapsulates all his thoughts in a few seconds of eye work. He feasts on the vision, yet the shine in his eyes melts into apprehension and guilt as he recalls both his wife and his broken arm. His eyes move through degrees of emotion in a matter of frames. He kisses his wife, who hauls him away, but his eyes engage in a postscript flicker that has not, despite all his disasters, vanished.

The pure Langdon moments are evident but brief, and except for them, any energetic Sennett recruit could have exercised the paces of the film. But Langdon owns this film in a unique way and adds a special comic tranquility to the slapstick. His style is not yet defined, but it is recognizably different—almost misplaced—in a Sennett comedy.

While making *Picking Peaches,* Harry formed a friendship that would last for the rest of his life. Vernon Dent, who played the store manager, was rugged and muscular and tended toward corpulence, yet he was decisive and graceful, like many overweight comedians of the day. Dent complemented Harry's pale, fragile frame in the tradition of other comedy duos such as John Bunny with Flora Finch, Roscoe "Fatty" Arbuckle and later Joe Roberts with Buster Keaton, and Oliver Hardy with Stan Laurel (decades later, Hardy and Langdon would team up briefly as a duo).

Vernon Dent was born on February 16, 1896, in San Jose, California, where his family owned prune and apricot orchards. His childhood was a difficult one, however, for his mother died when he was thirteen, and his father was killed by an irate husband. Dent drifted into show business after serving in the navy during World War I. He had a pleasing baritone voice and enjoyed harmonizing in a barbershop quartet while in the service. After his discharge, he joined a couple of friends on a singing trip. They played the Jewel City Café in Seal Beach, which was frequented by many people in the film industry. There, Dent was spotted by Hank Mann, one of Sennett's original Keystone Kops. Mann was starring in comedies at the time and engaged Dent as his second banana; Dent subsequently became a comedy heavy for actor (later director) Thomas Ince and finally joined the Sennett ranks. He played a foil for many Sennett comics, including Andy Clyde, Billy Bevan, and Chester Conklin, before being assigned to *Picking Peaches*. Langdon later said that Vernon resembled old Dutch Schultz from his medicine show days. In any case, the two men shared a chemistry and a gentle camaraderie, both onscreen and off, that connected them from the outset.[11]

Picking Peaches was directed by Erle Kenton, a ten-year veteran in the Sennett fold who had worked his way up from prop boy and bit actor and had several feature films to his credit. *Picking Peaches* was released with an intensive publicity campaign in both trade journals and fan magazines. Some enthused exhibitors remarked that this was the type of comedy they wanted for their patrons, who left the theaters smiling. Among the general raves for the film, an ad for *Picking Peaches* boasted that Langdon had brought two big assets with him from vaudeville: personality and popularity. *Picking Peaches* was, in short, "a great little picture comedy" and possessed all the elements of success. According to a press release, Langdon's success was almost guaranteed, as "Sennett goes so far as to say, 'he is Chaplin's equal.' Who should know better?"[12]

In one year, Harry's car had become an artifact of the past, and Harry Langdon had become a film star. His new "routine"—a slower-paced expressiveness conveyed by face and body instead of props—would be the foundation for his film comedy. Langdon was now being afforded the privileges of a veritable movie star, including an impressive salary, positive reviews, and fans' curiosity about his thoughts on filmmaking. His "voice"—whether of his own creation or molded by a publicity department—began to spout an offbeat, tongue-in-cheek philosophy of work and life, a strange hybrid of deep thinker and country bumpkin. This press release from December 1923 provides a hint of what was to come:

Hard work never hurts anyone, especially a young kid. Hard luck and a few bumps are an aid to knowledge in later years. A silver spoon should never be forced between the lips of a child, nor should a parent interfere with the wishes of its offspring, even if it craves matches or dynamite as its toys.

"Them's my sentiments," says Harry Langdon, new star of the Mack Sennett comedy forces, who has recently signed to a long and much-to-be-envied contract to appear in a special series of feature comedies.[13]

Tried-and-true Sennett formulas would be rehashed as new vehicles for the rising star and potential moneymaker. The camera lens would continue to scrutinize Harry Langdon, who was simply expected to produce the best.

Langdon was churning out a twenty-minute two-reeler every month for Sennett. To facilitate theatrical bookings, distributors preferred program fillers, such as two-reel comedies, to run between features, usually one per month from a given performer. This was the practice at Pathé Film Exchange, with which Sennett was associated from 1923 until the end of the silent era in 1928.

Following *Picking Peaches* was the March 1924 release *Smile, Please.* Ironically, any hint of the promising gentleness Harry exhibited through the slapstick of his first film was nearly annihilated in this short. Composed of two entirely unequal halves, neither gave Harry the opportunity to experiment with his brand of comedy. The film seems to be a compromise between two opposing factions on the Sennett lot—one that wanted a plot-driven story, and the other that preferred a static vaudeville routine on film. The director was Roy Del Ruth, who had joined Sennett in 1915; he wrote gags, prepared story outlines, and by 1917 had become a proficient director. This short also includes a cryptic credit line listing a "supervising director," which might explain the clash between the halves. This person was F. Richard Jones, Sennett's power behind the throne.

Langdon himself may have volunteered the vaudeville routine that makes up the first half of the film, which takes place in a photography studio. After all, for twenty years the stage had been his home. Sennett, for economic reasons (which were always crucial to him), may have decided that this full-reel routine could later be appliquéd onto another story line on some other reel. This practice of joining reels that were not made for each other seldom created a coherent two-reeler, but at least it did not waste any film, from Sennett's point of view.

In the first reel of *Smile, Please,* Harry plays a small-town photographer who doubles as the sheriff. His girlfriend is portrayed by Alberta Vaughn again, and his rival for her affections is Jack Cooper, one of the best supporting comedians on the Sennett lot. With Vernon Dent in *Picking Peaches* and now Cooper, Sennett may have been searching for a compatible partner for his rising star. The reel-length sketch is filled with clichéd gags centered around a photography session with a family posing stiffly before a huge box camera. Their delinquent toddler clambers into everything, including the camera, which becomes as much of a temperamental prop for Harry as his collapsible car had been. For example, the tripod caves in at inconvenient moments, a skunk noses into the camera box, and a beehive somehow finds its way into Harry's roomy trousers. Much of this business is, unfortunately, crude fakery that restrains Harry from taking advantage of his slow-paced, nuanced style. For example, in one gag, Harry sneezes and the entire rug rises from the floor and covers the family. In another gag, Harry crosses wires and electrifies the clan; in a particularly grisly scene, a bulb lights up in the patriarch's hand, with sparks spewing from his head and feet. A majority of the gags are physically impossible in "reality," and the use of suspension wires, reverse film, and process shots is painfully obvious, detracting from Harry's natural comic flair.

Still, most audiences liked the overt trickery. Moviegoers were engaged in the process of watching solidly established comedians like Charlie Chaplin graduate from crude slapstick to measurably superior gags constructed with ballet-like precision in his later films such as *Shoulder Arms* (1918), *The Kid* (1921), and *The Pilgrim* (1923). These films emphasized plot continuity, subtle mannerisms, and even emotional touches to convey an unexpectedly dimensional comedy with pathos. Harold Lloyd, another king of comedy of the mid-1920s and a former disciple of the Hal Roach studio, had shown audiences carefully developed thrill scenes in *Never Weaken* (1921), *Why Worry?* (1923), and *Safety Last* (1923). Buster Keaton, a perfectionist who had apprenticed under Fatty Arbuckle, one of Chaplin's competitors, also planted his indelible mark on the screen, despite his father's earlier protests that performing in film was an insult to stage actors. Keaton had already starred in a two-year series of short comedies under his own banner, Buster Keaton Productions. The sometimes visually bizarre and consistently intriguing gags were always performed in full view of the camera, and Keaton was well known for executing his strenuous, occasionally life-threatening stunts to drive home the "reality" of many absurd situations. When Langdon began working in film, Keaton was making feature comedies in which all the funny business was narratively motivated and carefully staged within a developed plotline. Almost as a challenge to the laughter, Keaton sometimes bordered on the intellectually tantalizing, far removed from his vaudeville and slapstick heritage.

In *Smile, Please,* however, laughs are derived from the elementary malicious pleasure of watching Harry suffer indignities and physical discomfort. One exhibitor implied that this malicious pleasure was an important criterion for successful comedy, noting how much his audiences laughed because of it. As for the skunk sequence—also involving the family dog, which holds its nose with its paws and faints, and a goat that inhales with disgust—the exhibitor remarked, "In the contest of odors the skunk defeated the goat by a wide margin." Some audiences clearly did not need much more than a skunk or two to feel they got their admission's worth.

While Harry does not play second banana to this menagerie, his mime talents lack an adequate showcase. Shaving off the thick layers of gimmickry, a perceptive audience might have recognized some Langdonisms, not only in the photography sketch but also when the short lurches into its disjointed second half. Harry executes a sturdy, slow-paced faint in reaction to the skunk and drags his camera down with him into an overpowered heap. A little Langdon also shines through during the high point of the routine when the woman tries to whack her husband. Harry quickly uses this situation to deliver a belated punishment to the annoying toddler by holding him in such a way that the child receives the whacks instead of the husband. With suppressed delight, Harry even smooths the kid's knickers to prepare for the spanking. Knowing that he is not meting out this punishment himself, Harry smiles beatifically, feeling compensated for his indignities. He is even generous enough to kiss the child in between the whacks.

The second half of the film is much looser, in contrast to the more confined location and feel of the photography session. Harry, who is about to be married, turns a gag into a gem of individuality by appearing before the minister with unusually broad shoulders; as he turns, he reveals that he has neglected to remove the hanger from his jacket. To keep from distracting the minister in a two-shot, Harry inches the hanger out but assumes an innocent pose each time the minister turns toward him. Later, during the inevitable chase scene, Harry holds his own against the racing dioramas of fake background landscapes, with an occasional indulgence in a frantic slapstick reaction. Contrasting the prominent slapstick found in many comedies of the time (especially Sennett's) with Langdon's more subdued mannerisms does not deny the success of one over the other. But recognizing this contrast acknowledges the gradual evolution of silent comedy as it integrated subtleties and narrative cohesion into two-reel films. This time of experimentation—presenting comic situations through the physical and eventually through the emotional and even intellectual—transformed caricatures and types into full-fledged protagonists in the hands of Chaplin, Keaton, Lloyd, and soon, albeit briefly, Langdon.

Sennett held off releasing *Smile, Please,* even though it had been filmed before *Picking Peaches.* The Old Man was shrewd: he realized that in *Smile, Please* Langdon was too immersed in Sennett's brand of comedy to exhibit his own unique style. Although broad slapstick was Sennett's default in filmmaking, he may have wanted to introduce Langdon's idiosyncratic comic mannerisms without interruption to test the reactions of audiences and critics.

The releases over the next few months alternated between Sennett's slapstick and Langdon's more leisurely style. Although these films received mixed reviews, the consensus on Harry Langdon was that he was a success, a special comedian. He was not yet being publicly compared with any screen contemporaries (although the Chaplin connection was never far from Sennett's mind), but he was singled out as worthy of attention. "Harry sure pleases and gets the laughs" was a good reaction for any veteran vaudevillian breaking into a new medium.

Shanghaied Lovers, a March 1924 release, was directed by Roy Del Ruth and featured Andy Clyde as the supporting comic for Langdon. His leading lady was Alice Day, who became Harry's regular partner for five films in a row, switching roles between wife and sweetheart. Harry himself would alternate between playing a married man in hot water with his wife and a single man trying to attain wedded bliss. In this film, Harry is a newlywed. Through a logistical mix-up, the couple lands on a ship belonging to an unscrupulous general from a small Latin American republic who is seeking to overthrow that government. The general forces Harry and Alice to sail with him to prevent them from divulging his plans, but they manage to elude him.

Harry on the set of *Shanghaied Lovers*.

The press kit for *Shanghaied Lovers* alludes to the nature of the early Sennett-Langdon relationship and reports that the comedy producer, always "alert for new types and faces," had been struck by the comedian when he saw him in Los Angeles playing the Orpheum circuit—thus reinforcing Sennett's "discovery" of Langdon and challenging other possible scenarios. According to this press sheet, Sennett had discerned Langdon's unique gifts during their first encounter, citing "his easy manner with saying things with his eyes, or a mere shrug of the shoulders or tilting of his head. His walk is even something to laugh at."[14]

Despite the praise of the studio publicity machine, *Shanghaied Lovers* garnered mixed reactions. According to one exhibitor, this was not an "average comedy" from Langdon and drew few laughs; another felt that it was not "as good as his previous ones." These reactions, though dismal, reveal how quickly Langdon was expected to perform at a certain level in only his third released short. They also illustrate how much of an impact Langdon's first release had made, leading to such high expectations. Langdon was no doubt used to fickle public opinion, even though his vaudeville experience had consistently been positive. Motion pictures, however, were widening his reach to larger audiences across the country, and the camera was impressing his work on their minds in both subliminal and conscious ways. His onscreen images were "larger than life" and "permanent" (that is, film was meant to be seen multiple times), making them more vulnerable to effusive praise or severe criticism. It was no longer possible for Langdon to pack up his props and start fresh at another theater with another audience if his performance had fizzled the night before.

Moreover, every film presented a new story filled with different skits and gags. Langdon had to insert his character into each new comic situation, react to it, bounce off it, and handle every variation. He no longer replayed the same routine with the same script. He had to understand that the same audience would come to the theater every month to see his new film, and they would be judging whether all the components—plot, gags, titles, characters—entertained them satisfactorily and surpassed the previous effort.

Another challenge for Langdon was that although he was a veteran star with a strong comedy background, he was a novice when it came to filmmaking. He was not alone in creating his act anymore; gag writers and directors devised and modified routines—sometimes spontaneously while shooting or editing. Langdon may have been unsure how to absorb and interpret such a mix of styles and material, making him feel as disoriented as his hapless characters. Like the proverbial square peg in a round hole, the good-natured Langdon tried to mold himself into whatever shape he needed to be. He was determined to fit by relying on his judgment whenever possible, unless he could find a set of like minds who would either support him or follow his lead, much as his vaudeville partners had.

Harry tackled each new challenge in turn. First, he concluded that it would be difficult to mold his acts based on audience reaction, because they were not present during shooting. Instead, he drew new ideas from the public success or failure of each film. He also recognized that the opinions of moviegoers and critics could be both hot and cold for the exact same film, so he had to average out those responses from opposite ends of the spectrum.

His next short, *Flickering Youth,* proved more positive; it was described as "extra good and better than his average comedies." Harry plays a bachelor—but not for long. He stops off for a haircut and shows the lady barber the engagement ring he bought for his girlfriend, but she thinks Harry is proposing to her. The film's working title was *The Lady Barber,* so she was obviously meant to play a larger role. Another Sennett stalwart, Charlie Murray, with a rubbery, forlorn face, plays Harry's lawyer; he secretly yearns for Harry's girlfriend and tries to marry him off to the lady barber. The whole affair ends up in court as a breach-of-promise case, and court procedures are mercilessly burlesqued. The film, directed by Erle Kenton, is generously spiced with the Bathing Beauties. The final title mocks a popular contemporary feature film, *Flaming Youth* (November 1923), starring Colleen Moore and Milton Sills. A number of Sennett titles teased current favorites through twists or puns, in the hope of cashing in on the popularity of the established hit. Sometimes these films were parodies of the original, such as *The Shriek of Araby* (1923), which Sennett made with cross-eyed Ben Turpin to take advantage of Rudolph Valentino's huge success in *The Sheik* (1921). Most often, though, there was no connection to the parent film other than the parodied title. *Flickering Youth* fits this category, as the actual release title was an afterthought.

In May 1924 Harry completed another Del Ruth–directed short called *The Cat's Meow.* Bachelor Harry is on the trail of a girl whose mother heads the town's Purity League. Unfortunately, he ends up at the Cat's Meow, a cabaret of questionable repute and the primary target of the Purity League. In eluding the dragnet, Harry's innocent behavior so impresses league members that they appoint him to be their law enforcer. Some audiences compared this short to *Smile, Please,* indicating that they recognized pure slapstick when they saw it and could even distinguish between good and limp slapstick: "Not nearly as good as *Smile, Please.* A very weak comedy," noted one critic. But another observation hinted that comedy in general— and Langdon's comedy in particular—was slowly transforming into a more stylized genre: "This fellow is genuinely funny. In a day when many of the comedies are just a collection of gags wherever you get them, he builds up his business cleverly and is making a name for himself." Although the days of guffawing at a skunk in a camera were far from over, subtlety was key for Langdon, who was consciously mastering it. Most significantly, *Moving Picture World* cited what would become a persistent parallel: the reviewer called Langdon's *The Cat's Meow* every bit as funny as Chaplin's *Easy Street*.

His New Mamma followed in June 1924. Harry's fourth offering under Del Ruth's direction had all the earmarks of a hit like *Picking Peaches*. Two strong comedy talents support Harry in this film—Andy Clyde and Jack Cooper—and the Bathing Beauties are again on parade. They "do their stuff," as one happy exhibitor remarked, and their stuff was selling. Here, Harry vacillates between the good girl next door (Alice Day) and the sultry siren (Madeline Hurlock). Clyde plays Harry's father, a rube who goes to town and brings home a Broadway chorus girl as his new wife. Harry is smitten with his beauteous stepmother, much to Alice's chagrin. Although *His New Mamma* is one of the few lost Langdon films that may yet be found and restored, reviews provide insight into some of the film's sequences and reveal an especially positive reception for the comedian's facial expressions.[15]

During the next six months and his next six releases, Harry Langdon's popularity rose steadily. His output kept pace with his developing mannerisms: his shyness and helplessness, his measured reactions to frenzy and absurdity. The films were designed in part to give Harry time to experiment with movement and interpretation. Slapstick was being subsumed by calmer, more plot-conscious pictures. Certain sequences began to feel if not tailor-made for Harry then at least molded to his style. His next films were purposefully constructed to convey the most complex situations to date, with Langdon as the sole interpreter.

Harry plays a newlywed again in *The First Hundred Years* (August 1924). His contentment and compatibility with his wife (Alice Day) are visually revealed as she holds out a dish and he, in matching apron, dries it meticulously. Then the new cook arrives—a cigar-smoking harridan (Louise Carver) who flings dishes onto the shelf with a remarkable pitching arm. Harry attempts to emulate her but stops midthrow, knowing that he will likely miss the target; unfortunately, the dish shatters when his heavy pocket watch falls on it. As man of the house, Harry bravely approaches the intimidating cook, but, child-man that he is, he backs off when she

Langdon on the Sennett set with Bathing Beauties Elsie Tarron and Thelma Hill.

heaves a meat cleaver. Harry then tries to fire the cook with the support of a ferocious bulldog, but the animal flees at the sight of her ugly face and drags Harry around the corner. The whole routine is linked with many gags, all highlighting Harry's henpecked demeanor in the shadow of a strong woman. The unity of the prolonged scene comes from each gag unveiling another facet of his personality as he reacts to his circumstances.

When the ugly cook is replaced by a gorgeous maid (reflections of *Picking Peaches* à la Langdon), Harry responds with the subtlety of a docile husband. He appreciates her flirtation but is uncertain what he did to deserve it. Harry characterizes this role reversal as a newly pampered man through increasingly satisfied expressions as the maid massages his feet. Harry gives a slight wag of his hand to his seething wife to indicate that she should watch and learn.

The plot swings into an unexpected haunted house theme as the maid warns Harry of danger and he becomes surrounded by mysterious characters who eventually arrest a dangerous crook in the house. As the focal point of these far-fetched scenarios, Langdon demonstrates his mastery of reaction. In one gag, Harry responds to a loaded pistol with a display of subtle shivers. He timidly observes the mysterious intruders in the house, but more often he complies with their presence rather than trying to escape them. His need to interact with these clearly unwelcome elements only fuels his naïve curiosity about the unknown instead of conceding to fear. Harry's instinct becomes his driving force, even though he does not always spring into action. His body reacts only when his face gives the signal. He makes odd movements like an overgrown child, stares widely, turns slowly. Harry's mouth seldom breaks into a wide grin; his smile resembles an upturned line in porcelain. When and if he utters words, his lips barely part. One can almost imagine hearing noises sotto voce as he moves—natural pops of surprise, sighs of wonder, gurgles of delight. His language is sound rather than word—a tour de force for Harry's visual agility, in that he can conjure aural impressions in a silent medium. Even later, when he communicates verbally in sound films, it seems as if he has only learned to form words and is fascinated by doing so. He often acts amazed that he has a voice in the first place.

Langdon's mannerisms were not lost on the critics; they were in fact highlighted as the secret of his success. Kenneth Taylor, reviewing *The First Hundred Years* for the *Los Angeles Times*, wrote, "Langdon can get over more comedy with one small motion of an eyebrow than some comedians can with a whole outfit of gags." *Motion Picture Magazine* featured an article by Tamar Lane that is worth quoting at length because it is one of the first published reviews to compare Langdon with Chaplin:

> It is only at very rare intervals that a really fine comedian arrives on the screen. Of mediocre buffoons we have always had large

numbers, but from the very inception of the silent drama there has been but a scant dozen of filmmakers whose work has been marked by any appreciable degree of originality and superior talent. . . .

And now we come to Harry Langdon.

This newcomer to the screen, in the few films in which he has appeared, gives every evidence of being the finest and most whimsical comedian that has flashed on the silver sheet since the arrival of Chaplin. He is droll, he is pathetic, and he has a most original and distinctive style of expression. But most important of all, the great percentage of his humor comes from within.

I do not say that Langdon has shown any brilliance to date, but he does appear to have tremendous potentialities and, with proper handling, should quickly establish himself as one of the most popular comedians of the day.[16]

A veteran stage comedian who had spent years on the vaudeville circuit both slow-reacting to a violent car and using it as a prop for slapstick, Langdon was now playing a consistent character in a palette of films. He was on the verge of defining the magical component that had caused his impressionable younger brother and his more discerning older brother to share genuine laughter at his reactions. Langdon was fleshing out a character and building a visual voice by which audiences would identify him.

Unlike the rough-and-ready types at the Sennett studio with whom the Old Man felt most comfortable, Frank Capra was a college graduate with a degree in engineering. He was one of seven children of Sicilian immigrants who knew poverty firsthand. He was also an adventurer. Since his discharge from the army in 1918, he had crisscrossed the West doing something of everything, including selling questionable mining stock and playing poker for a living. Before joining Sennett's studio, Capra had worked for a year and a half at a film lab as a processor and an editor, and for six months he had written gags for the Our Gang comedies under Hal Roach's supervision. There, he met Will Rogers, who recommended him to Sennett. When Langdon began making his two-reelers for the Old Man, Capra was still serving an apprenticeship as Sennett's gagman.

Around the same time, Arthur Ripley, who struck many people as dour and overly serious, was head of the editorial department and Sen-

Langdon surrounded by the Little Rascals.

nett's right-hand man. He had worked at Kalem in New York as a film cutter and editor in 1909, then performed similar duties at Vitagraph, Universal, Fox, and Metro. At the Sennett studio, Ripley had switched to writing gags and complete "scripts" by the early 1920s, although typical Sennett scripts were essentially just outlines of the main plot elements. Armed with a few suggested situations and gags, directors and actors improvised the film as the camera cranked. Despite his somber disposition, Ripley was considered a genius when it came to writing and developing gags; he had a knack for building well-paced, satirical comedy and proved that under his gruff exterior he had a keen, albeit somewhat black, sense of humor. He was living proof that comedy was serious business.

Canadian Harry Edwards, the third member of the Sennett team, entered the movie industry in 1912 as a handyman and worked his way up under the Old Man's guidance. Edwards was a steady, reliable director who could produce a quality picture; he had a calm, even-keeled personality that sat between the extremes of Capra's bright volatility and Ripley's cantankerous sternness. Edwards allowed his actors the freedom to work scenes their own way, in the manner they found most comfortable. Especially in silent comedies, Edwards wanted the comedian's artistic judgment to dictate the pace and tone of a scene.

This triumvirate of Capra, Ripley, and Edwards began to collaborate on Sennett productions around the time Harry Langdon made his first shorts for the company. They may have been three of just a handful of people to witness Langdon's film test with the vaudeville car. Sol Lesser's "white elephant," as it was known, had left them feeling a little numb, and they were eventually confronted with the possibility of directing and constructing gags for this latest Sennett asset. Capra, as gagman, had reservations about Langdon, which he voiced as kindly as possible in his 1971 autobiography *The Name above the Title*, written at a time when Capra was reviewing the milestones of his illustrious fifty-year career. The tone of his first encounter with Langdon is tinged with dismissiveness and resentment; he places himself in the position of fully recognizing the vaudeville comedian's limitations in film—even though at the time he had not yet directed. Given Capra's venerated, award-winning reputation as a director when his memoirs were published, it is not surprising that his description of their working relationship held sway. The Capra-Langdon collaboration had a sharp edge, and it ended bitterly, with unresolved issues between them. Capra's strong autobiographical voice eventually overshadowed any alternative truth because Langdon was long gone and could not challenge these perceptions. Capra's view of the promising star that Sennett wanted in his fold, his opinion of the filmed car routine, and, more important, his authority in deciding what would and would not work created the sense that Langdon needed extensive direction and molding that only Capra could offer.

In the reminiscences captured in his autobiography and in later interviews, Capra expressed the feeling that Sennett had "dumped" Langdon on him—a word that likely reflects memories sharpened by decades of brooding resentment. In *The Name above the Title,* Capra related the discussion among the group that convened after watching Langdon's filmed car routine. In this scenario, Capra was the one who made the connection that would create the new Langdon persona. He began by recalling Ripley's initial and not very generous reactions:

> "Now Langdon. What kind of magic could transmogrify that twirp? And since you're stuck with him, and my Aladdin's lamp isn't handy, I suggest prayer. Because at the moment I think only God can help us with Langdon."
>
> I nearly jumped out of my skin. "Wait—a—*minute,*" I said. . . . "I think Arthur's got something—"
>
> "Sure have—a pain in my chest."
>
> "No, no, Arthur. What you said," I enthused, "that only *God* can help an elf like Langdon. God's his ally, see? Harry conquers all with goodness. Sure! Like the Good Soldier Schweik."[17]

Capra was very secure in his understanding of what Langdon needed to enhance his persona, as well as what he innately offered his writers and directors to work with:

> What kind of material did we cook up for Langdon? Why was it *different*? Primarily, because it was based on a unique—but paradoxically, a universal—character. Langdon himself was at heart a child in real life. Now a child can be bratty, whiny, sulky, cruel. We gave the character the "fix" that made him appealing—a grown man with the actions and reactions of a trusting, *innocent* child.
>
> Langdon's material was non-violent. In a day when comics out-exaggerated each other—longer shoes, baggier pants, higher pratfalls, bigger "take 'ems"—Langdon played scenes delicately, almost in slow motion. You could practically *see* the wheels of his immature mind turning as it registered tiny pleasures or discomforts. Langdon himself was a virtuoso of flitting, hesitant motions. In the middle of extreme danger he could be distracted by a butterfly, or a spot of dirt on his finger.
>
> The "double-take" was a standard item in *every* comic's bag of

tricks. . . . But Langdon has mastered a *"triple-take"*—two long, beautifully timed, innocent looks at a lion, with plenty of time between looks, before convulsing the audience with his terrified third look—the "take 'em."[18]

Ironically, the disintegration of the Capra-Langdon relationship would eventually cause the embittered director to suggest that Langdon never understood his own abilities, had no qualities of his own, and needed someone to guide him through his helplessness.

The first step in forming the triumvirate was to develop even, consistent vehicles that pushed Langdon into stardom and created his unique character. Capra affirmed the view that if Langdon were to enter the realm of the reigning comedians of the day, he would have to do so with his own individuality. Chaplin was a quick thinker; Keaton was a deadpan acrobat; Lloyd was a speedy optimist.[19] Langdon would be different.

Capra's reflections on these events, seen through his own lens, underscored the tensions and power play that developed after both he and Langdon moved into feature films. His account spawned a persistent chicken-egg question of which came first and who created whom. Capra's successful career trajectory ensured that his "truth" about their working relationship would prevail over Langdon's. It would also ultimately shape and negatively reinforce Capra's *memory* of Langdon's helplessness—his difficulty in understanding his own character and his inability to navigate his own success without the director's firm hand.

At their preliminary encounters, Harry may have indeed been an enigma to Capra, yet the future director saw a resonance between the comedian and the *Good Soldier Schweik* protagonist. That novel, enormously successful in its original Czech edition and translated into many languages, was written in a refreshingly colloquial style; it used realistic settings and situations to depict the spirit of smoldering rebellion that the Czechs had repressed for many years. When Schweik is drafted into the Austrian army after the outbreak of World War I, he is appalled because, as a Czech, he hates the Austrian empire that kept his country enslaved for nearly three centuries. Since any open evasion of military service for the despised kaiser would result in death by firing squad, Schweik pretends to be feebleminded; he is excluded from regular training and is assigned to be an officer's orderly. He blunders through his time in the army not by refusing to follow orders but rather by following them so enthusiastically that he confuses the system and sabotages the original intent of the commands. Although the backdrop of war and political tensions had nothing to do with being a Sennett clown, Capra was fascinated by the essence of Schweik as an innocent. He saw Langdon's enigmatic mannerisms as those of an unconscious babe who survives mainly by fate and luck. The Schweik character as infused into Harry's character was not evident until the trio's third collaboration (*All Night Long,* November 1924), one of twenty-three short and feature films produced by the team.

In truth, Langdon was aware of his own "essence"—he had developed it in vaudeville. It involved exploring subtleties and mastering reactions, and his reviews affirmed its success. What became apparent, however, was that what had worked onstage was falling short onscreen, and Langdon may not have grasped the mechanisms at work. But Capra's suggestion that Langdon never understood his film persona is unfounded. Before Capra, Edwards, or Ripley had ever worked with the star, Langdon's "essence" was already pervading his first films for Sennett—simmering beneath the slapstick, bridging the blatant and the subtle. Nevertheless, Langdon's timid character, the slow reactor, had the best chance of thriving with a unified cadre of creativity—namely, the Capra-Ripley-Edwards team.

Before *All Night Long,* Langdon had completed two other films with the trio. This first group effort, *The Luck o' the Foolish,* was shown to key people at Sennett headquarters. In his memoirs, Capra deemed it a winner. Now the triumvirate felt they needed to be with Langdon on set, not sequestered in the "Tower" where Sennett's gag writers usually worked in isolation. Edwards had asked permission to have "the boys" with him to think up "little goodies on the spot," and Capra supported him: "This Langdon's something else. He's a gold mine. We'd like to dig into him, study him. We can't do that cooped up in the Tower." Sennett retorted impatiently that Capra was eager to be on the set only because he aspired to be a director himself. Then Ripley joined the chorus asking to be liberated from the Tower: "The key to Langdon is innocence. That's a mighty frail reed, Mr. Sennett, not understood by many—not even by Langdon—not even by *us* really, yet. Monkey around with that frail reed and this guy could easily revert back to a small-time comic. That's the reason we'd like to study him." Sennett reluctantly conceded: "Aw, to hell with you guys. . . . You're all goddamn lawyers. All right. Get out, get out."[20]

The Luck o' the Foolish finds Harry and Marceline Day as a down-on-their-luck married couple hunting for work, she as a cleaning woman and he as a policeman. A bomb sequence in the film is ingenious in its gag construction, hinting at the Schweikian innocence of the character. As the title implies, Harry manages to survive such catastrophes by luck rather than cleverness. He scales the side of a house to reach the balcony outside the room where he suspects his wife is cheating, but drops into a swimming pool below. Just then, a thief in the room hurls a bomb that lands in the pool and flings Harry into the room he wanted to enter. Harry triggers another bomb that dispenses with the crook but propels himself out the window and onto a utility pole. Harry's charming clumsiness cuts through the slapstick with blinking starts and stops at each situation—a trait that was becoming uniform in this film. Perhaps the clearest sequence capturing his puerile reactions is when Harry demonstrates to the police chief how diligent he is. Harry prances across the street, adjusting his stride to his superior's and signaling his attention, but the chief does not even notice. Remarkably, Harry is capable of appearing so insignificant in his purposeful gestures that he can be overlooked by someone staring directly at him.

Another gag involves a plug of chewing tobacco that a lineman drops from a utility pole onto Harry's open sandwich. Obliviously, he bites in, but rather than exhibiting disgust, he simply lowers his eyes, twitches the corners of his mouth, and creates the illusion of drifting through time, hoping the ill effects will pass. As he stands, his legs collapse in slow motion. He crawls across the street, staggering between the onrushing cars. Overcome by the vile taste, Harry stops to nap mid-traffic, bending forward on his knees and resting his face on his hands. The tobacco gag struck Thomas C. Kennedy of *Motion Picture News* as a "piece of pantomime which registers excellently." He noted that Langdon's "individualistic style . . . is bringing into comedies something which is a bit out of the beaten track. His eloquent facial expression never fails to amuse."

The Hansom Cabman (October 1924) shows the Langdon-Capra-Ripley-Edwards team exerting control and repeating a formula that Sennett's comedians excelled at, but one that had not been used in a while: a thrill-packed Keystone Kops comedy with a breakneck chase involving cops, crooks, and cuties. The experiment backfired, however, because Harry was allowed to contribute relatively few of his special talents. The team was likely trying to determine how much Harry could do with such material. The laughs belonged to the gagmen rather than to Harry, and interestingly, these madcap antics were never used with Langdon again. Given that the chase was the focus of the film, it became the only logical sequence in an otherwise confused plot. In it, Harry shines fleetingly in a number of eye-catching moves: for example, he steps back and forth over a distance of two feet, concocting much perplexity in just a small space. As he runs, his feet dart to the sides, creating the effect of an overgrown toddler who is able to run but is unaccustomed to the effort, much less its purpose.

Critics and exhibitors had mixed feelings about *The Hansom Cabman*. The *Cleveland Plain Dealer* called the ending "blah" but credited Langdon for making the film funnier than it deserved to be. Most strikingly, reviewer W. Ward Marsh pronounced Langdon one of the top three comedians: "Langdon's face is not so sensitive as Chaplin's, nor does his style have the flexibility and pathos of Chaplin's, but as a comedian Langdon is infinitely better than Harold Lloyd. In the race which this column sees, the newcomer and Keaton are neck-and-neck at this minute—and Langdon hasn't made a feature comedy yet!" By contrast, an exhibitor with a small-town patronage in Wisconsin lamented, "This bird may be a knockout on the stage or in some places, but he hardly ever gets a titter around here. His stuff moves too slow. He tries to put his stuff over by making faces at the camera." The scale was tipping in favor of Langdon's stature as a top comedian, but dissenting voices clearly offered their opinions.

In Langdon's next vehicle, the oversized child puts on a soldier's uniform, creating a startling delineation between an infantile caricature embroiled in Sennett mayhem and a fuller character that pushes beyond stereotype. Harry had already toyed with peculiarities that bored through the density of slapstick, but in *All Night Long* he finally reaches the apex of characterization and commands the entire picture.

In the film, Harry awakens from a nap in a movie theater to find that he is alone. On his way out, Harry greets his image in a mirror with a small, happy kick. Then he stumbles onto a team of safecrackers in the manager's office. There is an unexpected flash of recognition between Harry and one of the thieves—it is Harry's old sergeant (Vernon Dent) from World War I, now fallen on hard times. While the accomplices work on the safe, Harry and the sergeant reminisce. Harry's reaction to this odd encounter is a combination of fear and doubt, coated with naïveté. The setting is ripe for flashback, which provides a new identity for Harry: as a hapless KP, he peels away at a mound of potatoes that dwarfs him into insignificance. His futility in this sight gag is further emphasized by a

was also buried in the blast. The sergeant then banishes him to Suicide Post, and Harry leaves with a feeble handshake and a look of nausea. Next, he is on guard, perched on a pole, when a flying bomb carves out one side of the pole, which he conveniently uses as a foothold. Three more bombs knock him onto a colonel, whom he inadvertently saves from danger. Harry's promotion is revealed when Nanette opens a door and finds him standing in his new uniform; the sharp door frame only emphasizes how puny and pathetic he looks in his baggy clothes.

The flashback concludes and the action returns to the present as the police enter the theater and the dynamite explodes. Abruptly, Nanette accompanied by three children pushes a baby carriage away from the camera. When the view is reversed, a well-bandaged Harry and Vernon are seen sitting in the carriage side by side. Harry notes that he and Nanette named one of their children after the sergeant. The film ends with a patriotic veterans' parade, and Harry stands to salute, although his wounded leg is in a sling tied around his neck.

All Night Long was highly satisfying across the board. According to a notice in the press, there was an unusual advance response to the film. Learning of its wartime setting and doughboy characters, heads of the American Legion and other soldier organizations wrote to Langdon to voice their support. Concerned about the verisimilitude of the battlefield scenes, Langdon and Edwards reportedly consulted many ex-servicemen to ensure they depicted the proper atmosphere of a battlefield "over there." There was even a sense that the bumbling antics of Langdon's doughboy would provide cathartic relief for the ex–fighting men.

After its release, exhibitors noted audiences' positive reactions to "one of the best comedians in the business." One theater manager pleaded, "Give us more of Harry's stuff." *Moving Picture World* extolled Langdon's knack for turning the "thread of an idea" into "two reels of side-splitting fun." Harry was finally carving out a secure niche for himself in film; even though he was starring only in shorts, which were the testing ground of all comedians, he was in great demand. The character in *All Night Long* may have drawn from Schweik, but Langdon had created his own version of a man-child identity. More importantly, he had found critical acclaim, and his name was now regularly mentioned in the same breath as those of his more famous contemporaries. A short time after *All Night Long* was released, the *Film Mercury* reflected on top stars Chaplin, Keaton, and Lloyd, as well as Larry Semon, a pasty-faced, expressive comedian with a vaudeville background who had been contracted to work for Vitagraph Studios in 1915. Semon had starred in numerous short films with wacky alliterative titles such as *Noisy Naggers and Nosey Neighbors* (1917), *Hindoos and Hazards* (1918), *Bathing Beauties and Big Boobs* (1918), and *Huns and Hyphens* (1918) and longer films such as *The Sawmill* (1922) and *Wizard of Oz* (1925). When he produced his own films, as most stars eventually did, Semon was too extravagant, went bankrupt, suffered a mental breakdown, and died of tuberculosis and pneumonia in 1928 at age thirty-nine. Yet his body of work, at least according to the *Film Mercury,* ranked him among the best. For Langdon to be included in this clique as "the maharajah of mirth" was a coup, especially as the article devoted to Langdon was titled "The Greatest Comedian on the Screen Today."

One perk of stardom was being prominently named in the headlines of fan magazines. For example, *Motion Picture* published an October 1924 article by Dorothy Herzog entitled "The Wistful Mr. Langdon: What He Craves Most of All Is to Be Left Alone." It highlighted the comedian's intense preoccupation with filmmaking, to the exclusion of everything outside the studio. As Herzog reported, "He lives, sleeps, eats, and indigestions over flickers." She leveled the highest praise possible at this time—near-equal standing with Chaplin—and even indulged in the word "genius." Such adulation, in combination with Langdon's withdrawn wistfulness, seemed to trigger a shift in attitude within the comedian himself. Formerly dependent on filmmakers to help him navigate through a young business, he was feeling newly liberated and perhaps even a little superior, since he had achieved a status he had never known in vaudeville. No comparison to giants of the stage had tantalized his thinking about himself. Now an entertaining news item from the *Portland Oregonian* personified Langdon's "graduation" in his career, jokingly referring to his education with Sennett: "It took him a year to master movie vocabulary but he feels [he] is qualified to receive a diploma from the hands of President Mack Sennett, head of Sennett University of Comic Expression." Taught such useful terms as "Hittem" (turn on the lights), "Take it" (blink your eyes and fall on your face), and "Clinch" (hero and heroine embrace), Langdon was ready for his commencement ceremony and to start his life beyond "school." The tongue-in-cheek article tapped into Langdon's aspirations far more accurately than it might have intended.

Herzog's article was also a rare exploration of Langdon's offscreen persona from a "psychology" perspective. She alluded to the effect of negative reviews on his sensitive nature, distinguishing between "constructive criticism," which Langdon welcomed, and the type of commentary that "allows wrinkles to exercise when he learned he is a 'male Lillian Gish' to some and Charlie Chaplin's successor to others." Work itself became Langdon's comfort, to the point of "inversing" him into solitude. Herzog presciently identified a temperament in this "funny little feller" who was prone to extreme reactions: "He's a whole-hearted emotionalist who soars to the top and thuds to the bottom with unexpected changes of gravitation."[21]

This internal shift was a curious observation, but it became more obvious as the publicity surrounding Langdon's stardom intensified. It seemed that the demands of producing consistently successful work to meet distributors' and audiences' expectations affected Langdon's approach to and attitude toward working. As a stage star, he had primarily figured out routines on his own, isolated from almost everyone. Yet the teamwork that went into his films was ensuring his fame, and he would be wise not to challenge it. How much each party in any collaboration actually contributes to the success of the final product—and the emergence of its star—can never be measured accurately. The product is always a *blend* of mutual ideas and creativity. Only in hindsight does confusion arise over the "degree" of creativity emanating from each collaborator, and both Capra and Langdon eventually needed to claim that highest degree to satisfy their own egos.

For the time being, however, critical acclaim was forecasting only the best for this new comic genius. The Sennett triumvirate had gained solid insight into their new hero with *All Night Long* and would rely on it as a template for success. Langdon was now their spokesman, imbuing life into a child-man in a baggy outfit. The face that would launch a thousand expressions—and the team behind that face—would create the perfect comedy.

Over at last were the days of Rose's "grouch bag," in which the Langdons kept all their spare cash. They had very little in the bank when Harry ventured into film. Money earned from twenty years in vaudeville evaporated rapidly to meet the needs of their large families. But events were moving so quickly in the movie world that it was difficult for Rose and Harry to keep up with them. Within one year of signing with Principal Pictures, Harry, good to his oath, had become a movie star. Sennett had started him at $150 a week, less than his vaudeville salary, but within months the new star was earning $1,000 a week—more money than the vaudevillians had seen in their lives.

To mirror their rocketing lifestyle, Harry and Rose purchased a two-story stucco manor, the first permanent residence either of them had had since their teens. The house at 1729 Canyon Drive reportedly cost an exorbitant $25,000. Rose, who had resigned from show business and had little to do, was feeling lonely, so she invited her niece Mary and Mary's husband Gene to live with them. She felt the house was too rambling, and she needed them not only to shop for furniture and to run the household but also for company. With Harry working so intensely on the Sennett lot every day, producing shorts with machine-gun speed, he was rarely home.

For Harry, December 1924 provided a perfect cap to an illustrious year with the release of a short called *Feet of Mud*. He plays a total washout of a college football player whose pathetic little body is lost in the spaciousness of his uniform, which he futilely puffs up with pillows. When a football flies toward him, Harry stretches out his arms like a toddler reaching for his mother. He inadvertently wins the game when the ball lodges in his uniform and he runs over the goal line because he is afraid of the two teams pursuing him. A college coed (Natalie Kingston) is impressed and considers Harry's marriage proposal, but her tycoon father insists that Harry work, and he does—as a street cleaner. In a long shot that instantly epitomizes the futility of his job, Harry stands on a heavily littered street as the unwitting victim of his environment—a new dimension to his character. He robotically picks up the litter with his spike and unintentionally pokes a cop's shin. Typical of visual comedy playing on spatial surprises within the camera's frame, neither Harry nor the audience has seen the cop. When Harry realizes what he has done, he sympathizes by limping. As the film progresses, Harry becomes the victim of another unusual environment—Chinatown—where he inadvertently triggers a tong war and is carted off to an opium den.[22] There, his saucer-like eyes are shown to great advantage as he inhales the smoky air: first they convey irritation, then relaxation, and finally sweet euphoria. Incredibly, before the film ends Harry also manages to rescue Natalie, who has been kidnapped and stuffed in a mummy case, and her father permits their marriage.

Like *Smile, Please*, this film is composed of two distinct one-reel comedies: the college story and the Chinatown sequence. Here, however, the two reels are linked more skillfully by the uniformity of Harry's mannerisms throughout the scenes. In addition, the environment is a new element

Cleaning up in Chinatown (*left*) and saving his girl (*right*) in *Feet of Mud.*

that collaborates with his persona to present a broader thematic conclusion about what the Langdon character represents. Harry was now moving in a more defined direction to fine-tune his character, becoming, as the *Columbus (Ohio) Journal* suggested in February 1925, eligible for that "select class of super screen comedians, limited to Charlie Chaplin and Harold Lloyd." There was the inevitable grumble from some exhibitors, however, who thought Langdon was overrated and should remain in two-reelers.

Coincidentally, Lloyd's film *The Freshman,* released nine months later, is based on a similar premise as *Feet of Mud.* Lloyd often expressed his admiration for, as well as his "discovery" of, Langdon, and *Feet of Mud* may have supplied some inspiration for Lloyd's feature. Both Lloyd and Langdon are rushed into a football game as a result of key players' injuries. But while Harry wins by chance, Harold wins by superhuman effort; while Lloyd's film ends with the crucial game, Langdon's shoots off to an exotic location.

Another comedian ambling up the ladder of cinematic success at this time was Stan Laurel. Like Langdon, he too played a giddy street sweeper in *White Wings,* released slightly before *Feet of Mud.* Coincidentally, a little more than a decade later Langdon would become a screenwriter for the comedy team of Laurel and Hardy and briefly "fill" Laurel's shoes.

Not surprisingly, the odd title *Feet of Mud* was a parody, this time of the Paramount feature *Feet of Clay,* released in September 1924 and starring Rod La Rocque and Vera Reynolds. It is a tearjerker about a young couple fighting for happiness against stiff odds. Harry's film had no relationship to the feature, and perhaps the only parallel was that Harry faced many odds in his own films and managed to spin his circumstances into whimsical comedy instead of tragedy through the simplest of gestures.

Harry christened 1925 with a Scottish yarn called *The Sea Squawk.* The title was another spoof, this time of *The Sea Hawk,* an Associated First National adventure saga starring Milton Sills and Enid Bennett that had been shown around the country the previous summer. Its swashbuckling heroics had nothing in common with Harry's saga. Harry plays a kilt-clad Scotsman traveling to the States aboard a ship that is also carrying a Hollywood star in possession of a large ruby. During the voyage, a jewel thief (Vernon Dent), who is also Harry's cabinmate, steals the gem and, of course, involves Harry.

Langdon performs some of his best mime in his naïve reactions to the thief's gun. Harry pulls a little pistol from his kilt, twirling it nervously. One close-up of the two guns—Harry's puny pistol and the thief's larger one—instantly captures Harry's psychological and physical relationship to his cabinmate. Confronted with danger, Harry responds by breaking into a fit of trembling before curling up and playing dead. The thief forces Harry to swallow the ruby, and he is mortified when the police search him. He manifests a look of ravished innocence and that of a child who has swallowed cod liver oil. As he is flung about, he either flails his legs or freezes into the fetal position, as though no other poses of defense are possible. But even a baby can muster the courage for self-preservation: Harry quietly removes his shoe to hit an opponent on the head, ensuring his escape, thanks to personal ingenuity.

The kilt adds a helpless, girly air to Harry, and the convenience of a masked ball on the ship allows him to tackle a popular trend that all the major comedians indulged in: cross-dressing. He uses a handy hooped skirt and curly tresses to make his escape. Wisely, there is no attempt to make Harry look like a real girl; instead, he caricatures one, creating an illusion of coy flirtation while still drawing on his masculine side when he needs to hit someone. The 1890s-style skirt, much like the box camera in *Smile, Please,* becomes a typical Sennett excuse to insert crazy props that, like a deus ex machina, surface at opportune moments to make the gag work, however illogically. This time, a monkey hides in the folds of the

Langdon, in a kilt, between takes with Vernon Dent on *The Sea Squawk.*

skirt, triggering Harry's jerky movements, twitching shoulders, and harried looks. His fringed pantaloons provide the means for an uncomfortable sight gag that is repeated three times without variation: the patently fake monkey's tail protrudes from under the skirt to tickle the face of a nearby musician. Unfortunately, these physical-discomfort gags were de rigueur—the Old Man loved them, and they were sprinkled into each script with his approval.

Despite these drawbacks, *The Sea Squawk* was well received, in large

Dress used as a prop in *The Sea Squawk*.

measure because Langdon made even the bad gags work. His whimsical approach cut through the slapstick in a way that disarmed the audience. Some reviewers noted that Langdon had already abandoned slapstick, even though others in the cast indulged it. In a fine compliment, the *Pre-View* commended Langdon as a two-reel comedian who can "really act." For the first time in a Langdon short, director Harry Edwards, supervising director F. Richard Jones, and J. A. Waldron's titles were acknowledged for creating this clever comedy.

Encouraged by such positive responses, Harry stepped lively into his next short, in which dealing with women would threaten both his physical and his emotional equilibrium. *Boobs in the Woods* (February 1925) was

Arthur Ripley's first screenwriting credit on a Langdon film. The title, a twist on the phrase "babes in the woods," provides an interesting example of the gag-writing process at Sennett's studio. Other titles under consideration included *Lumber Limbers, The Lumber Ox, Up a Tree, Timber Twisters, Buzz Saw and Buckwheat, A Buzz Saw Romance, Busy Buzz Saws, Buzzing Around, The Saw Dust Trail,* and *Chips and Shavings,* but *Boobs in the Woods* had been circled in pencil as the preference. The same selection process applied to the many intertitles that provided commentary and dialogue. The Old Man insisted on close communication with his writers and controlled much of postproduction. He was picky about the intertitles and often studied the long lists his titlers provided. An amusing selection of snappy descriptors and tongue-twisting titles to introduce the setting of the lumberjack camp included the following:

> In the Hermitage mountains, where the men are so tough they steal wood alcohol from the trunks of the trees. . . .
> In the wild Kilmenny Mountains, where the lumbermen break saplings and saps with their bare hands. . . .
> In the Northwoods, where even the jack rabbits chew tobacoo [*sic*]. . . .
> In the Northwoods country—where men play mumblety peg with double bitt axes. . . .

Sennett's "winning" title was: "In the great Northwoods where Nature makes any family tree look like a daffodil."[23] Wimpy Harry, whose family has sent him to lumberjack camp to toughen him up, fits right in.

In addition to facing the dangers of Mother Nature, Harry fends off the bully (Vernon Dent) who runs the camp, acquires a reputation as a fast gun, and wins the girl. The characterization that supersedes this tough terrain, however, is an unusual one for a comedy: Harry, a boy on the brink of adolescence, is engaged in an inner struggle. He is interested in the girl but unsure and wary of her intentions. His mannerisms cover a spectrum of curiosity, doubt, reluctance, and eagerness about starting a relationship, yet being a full-grown male—at least physically—he knows he must be dominant. When Harry sees the girl, his smile is shy, his greeting tentative. She understands the cues and allows him to advance, hiding behind a tree to perpetuate the allure. As long as the game is played on an adolescent level, Harry enjoys it. Once the girl pursues him, however, Harry assumes

Study in lumberjacks: shooting *Boobs in the Woods.*

a defensive stance: he wields a hatchet—a tool of the macho lumberjack trade—but it is a tiny one that he evidently carries to protect his virtue. His playful movements and facial messages are cues of a budding adolescent, but he is shocked when the girl dares to behave like a grown woman. Yet he would never use his hatchet with vengeance; it is a mild warning, and the girl is never in danger. As in *The Sea Squawk,* any weapon Harry holds will never be used for its intended purpose, for he is incapable of it. If anything lethal does result from his halting gestures, it will happen through fate, and Harry will be the most frightened of all.

Langdon was now using a minimalist approach in situations that bordered on emotional responses such as love and fear. *Film Daily* made special note of Langdon's "lip pantomime" as the "perfect barometer of his varied emotions. We can recall no other comedian who does so little to express so much." Although the Sennett triumvirate was working behind the scenes as a unit to create these films—and their work was finally garnering some public acknowledgment—Langdon was still the sole representation of that collaboration and its tangible manifestation onscreen.

Langdon was justifiably rewarded for his unique presence in silent comedy as he merged artistic and financial success. Confined to the company of fellow vaudeville actors for most of his life, Harry now expanded his social circle to include famous celebrities; he received nationwide publicity, played golf with film executives, and entertained a bevy of "pretty peaches" who sought fame and money in Hollywood—or, more accurately, a man with fame and money. Harry's onscreen characters may have been timid when grappling with the opposite sex, but offscreen, Langdon had little difficulty succumbing to temptation, and as the saying goes, he began "seeing other women."[24]

Rose sensed that this heady mix of fame, independence, and fortune was changing her husband into a more self-possessed man, and he may have felt entitled to all this attention after decades of hard work. She had become an outsider to him—not only as a business partner but also as a life partner—even though he was still providing her with a lavish lifestyle. For years, she and Harry had bickered over a lack of money or how to play a routine onstage, but their union had been secure. Their small world had consisted of long road trips and changing venues, and nonstop traveling and sharing the spotlight had been the glue between them. Harry's film work excluded her, and now their fights sprouted from trivialities, with every new argument dissolving their bond a little more. For Rose, her long marriage and financial security were at stake, and finding a way to hold on to Harry was imperative.

Ironically, Langdon's next film was titled *His Marriage Wow,* in which he plays a bridegroom who has second, third, and fourth thoughts about marrying. The title obliquely refers to Warner's July 1924 feature *Her Marriage Vow,* about a neglected wife who strays, starring Beverly Bayne and Monte Blue, but there is no other similarity. For the first time, Harry's character, who shivers from a severe case of cold feet, is given a name: Harold Hope. His situation, however, is anything but hopeful: he appears at the wrong church for his wedding, misplaces the ring, and is abducted by a crazed guest, Professor McGlumm (Vernon Dent), who reminds Harry that he should flee married life while he has the chance.

Although Harry does eventually marry, McGlumm convinces him that his wife is after his money (not necessarily unrelated to Rose's desperate desire to keep Harry close). This premise spawns a lengthy routine in which Langdon's frightened-child mannerisms explode into action when he thinks he has been poisoned. He has only drunk some foul-tasting coffee, but his imagination has conjured up the worst: a slow glaze covers

Hapless bridegroom in *His Marriage Wow* with Natalie Kingston.

Harry's face, his lips droop, his mouth twitches. He stumbles from the table to submit to a creeping death and sinks into his trademark fetal position. Clearly, Langdon is adding subtle embellishments to his basic foundation of a reaction. McGlumm helps Harry escape, and the manic driving,

Langdon with a "McGlumm" Vernon Dent readying for the race, with Harry Edwards standing at the side giving direction.

gags, and stunts elevate this car routine beyond the typical Sennett-style pursuit. The focus is on Harry's inner turmoil as he recovers from his stupor to find that his life is now threatened by a lunatic driver. The sequence and the film end with the inevitable crash and Harry coiled into a virtual knot—a symbol of how tying the knot got him into this mess.

Langdon's work here garnered a definitive "here to stay" appraisal from *Motion Picture News* reviewer T. C. Kennedy, who would follow Langdon's career with enthusiasm and, later, sincere concern for the twists and turns it took. But for the present, Langdon basked in hearing such descriptors as "skillful," "eloquent pantomime," and "most promising." He could not imagine what other possibilities might affect his upward mobility.

Langdon's life at home, by contrast, was poorly scripted. Any contribution Harry might have made to resolving his marital woes was diverted by work. Rose knew that one of Harry's desires was to be a father, but as a young married couple they had thought better of exposing a child to their itinerant existence. Now, with time and money to spare, Rose was willing to risk a pregnancy, despite being over forty. Harry must have been swayed because, in the spring of 1925, Rose announced that she was pregnant, and they were both overjoyed. They bought a larger house at 7206 Hollywood Boulevard, even though they had spent barely a year in their first home. Rose assumed that Harry's excitement at being a father would encourage him to settle down, accept his domestic responsibilities, and end his flings with starlets. The child's name would be Francis or Frances so that, boy or girl, Rose's real first name would be preserved.

Temporarily appeased on the home front by this good news, Langdon sped through a relentless output of short comedies. Released on March 29, 1925, *Plain Clothes* stars Harry as a down-on-his-luck private detective who is hired to retrieve a stolen necklace. A Keystone Kops–style sequence full of shootouts and a climactic confrontation between Harry and the thieves ensures his victory at the end of the film. This proved to be a surprising regression to Sennett's earlier madcap style, a template that sometimes resurfaced out of habit, if not necessity. It is salvaged by Langdon's solo routines punctuating the longer scenes. In showing off his detecting skills, for example, Harry tracks a man, surreptitiously measures his height with a pocket tape, and compares his likeness to a photo. Like a tot who knows his parents will be proud of his efforts, he is about to arrest the man when he discovers that the suspect is a detective. In another scene, Harry tries to asphyxiate a crook by breaking the glass of a gaslight fixture over his head but manages only to incapacitate himself. He falls like a plank and then, in an afterthought, rises slightly only to faint again. Langdon was establishing a pattern of accessorizing his babylike gestures with repetitive afterthoughts—evidence of his skillful use of beats to reinforce his mannerisms and enhance the comedic business. These traits were becoming the defining characteristics of his persona.[25]

Loyal reviewer T. C. Kennedy lauded the richness of Langdon's pantomime, as well as the clever timing and "subtle play of humor and pathos." Chaplin was now the only standard used when referring to Langdon because, according to Kennedy: "He is more than a 'silent actor' employing gestures and grimace as a substitute for words. He not only registers emotion, but projects it with an ease and grace which remove from the business of acting all obviousness and effort." It seemed that Sennett's slapstick formula was now intruding on Langdon's brand of comedy. In fact, the Sennett style was becoming obsolete in the face of Langdon's skill with more sophisticated alternatives. Langdon was no longer relying on slapstick as a synonym for his comedy.

While *Plain Clothes* was played strictly for laughs, *Remember When?* became a turning point in the treatment of Langdon's character and situations and the atmosphere they created. With its poignant and romantic tone, this April 1925 release was a firm move by Capra, Ripley, and Edwards to give the star a more dimensional story instead of a string of gags in the ill-matched halves of a two-reeler. This short film, set in a circus, also became a touchstone for Langdon's embrace of his own self-importance. Fan magazines were seeking him out as a "consultant," asking him to tell their readers how comedy was constructed effectively. Whenever his "voice" appeared in print, however, it assumed an air of stiff authority on the subject, strangely at odds with the near wordlessness of his screen character. This was, of course, the man, the artist, the acknowledged comic genius speaking in pedantic sentences about what he referred to as his "study" of how to get laughs on both stage and screen.

Langdon also admitted that the best assets in comedy are good gagmen. His words were substantiated by the films that propelled him to stardom. The gags in his shorts, especially those resulting from the official union of Capra, Edwards, and Ripley, were more finely woven into the fabric of both comedy and character. It was as if Sennett's productions, at least those involving Langdon, were growing up to meet a more mature audience. It was also ironic that Harry's "child" was engaging this older audience—as though this character required parents who could understand the intended meaning behind their offspring's obscure communications.

The script of *Remember When?* is credited to Arthur Ripley and Clyde Bruckman. Capra seems to have distanced or removed himself from this venture for reasons that are not clear. He may have been preparing a script for a feature film, as Langdon was on the brink of shifting from shorts to features—or so he thought. It is interesting to compare this plot with those developed by the triumvirate and to observe the differences produced under the dominant hand of Arthur Ripley. He had a reputation for being sardonic and bleak, yet he was also keenly aware of the "other side" of comedy—the robustly funny side that was succinct, subtle, and precise in its visual and verbal tensions. *Remember When?* is brimming in pathos with an edge. One can only wonder how different the plot would have been if the more upbeat and optimistic Capra had worked on this project.

The poignancy is immediately established in the first scene when Harry and Rosemary (Natalie Kingston) are identified as childhood sweethearts in an orphanage. A young boy actually plays Harry as a youngster,

Rave reviews publicized in a *Moving Picture World* advertisement.

but it is unmistakably the man-child Harry would grow up to be—a mini-version with his trademark baggy sweater and hat. When Rosemary is adopted, little Harry runs away, carting all his worldly belongings in a ker-chief tied to the end of a stick. He cuts a heart-rending picture as he shuf-fles down the road, away from the camera, reminiscent of Chaplin's Tramp figure. Indeed, when the boy becomes a man, his wardrobe and destiny have not changed. Still lugging the same sack on a stick, Harry is shown traipsing down the road in an extremely long overcoat. His desperate hunger is the source of several extended routines specializing in Langdon's slow pondering. For example, sitting at an abundantly laden picnic table, he takes so long to decide what to eat first that the picnickers return and cart off their belongings, leaving Harry as famished as ever. He then kidnaps some live chickens by coaxing them to jump into his overcoat. Many throttles and chickens later in this repetition-with-variation gag, Harry is ignominiously kicked away by the sheriff (the chicken routine impressed at least one reviewer as being expertly acted). Harry's woebegone adventures ultimately lead him to a circus, where the owner (Vernon Dent) hires him because of his peculiar acrobatics while fending off some angry bees. The thread linking the first and second reels is the bearded lady in the circus—none other than Harry's childhood sweetheart. But Harry does not notice because he is too busy with Minerva the elephant, who wreaks havoc with some suitcases. Interestingly, contrary to Langdon's sage advice on comedy construction, this part of the routine is strictly mechanical, and his actions are noticeably forced. No suitcases are actually dropped onto Harry's back; the routine is manipulated by trick photography (reversing the film) and lacks the natural gravity that would suspend disbelief. However, Harry compensates with a topper gag: after each haul, Minerva straightens out Harry's curved back with a hefty step of her foot.

When Harry finally spies the bearded lady, he is appalled and offers her a cigar, yet he recognizes something familiar. For the first time in a Langdon short, a flashback is used to insert a moment of pathos and sentiment: he recalls a time when two youngsters in love played contentedly on a swing. Harry is puzzled by this sense of déjà vu, flips the lady's beard, and stares at her with great confusion. She also has a tremor of recognition, so she sends Harry to the orphanage with a note inquiring about her former sweetheart. When she learns that it is indeed Harry, they kiss tenderly, but her fake beard sticks to Harry's chin. It is a subtle gag—a bearded lady ends up giving Harry his first facial hair. He strokes her clean-shaven cheeks with relief and wonder, along with traces of a love that has never faded.

This pathos, percolating under the surface of Langdon's previous films in sparks of childlike contemplation and amazement, fully blossoms in this story that begins with the premise of a young love lost. The outcome of this story—a comedy, which usually ensures a happy ending—adds an emotional layer to his innocent character, giving it a different resonance and interpretation. This film also solidifies the physical trademarks of clothes and gestures that represent a spirit caught between childhood and adulthood. Here, Harry's emotional side has breathing space, and Langdon uses it to his advantage. *Remember When?* finally encourages the sentiment behind the comedy. But instead of a heavy-handed message of love lost and regained, comedy keeps the emotions light and airy.

Other comedians handled the tricky field of emotions differently. Keaton tended to cut his sentiments short; the images, though poignant, often kept emotions at arm's length. Chaplin veered in the opposite direction, with strong, intentional wrenches at the heartstrings. Lloyd worked the middle ground, with simple, wholesome, uncomplicated boy-meets-girl sentiments. Langdon, who began his film career after these other stars had settled into their respective personas, seemed to combine all three, yet he interpreted their styles with a novel spin. Instead of withholding too much sentiment as Keaton did, Langdon dwelled on it just enough to tug at the heartstrings as Chaplin did, before resolving the dilemma straightforwardly as Lloyd did. Langdon offered a simple explanation of his style: "All I ask of a scenario department is a light story into which has been introduced a love interest, a sprinkling of romance and a little adventure; and with my director and good gag men, we will inject as many laughs as it will hold." But the complex, fragile balance between too much sentiment and too little was one that Langdon—through instinct as well as the guidance of Capra, Ripley, and Edwards—was mastering more skillfully with every film. Harry referred to this balance as early as October 1924 in a fan magazine:

> I believe that the comedy which is wholly human has the best chance of appeal to the masses as well as to the classes. We are all brothers—as well as sisters—under the skin. Humor can be appreciated by all sorts and conditions of men and women. . . .
>
> I am to create roles that are just sufficiently away from the ordinary to be interesting, yet which partake so strongly of realism that they will be acceptable to the man in the street or the more pedantic type who finds his relaxation in humor.

Some were beginning to recognize the wholesome human comedy, blended with Langdon's style, as unique. It was lauded and sought. It also needed room to grow.

Langdon began to feel that he had outgrown Sennett. Despite claims to the contrary, the stubborn Sennett did not completely understand Harry's brand of humor, even though he always encouraged him and believed that, in some of his "pathetic scenes," he was as good as Chaplin. But the Old Man was shrewd enough not to argue with financial success, and he intended to keep Langdon starring in two-reelers. Sennett raised his salary, as stipulated by Langdon's contract, which ran until December 31, 1925, but he did little to grow his films along with his fame.

Langdon wanted to make features. All the other major comedians—Chaplin, Keaton, Lloyd, and Semon—had already switched to the feature format to ensure their popularity, importance, and longevity. Story and character could be developed more fully in a feature than in a confining, split two-reeler. Features provided broader avenues to experiment with context, costume, and plotlines that were not easily approached in short films. Keaton, for instance, dove into period pieces (*Our Hospitality*, 1923; *The General*, 1927), and his character fit into them with ease. Chaplin wove his persona into extended tales of poverty and endurance that became social commentary; even after talking films debuted, Chaplin continued to use silence to convey his message with iconic images (*The Kid*, 1921; *Modern Times*, 1936).

Mack Sennett, however, had a negative attitude toward features. He was strikingly stubborn on this issue, although it was partly understandable, given that Sennett had pioneered the short format in comedy in 1914, at a time when exhibitors thought audiences could not endure more than twenty minutes of comedy at one sitting. Some dramatic exceptions had succeeded and were considered major uplifting events: Sarah Bernhardt's *Queen Elizabeth* in 1912 and D. W. Griffith's *Judith of Bethulia* in 1913, among others. Full-length comedy, however, seemed like a frivolous waste of time and money; it was also difficult to sustain a long comedy because it was, by nature, based on speed and repetition that might wear thin if prolonged.

Sennett had experimented with the feature *Tillie's Punctured Romance*, released in 1914. For six months he tried to persuade exhibitors to show the film, and when he finally succeeded, Chaplin became a major star and left the Sennett studio soon thereafter. Two years later, Sennett made *Mickey*, a full-length comedy with his girlfriend Mabel Normand, lavishing nearly a year's work and a quarter of a million dollars on it. *Mickey* was shelved until a theater finally played it in 1918 as a substitute for a film that had not arrived. This venture proved to be a complicated enterprise for Sennett. *Mickey* captured Normand's gifts as a comedienne in a way that

Sennett's slapstick shorts had not, and a veritable *Mickey* craze turned her into a star. Normand railed against Sennett's controlling nature during their tempestuous relationship and moved on to Sam Goldwyn. This left Sennett with a bitter aftertaste once they had separated both personally and professionally.

Having lost two of his most important moneymakers and close allies because of features, the Old Man may have considered long films a jinx, and he was reluctant to try a third time. Moreover, he had an agreement to supply a steady stream of two-reelers to all his regular distributors, including Pathé. Features were unquestionably risky: if successful, they could draw lucrative returns but might drive a star away; if they flopped, they could bankrupt a studio with a shoestring budget. Shorts were safer for Sennett's purposes.

Langdon felt loyal to Sennett, who had provided him with a talented creative team and stardom, but he was torn. To maintain his lifestyle and support a new baby, Harry needed more income. Even brother Tully, who had reentered the picture, encouraged Harry to form his own unit so they could work together again, as they had in vaudeville. Ripley and Capra sided with Langdon because they were eager to turn their talents to full-length stories. Only Edwards remained noncommittal and was content with either format. News of this conflict filtered into Daisy Dean's column "Notes from Movieland," and she reported in March 1925: "'Tis said that Harry is becoming such a favorite with the fans that they are demanding to see him in longer films. So when Harold Lloyd leaves the Pathé organization for the Paramount lot, Langdon will take his place in feature-length pictures." This was news to Sennett, who felt that he had earned the "king of comedy" reputation—at least on his own lot—and had little tolerance for opposing views. Some staff members, such as F. Richard Jones, knew how to smooth-talk Sennett into believing that whatever happened had been the Old Man's idea. Langdon, however, did not. Instead, he demanded a new contract that promoted him to features, with more money and more autonomy. Sennett's counteroffer was a renewal of the existing contract. Langdon refused to budge, and Sennett told him what he could do with his demands. Langdon promptly announced that he was leaving.

Ultimately, cooler heads prevailed, but not before the Hollywood grapevine learned of the dispute. The *Film Mercury* of April 17, 1925, reported that the differences between Langdon and Sennett had triggered an "avalanche" of offers for Langdon, including a generous one from Har-

DRESSING ROOM

CHARLIE CHAPLIN
BETTY COMPSON
FORD STERLING
SYD CHAPLIN
CHAS MURRAY
BEBE DANIELS
HAROLD LLOYD
GLORIA SWANSON
HARRY LANGDON

Harry inheriting Sennett's famous dressing room.

old Lloyd himself, who wanted to produce Langdon features as part of his own company. It was, in the newspaper's view, "the first time in film history that one star has sought to get control of a dangerous rival." Other rumored offers came from Metro Goldwyn for a flat salary, Famous Players–Lasky, and Warner Brothers, which proposed a dazzling figure for six productions. The report implied that Sennett had a reputation for creating stars and then losing them when others offered more lucrative deals. Sensitive about this public image, Sennett refused to rescind his decision. Jones gently suggested a compromise: Harry would star in a feature, but he would also continue to make two-reelers for the remainder of his contract. Harry agreed, but only if he could make three-reelers. Jones then proposed a mix of two-reelers and three-reelers, and the two men finally settled on this deal. The "avalanche" of outside offers must have persisted, however, as Langdon continued to negotiate privately, even while working on his initial feature for Sennett, *His First Flame*.

On one exceedingly hot day in late May, California was hit by a tremor. No major damage occurred in the Langdon house, although pictures swayed and china rattled. But Rose suffered a miscarriage. She sank into an extended period of mourning and depression, lighting votive candles around the house and secluding herself. The rift between Rose and Harry created by ambition and money—as well as his infidelities—only widened with this loss. As Rose's relatives rushed to her side, Langdon began to feel uncomfortable in his own home and escaped to the studio to pursue bigger movie ideas and fulfill greater ambitions.

The Capra-Ripley-Edwards team spent more than two months on Langdon's first feature film. When *His First Flame* was finally in the can, however, Sennett strategically chose to delay its release. But Langdon's insistence on doing longer work had left the Pathé Exchange in a quandary. Exhibitors were accustomed to receiving one Langdon comedy per month, and no shorts were forthcoming because of his work on this feature. To meet the quota, Sennett decided to release the two shorts Harry had made for Sol Lesser at Principal Pictures two years before, which he had acquired as part of Langdon's contract.

Horace Greeley Jr., directed by Alf Goulding, was released in June 1925. In it, Harry concocts a romantic image of the Old West from reading dime novels and decides to explore it. This basic premise is reminiscent of one of Douglas Fairbanks's most successful early films, *Wild and Woolly* (1917), in which he plays a naïve New Yorker with no idea that the West has already been tamed. However, *Horace Greeley Jr.* most closely resembles the second half of Langdon's *Boobs in the Woods*. By dumb luck, Harry earns an undeserved reputation for toughness and wins a pretty girl's affection. The title *Horace Greeley Jr.* was another attempt to exploit a popular film of the previous year, Keaton's *Sherlock Jr.* The ever-perceptive reviewer T. C. Kennedy, who thought the film had some effective scenes, also recognized a difference between the old (good) Langdon and the new (great) one. This was, chronologically, only Langdon's second film after twenty years of vaudeville. Thus, it did not reflect how Langdon's comedic style and persona had evolved since his first screen appearance in *Picking Peaches*. Although Sennett released this early effort out of financial necessity, he inadvertently provided a measure of how far Langdon had come since his initial screen appearances.

To keep the Langdon flow going in July, Sennett released the second Principal short, *The White Wing's Bride,* also directed by Goulding. The plot of this film may have been worked into the later Sennett short *Feet of Mud,* given that Harry plays a street cleaner in love with a socialite, and much of the plot concerns his efforts to hide his lowly profession from his prospective in-laws. "White wing" was 1920s vernacular for street cleaner because of the white uniform. The title may have been another attempt to parody a current hit: a Universal release circulated in 1924 titled *A White Wing Monkey,* starring a chimp named Joe who plays a street cleaner in Jungletown and rescues a baby from lions. Almost routinely, reviewer Kennedy labeled this "conventional slapstick" and noted the difference between this earlier jaunt and Langdon's later work. Although the film showed that Harry's trademark pale makeup, giant coat, and small-size hat had already emerged at this early stage, clearly this short could "not bring the laughter which is now expected of Harry Langdon comedies."

Nevertheless, these two shorts filled the gap until August 1925, when Langdon returned to a regular work schedule. His release that month was *Lucky Stars,* in which he plays another aptly named character, Harry Lamb, who is meek and mild and, as an intertitle describes, "TRUSTING AS A BALD MAN WITH HIS FIRST BOTTLE OF HAIR TONIC." Lured by a quack doctor named Hiram Healy, played vigorously by Vernon Dent, Harry seeks his "lucky star" but finds only trouble, especially as Healy is interested purely in money. Langdon must have enjoyed reenacting his medicine-show days under Dutch Schultz (whom Dent may have resembled). As the real Harry did in those days, the film character Harry Lamb entertains the poor suckers and persuades them to buy the phony elixirs. Natalie Kingston appears as the daughter of the town pharmacist, and Harry is drawn to her beauty, believing she is his lucky star. He is unaware that her father has asked her to get rid of the competition. The "Lamb" is continually duped by the quack doctor, his love interest, and even the suckers: Harry is simply unable to understand the cruel side of life. The complete innocence of this character is demonstrated by minute movements and expressions, such as

There He Goes.

listening to Natalie's heart with a stethoscope but then cuddling up against her like a child with his mother, even as she readies to stab him in the back. The subtlety of the "Lamb" is almost lost in the rampant slapstick, although the pathos of the Langdon theme—child against cruel destiny—becomes vividly evident by contrast.

Despite these story flaws, the onscreen trio of Harry, Vernon, and Natalie was moving like a well-oiled machine, just as the team of Capra, Ripley, and Edwards did so offscreen. A little more than two weeks after *Lucky Stars*, Pathé released *There He Goes*, the first of the three-reel shorts Langdon was supposed to film that summer. It was launched with surprisingly little fanfare, contrary to what one would expect with a new format. Harry's role as a racing car driver spoofed the 1924 Universal release *Sporting Youth*, whose working title had also been *There He Goes*. Harry's famous stage routine "Johnny's New Car" had finally been symbolically integrated into the plot. But despite Langdon's popularity with his fans, *There He Goes* was treated cavalierly. Sennett knew Langdon was not intending to renew his contract and had chosen to work for First National instead. The Old Man saw no point in spending good money to promote a disloyal employee.

The dismissive publicity for the film, in conjunction with its chaotic slapstick plotline, fueled the exhibitors' disappointment. *There He Goes* came and went quickly, almost unnoticed in the newspapers. The film was the listless swan song of a promising collaboration that had run its course. Sennett watched yet another of his stars defect to a rival company. Meanwhile, Langdon's dream of making independent features was materializing, and he was on the threshold of limitless promise. He was ready to grasp all that film stardom had to offer. Harry Langdon—and his latest alter ego, Harry Lamb—were fully prepared to find their lucky star, searching for it with both eyes closed and hope in their hearts.

According to his contract with First National, Langdon would "deliver a minimum of three feature films at a budget of $250,000 each ('A' pictures), with an option for more at the same budget.... First National would eventually put up a total of $1,000,000 plus $6000 a week salary for the comedian, plus 25 percent of the profits."[26] Langdon's business manager, William H. Jenner, and his attorney, Harold Lee "Jerry" Geisler (who would attain a reputation as "lawyer to the stars"), handled the negotiations.[27] Moreover, Langdon would have his own production unit, with the freedom to choose his own writers, directors, and supporting stars. More exactly, the contract set out the preeminence of "'Harry Langdon's judgment, management, supervision and control, solely, exclusively and uninterruptedly exercised by him at any and all times and places and in the manner determined by him alone,' including the 'employment, discharge, control, direction and action of directors.'"[28]

Given the press reports of numerous lucrative offers (or rumors thereof), it is unclear why Langdon chose First National. It is possible that Sol Lesser reentered the picture, now kicking himself for letting his "white elephant" slip through his grasp. Lesser was an entrepreneur with many interests, and Principal Pictures was merely a side venture. He had helped organize Associated Exhibitors, then bought out P. L. Talley, one of the original founders of First National Pictures Corporation, and merged the two into Associated First National. The company was principally a distributor, but it also financed the production of films it wanted to distribute. Acting in the company's behalf, Lesser had, for instance, signed up child star Jackie Coogan, who had achieved fame in Chaplin's *The Kid* (1921); he established Jackie Coogan Productions and made six films with the youngster, including the successful *Oliver Twist* (1922). Thus, Lesser was experienced in setting up a star's autonomous production unit, with First National as the backer, in return for the right to distribute the films. If he was indeed the catalyst in this deal, Lesser may have used the same strategy to lure Langdon to First National, which would have been easy, given their previous relationship. The deal with First National was reached on September 15, 1925, a year after Langdon had first been approached to work in film. He was now in charge of his own features under the new Harry Langdon Corporation banner. A formal announcement appeared in the *Los Angeles Times* on November 9: "Harry Langdon and his staff have moved bag and baggage to their new quarters on the United Studio lot where First National makes its headquarters."

Once settled, Langdon organized his own team. He hired Harry Edwards at $1,000 a week to direct and Frank Capra at $750 a week to act as assistant director and screenwriter. Also joining the team was Elgin Lessley, who had apprenticed in 1911 with the old Méliès Star Film Company and was recognized as a top cameraman in the comedy field, having worked at least ten years for both Arbuckle and Keaton, among others. Arthur Ripley later reunited with his old teammates on Langdon's second feature film.

This leap into "independence" created fodder for the media to speculate about the "real reason" Langdon left Sennett, and the fan magazines rarely skimped on theories and opinions. A cartoon in *Motion Picture Magazine* drawn by Chamberlain depicted Langdon in a clown outfit strolling off with his First National contract in hand and looking over his shoulder at Sennett, who is standing agape in a baker's outfit and tending a cart with a sign that reads, "Custard Pies Mack Sennett." A cynical "nursery rhyme" tops the drawing:

> Simple Simon left the pie-man,
> Not because he was not fair,
> "But," said Simon to the pie-man,
> "I can make more jack elsewhere."[29]

Given all the hoopla over the breakup, Langdon felt compelled (or perhaps was advised) to make a public statement to assuage any notion that the separation was the result of ego, resentment, or bad feelings. Langdon called these erroneous perceptions unfair to both Sennett and himself. He lauded Sennett's "genius and uncanny ability as a producer of comedy entertainment," which had in fact helped Langdon achieve his present status. Langdon assured the public that the contract in place would allow him to continue enjoying "Mr. Sennett's cooperation for many months to come." Moreover, until there was a more formal announcement directly from Langdon's office, he asked everyone to stop spreading rumors.[30]

Langdon was now in charge of dictating his position, his allegiances, and his future. He also shared some of his newfound wealth with his relatives. Brother Tully was hired as an "adaptor," essentially an honorary title. Youngest brother Claude, who was married and had an infant son, moved from Iowa and was put on the payroll as a "confidential secretary and consultant." This nepotism might have offered Langdon moral support, but he frittered away a good portion of his $6,000 a week on these "employees." Harry, however, considered it necessary and reasonable to support his blood relatives in this time of great professional success. Meanwhile, his relationship with Rose and her extended family was disintegrating, and his personal life was becoming more challenging, given Rose's emotional demands. He needed to focus on the one aspect of his life over which he could exert full control. Langdon had always been comfortable working and reworking a surefire routine, so now he would rework his films. He knew on some level that his new autonomy and the public's acceptance of him as a comedy "expert" were guarantees that he could not fail in this arena. All else was, by contrast, unworthy of his attention.

In her isolation, Rose still pined for her stillborn son, and her remedy for grief and depression was to host extravagant parties for Hollywood's upper crust. Despite being a public figure, Langdon was an intensely private man. Partying triggered his extreme shyness and added to his resentment over having so many "strangers" in his home, including his in-laws, who had challenged him for decades over Rose's well-being. Interestingly, Langdon's marital woes were paralleling those of his peers. Both Chaplin and Keaton had troubled or broken marriages and had been involved in scandals; only Lloyd seemed to have found wedded bliss. After avoiding his marital problems by working late hours, Langdon finally decided to move out officially after one particularly bitter argument with Rose.

By now, Langdon was willing to extricate himself from what he considered a suffocating bind. In a property settlement reached on December 26, 1925, Harry instructed his lawyers to give Rose whatever she requested. Harry kept for himself only the stock in his filmmaking corporation, some personal possessions, and a small car. Rose got the house, a Lincoln sedan, the property on Hollywood Boulevard, and several pieces of real estate they had acquired in Los Angeles and Milwaukee during their marriage. Rose was also to receive $25,000 for each film Langdon made at First National and 20 percent of all his earnings up to July 21, 1933. Rose made sure she benefited from the collapse of her marriage, and out of desperation, Langdon hastily conceded. The gossip columns called it an amicable divorce and even made light of the outcome—no doubt feeling that a comedian's marital difficulties warranted some levity: "Under the peace terms Mrs. Langdon acquires their Hollywood home and numerous skits and other odd bits they possessed when the Langdons were in vaudeville and thought celluloid was only used for collars. Harry, for his share, gets the air and the gate."[31] Langdon likely did not see the humor in the situation, but given the security of his corporation and his anticipated success, he had no problem paying an exorbitant amount of alimony. From that point on, Harry and Rose ceased all communication except through the courts.

While Langdon was ending his marriage at considerable cost, Sennett was still gathering the loose ends of his own relationship with Langdon and trying to recoup his losses. Although they had separated amicably—at least according to Langdon's public statement intended to squelch rumors to the contrary—Sennett found a way to profit from Langdon's early work. While Langdon was developing his first feature for First National, *Tramp, Tramp, Tramp,* Sennett decided to dust off Langdon's three unreleased shorts—*Saturday Afternoon, Soldier Man,* and *Fiddlesticks*—as well as his first feature comedy, *His First Flame.*

When *Saturday Afternoon* was distributed in January 1926, Sennett must have felt fresh pangs over losing Langdon. The film approaches comic perfection, and its three reels are packed with generous helpings of Langdon's screen repertoire. Harry plays a classic henpecked husband, but he also enjoys his transgressions with pretty girls (mirroring Langdon's personal experiences at the time). However, his efforts to be a cheating playboy are filtered through the lens of a young boy, and Harry is full of anticipation as he experiments with sideways glances, winks, and other flirtatious mannerisms. Yet when a girl touches a button on his overalls, Harry snaps to defend against physical intimacy—ironic, considering that he is playing a married man. One can only conclude that he is not really a husband but a child pretending to be a grown-up. He is not an ordinary guy seeking extramarital fun; he is a female-dominated innocent hoping to prank his dragon of a wife. Likewise, during fisticuffs with a rival (Vernon Dent), Langdon refines his concept of boy-man bravery. He is neither a coward nor a weakling; he willingly leaps into the fray and assumes the proper threatening postures of a man. But clearly he is not a man, and all this motion is ineffective. Harry's reaction to brutality is exquisite. Felled by a mighty blow, he is more surprised than pained. He simply sneezes and curls up into his favorite fetal position.

If *Saturday Afternoon* had been released when it was made, it would have been a portent of Langdon at his best. With expertly measured pacing that enhanced Langdon's routines, this new style of comedy omitted the traditional Sennett slapstick. The controlling force in this vehicle was not Sennett himself but four of Sennett's best minds pooling their talents.

While the Old Man was planning to release the last of the Langdon gems in his collection, the public was about to witness the first film produced by the Harry Langdon Corporation and the first six-reel venture for the comedian. It was the result of the same four minds in full gear, but completely independent of Sennett. Although the old trio and their star were confident that they could not fail, more objective reporters were waiting to see their output before pronouncing the verdict. The *Film Mercury,* which had reported the Sennett-Langdon breakup a year before, had uncannily predicted the great expectations surrounding the comedian's new work:

> As the first publication to appreciate the real genius of Langdon and forecast for him a success equal to Chaplin and Lloyd, the *Film Mercury* advises the comedian to think well before jumping and above all things be sure that the producer he does [work] with is capable of providing him with an organization that can make good pictures for him. Most of them are offering him money but no assurance of a first grade line of comedies. And without good pictures Langdon can never get into the big league of film stars.

Langdon felt that his reputation had been solid for at least a year. Now that he was his own producer and had a solid team behind him, he could expand his character and his stories to give his fans and critics only the best. Langdon had been moved and influenced by the high praise lavished on him. As early as March 1925, Harry Carr of the *Los Angeles Times* had declared Langdon the funniest in Hollywood. According to Carr, the inevitable comparisons to Chaplin had elements of validity—the same undercurrents of pity mixed with humor, the delicacy of technique, the "shades beyond shades." But Carr's words elevated Langdon to an echelon of his own, where he had no peer: "I say 'like Chaplin,' but the fact is he isn't the least like Chaplin. He is like no one the screen has ever seen before—or is likely to see again. He is just Harry Langdon." This lofty estimation signaled the expectation that each Langdon film would outdo the last. Even allowing for an occasional flaw—even the best films have weak spots—Langdon concluded that he was meant to follow the same direction that had led him to this pinnacle. He felt invincible simply because he was like no one else.

The reviews of *Tramp, Tramp, Tramp* were virtually unanimous: "Harry Langdon exceeds expectations. We thought he would be good. Now we know that he is great." So declared the *Lewiston (Idaho) Tribune*. *Variety*, the industry standard, praised Harry in his first independent feature: "Aside from the expert handling of all the gags assigned him, he does several very long scenes in which facial expression is the only acting. . . . If Langdon can follow it with something as good or better, he is automatically installed as a pretty high muckety-muck among the Chief Screen Comedians." The Kansas City Mainstreet Theatre reported that "customers tramped through the entrance for the biggest week [a gross of $18,000] the house has had this year."

Austere Mordaunt Hall of the *New York Times* caught the film's premiere at New York's Mark Strand Theater on March 21, 1926, and concluded, based on audience laughter, that it was "jolly entertainment." He drew typical parallels with Chaplin, citing *The Gold Rush*, but actually thought that Langdon's episodes suffered by comparison. However, he attributed this "fault" not to Langdon but to those "half dozen authorities who contributed to the gags in his story." Langdon might have interpreted this critique to mean that he, as the star, had made the best of some inferior material and that his efforts alone had saved the show. It was important to Langdon that he continue to shine, despite any flaws in the script penned by his paid writers.

Tramp, Tramp, Tramp is another story of hapless Harry seeking fortune and love. His innocence merits him both, yet his bumbling casts doubt on whether he will achieve them. Curiously, the film opens with a dramatic situation involving small versus big business; in this case, Harry's father is a shoemaker being overwhelmed by a corporate manufacturer, Burton Shoes. The struggle is soon reduced to the familiar conflict between Harry and the rest of the world—like a tiny planet threatened by the kismet forces of the solar system. Burton himself has plastered the town with posters of his daughter Betty (played by an ambitious starlet named Joan Crawford) and is sponsoring a transcontinental walking contest to advertise his footwear. Although the opening sequences refer to this drama, the appearance of the humorously pathetic figure of Harry translates all dramatic possibilities into a strange mix of seriousness and levity, complexity and simplicity. Langdon's costume provides an instant sight gag and fashion statement whereby clothes make the man (or man-child). His work apron must be worn over his full suit, while his fat cloth hat stands at attention like an exclamation mark. His response to his father's crisis is to inquire, "Does that mean I don't get my bicycle?" This query does not make sense coming from a grown man, yet it is oddly convincing because Harry's naïve expression and pillowy clothes are persuasive of a child's logic. He aspires to growth, as do all children sooner or later, and announces that he will raise money to help his father "in three months if it takes a year." To the extent his brain can grasp reality, this bizarre calculation makes complete sense. He is at least cognizant that winning the walking race might earn him $25,000, and he is motivated probably as much by the desire to help his father as he is by the desire to get his bicycle.

The rest of *Tramp, Tramp, Tramp* chronicles Langdon's encounter with the reigning champion walker Nick Kargas (Tom Murray—a Vernon Dent look-alike); the poster girl Betty, on whom Harry has a major crush; and his oddball predicaments on the way to winning the competition. Earlier in his film career, Langdon had been restricted to the testing ground of twenty minutes or two reels to deal with love interests and catastrophes. Now he had at least an hour to indulge in nuances. Yet Langdon, or director Harry Edwards, still needed to recognize the limits of excessiveness; the film should sate the audience but leave them craving more. Langdon's rapport with stage audiences had given him the hard-earned license to convey them just so far; what worked in one town he could replicate in another town, or he could modify whatever had not worked. Now his "invisible" audience expected fresh new films. While shooting, he had to measure what was comic enough or serious enough for this mass appetite, and it was a time of experimentation with new possibilities.

For example, in one sequence, Betty has been watching Harry's shy demonstrations of affection toward her poster, and he starts a lengthy but well-paced exposition of coping with her physical proximity. He dodges and scampers toward the protection of the trees. He compares the billboard face with the real face. Afraid to touch her, he reaches to within millimeters of her body. His glances are purposefully out of sync with hers. There is little dialogue, but Harry's communication is clear. He cannot forge a mutual relationship; he is capable of only a Harry-centered relationship with a human prop to which he reacts. It is a showcase for a one-sided language of quandary. The human prop finally provides the terminal punctuation to Harry's dawdling sentence: when he braces himself to kiss Betty's hand, she gives him a pair of Burton shoes and leaves.

Love, in short, makes Harry goofy. He has pasted poster cutouts of Betty's head on the walls of the hotel room he shares with Kargas, leading to a series of gags—which include breaking the bed and ripping up feather pillows—that tax the champion's patience as he tries to sleep. To silence Harry, Kargas feeds him a fistful of sleeping pills, culminating in two lengthy routines in which the only movements are Langdon's leisurely facial and bodily expressions. The drug's languishing effect creeps meticulously over Harry's face, setting off hand flutters and lip tics. He exhibits a remarkable spectrum of sleep states in close-up. He reaches for a pitcher of water that sits across the room, yet to him, it seems to be only an inch away. Unlike his stupor in *All Night Long,* which contains a manipulated slow-motion traipse, Harry now creates slow motion with real-time fluid body movement. Like a juvenile ballet dancer winding down the dance of the dying swan, Harry floats toward the pitcher but sinks drowsily to the floor, his body propped into a triangular shape. This unusual pose becomes an after-gag in the transition to the next day: the race is about to start, the crowds are cheering, and—with a cut back to the hotel room—Harry is still a triangle on the floor.

The second routine flows naturally out of the first as an assistant comes in to help Harry dress. Of course, the Burton sweater is oversized. As the assistant tosses him about like a rag doll, Harry erupts into laughter at being tickled and drowsily wags a reprimanding finger. Every attempt to bring Harry to the starting line is hindered by his physical hems and haws. Still sleepy, he sinks into a crouch to survey his predicament, almost forming a question mark that punctuates his opponent. When the assistant rolls up his sleeves to knock some reason into him, Harry groggily imitates him

Harry waiting for his billboard girl to see him race in *Tramp, Tramp, Tramp*.

but then becomes more intrigued by a coin he has unearthed from his baggy sleeve.

Once the race begins, *Tramp, Tramp, Tramp* is an episodic recounting of Harry's problems. Kargas tries to eliminate Harry, who continues to stroll along with an indomitable spirit and uncanny luck. Kargas sends Harry crashing down a steep cliff, but fortuitously his sweater catches on a retaining fence and leaves him hanging. However, his illogical efforts to secure himself to the fence rather than climbing to the other side only loosen the fence, so that he dangles more precariously until he toboggans down the slope. Harry executes the routine well, but its main drawback is the scene's poor editing. The original shot establishing the steep drop is unevenly matched to the next shot of the gentler slope down which Harry slides. Nonetheless, one might choose to overlook this editorial defect because of Harry's insanely perfect luck, which preserves his innocence and lands him in first place.

Langdon later reflected on this scene in a 1927 article he wrote for *Theatre Magazine* called "The Serious Side of Comedy Making." He points out that "tragedy frequently stalks" the making of comic successes, "for an essential element of successful comedy is thrill, and thrills are seldom obtained without some actual physical danger." Langdon recalled that no one in the company wanted him to do this stunt—he was not a hardy athletic type like Keaton, who single-handedly executed many extreme stunts. But lacking a stuntman, Langdon chose to do the feat himself. He was concerned that "there hadn't been a titter from the crew" as he coasted down the precipitous drop, because he was convinced that the only way to "judge whether your stuff is funny [is] by the reaction it gets from your impromptu audience. When I got off the fence I met nothing but blanched faces and silence." Fortunately, the stunt elicited laughter from audiences, who had not witnessed its dangerous execution.

The film marches on with a redundant title that appears twice: "Tramp Tramp Tramp / The Boys Are Marching." In addition to justifying the title of the film, the statement alludes to a popular song of the day. Langdon may have volunteered this verbal gag, given that he compiled the thematic music cue sheet for the film. He also included such ditties as "Dear Little Boy of Mine" for his father's appearances, "Stay in Your Own Backyard" and "I'm Sitting on Top of the World" for the fence routine, and a variety of "Airs de Ballet" to accompany his limber moves. The "race" has now taken detours that fill screen time but shift the focus of the action to Harry's idiosyncrasies. He amuses himself by stealing fruit and is caught with his rubbery face painted dark with fruit stains. In addition, a watermelon slips out of his billowy sweater, rolls down to a lower road, and knocks out Kargas. Inexplicably—but with the logical illogic of comedic plots with gags for their own sake—Harry falls in with a chain gang, adding a new twist on the title "Tramp Tramp Tramp / The Boys Are Marching." Harry replays some familiar gags: he finds a junior-sized sledgehammer, strikes a rock, and patiently waits for the effect. His confrontations with the chain gang emphasize his ineptitude with weapons: firing a gun scares him, so he uses it as a sledgehammer. Although the prison setting has no purpose in the plotline of the race, one might excuse it as Langdon's chance to mine his character's development as a helpless babe and, ultimately, an opportunist. Having acquired an iron ball chained to his leg in the prison fracas, Harry escapes on a train, but his shackled foot drags on the ground; forty miles later, he is ahead of his competitors without technically cheating because one foot has never left the earth. Strange creature of habit that he is, Harry never notices that the train wheel has cut through the chain, and he continues to carry the ball with him in lockstep.

The climax of the film and the race is a cyclone.[32] The cameramen who shot this sequence had to be lashed to trees to avoid being blown away by the wind machines. Keaton also shot the iconic scenes in his short *One Week* (1920) and his feature *Steamboat Bill Jr.* (1928) standing against fierce winds at a forty-five-degree angle. Harry's encounter with wind gusts is less extreme, yet he choreographed it to suggest a mental conversation with nature. After being blown back several times, he throws objects at the wind; when a newspaper flies back at him, he jumps in fright. Finding himself in a vacant barbershop, Harry decides to wash up; as he removes each article of clothing, the wind sweeps it away piece by piece. When he reappears wrapped in the shower curtain like swaddling, he wonders where his clothes went. The cyclone also spins a bedraggled Kargas into the area, and he pleads with Harry, of all people, to rescue him. Horrified, Harry responds with the same nearly effeminate outrage displayed in *The Sea Squawk*. Unlike Keaton—who by the end of his films is honed into an athlete of impressive strength and bravery, despite his initial clumsiness—Langdon never undergoes a mature transformation. He remains a child and faces calamity with this mentality.

Despite his immaturity, the final scene of *Tramp, Tramp, Tramp* reveals that Harry and Betty have married and are parents. Thanks to oversized furniture, Langdon plays his own infant. The quirks of fluttering, staring, and gurgling, with and without baby bottle and ball, perfect Harry's regression from child-man to total baby. Now Langdon has the chance to be a pure unadulterated baby without compromising to adulthood. Whether teething on his crib or swinging the crib until he is dizzy, Harry is a baby from another planet. A review in *Picturegoer* attested as much: "It seems incredible but he really is a baby . . . a changeling, maybe . . . with all the baby attributes you can imagine. He must have studied babies by the hour to have achieved it." Or else the baby embedded in Langdon all this time had finally surfaced in unharnessed perfection.

Tramp, Tramp, Tramp solidified Langdon's critical reputation as a comic wonder boy, a prediction made by *Photoplay* in March 1926, when it named him Hollywood's favorite comedian, and confirmed in its August review. Referring to the link between Lloyd and Langdon, whose chance to collaborate was now just a distant memory, *Photoplay* proclaimed: "Ask Harold Lloyd who gives him his biggest celluloid laugh. Ask any star. They will all say Langdon." The fan magazine applauded the fact that this "doleful face and pathetic figure" was finally out of the two-reelers and called him "a worthy addition to a group of comedy makers of which we have entirely too few."[33]

Harry as his mini-me in *Tramp, Tramp, Tramp.*

Unfortunately, some reviewers were harsh. W. Ward Marsh, writing for the *Cleveland Plain Dealer*, stated on April 19, 1926, that fans had witnessed Langdon's metamorphosis from "an expert two-reel comic to a fair-to-bad feature length comedian." Likewise, exhibitors based their negative responses on audience reactions, calling the film a "grand and glorious flop." One exhibitor clearly did not think too highly of Langdon's subtle comic style, complaining that "standing around and looking foolish isn't comedy." As a result, box-office receipts were disappointing, and the film barely broke even.[34]

Although some exhibitors griped, one person who could not control her laughter at Langdon's expressions and clumsy gestures was his costar Joan Crawford. Langdon alluded to her lack of acting discipline in a 1929 interview. He said she never caused him trouble except for laughing so hard that he had to redo scenes multiple times.[35] In trying to restrain herself, however, Crawford also seemed to restrain her acting, for she is stiffly adequate as Betty, and the role is meager for a feature-length love interest; however, this served to put the focus on Langdon. *Tramp, Tramp, Tramp* was actually Crawford's eighth picture, but the previous seven had all been shot the year before, so she had not been a screen actress for very long. She had come to film directly from the chorus line; her first interest was dancing, and she had no formal stage training. She had been loaned to First National by MGM, which was grooming her for more important vehicles. Langdon claimed that he had arranged her loan-out, but both Edwards and Capra said the same.[36]

The dispute over who had obtained Crawford was minor, however, compared with the larger issue of who actually directed *Tramp, Tramp, Tramp*. Edwards was credited as director, and Capra, assisted by five gag writers, was credited with writing the story. But Capra was on the payroll as assistant director, and with all his apparent contributions to "directing" the film, he may have felt double-crossed at credit time for not being acknowledged as such. Given his obsession with detail and his prior editing experience, Capra would not have permitted the slipshod matching of shots in the cliff scene, whereas Edwards was less concerned with such details. Capra, who had always seen Langdon's persona as a grown-up innocent, may have injected some subtle touches—or at least suggested them—to enhance Harry's character in *Tramp, Tramp, Tramp*. For example, when he pretends to be casual with Betty but succeeds only in looking awkward, Harry is framed entirely over her shoulder. This may have helped camouflage Crawford's incessant giddiness, but the technique also zeroes in sharply on Harry. Such an inventive use of camera work was more likely to be devised by Capra than Edwards.

Long after its American premiere, an article by Don Eddy in the May 1, 1927, edition of the *Sioux City Sunday Journal,* curiously entitled "Harry Langdon Stirs Bushmen," related excerpts from three letters from around the world reacting to *Tramp, Tramp, Tramp,* indicating Langdon's global stardom. In one letter (which took sixty days to arrive in Hollywood), a woman who lived in a village in New Zealand noted that she could not enjoy the film "because of the screaming and shouting of the natives" in the theater. In a village in India, the theater was "a circular stockade of thornbush inside which the natives squatted on the ground." The letter writer and her husband enjoyed the film because it had English subtitles. An interpreter translated for the rest of the audience, who laughed continuously even though they were usually quite reserved. Finally, in Switzerland, the Kulm Hotel advertised a showing of the film on a little slip of yellow paper attached to the restaurant's menu, announcing "a grand cinema performance . . . in the grill room tonight after dinner at 9½ p.m.," with tickets "available at the concierge and by the entrance."

Based on both his recent critical fame and his lifelong experience in stage comedy, Langdon became more confident when sharing with the public his expertise on comedy. In the 1927 article for *Theatre Magazine* cited earlier, Langdon expressed his understanding of the dual nature of the comedy genre. This no doubt justified his persona as both tragic and comic—as he saw it, as it was being developed by his creative team, as it was perceived by audiences and critics alike, and as it was compared and contrasted with his peers. Langdon composed (either on his own or through his publicity machine) a very "serious" consideration of funny business; it included intriguing pearls of wisdom—culled from classic literary references—that (despite his earnestness) would not always match his output in later films. A lengthy excerpt from that article permits us to "hear" the voice he chose to make public in the silent film era:

A despondent man goes up to leap to his death from a high building; his coat catches on an awning and he dangles in midair. It is tragic to him, but the audience screams. A man is in love, the girl rejects him for another. That is tragedy, but the things the comedian does are funny. A man buys a new hat, it blows off and a horse steps on it. It is a calamity to him, but a howl to an audience.

Have you ever analyzed why you laugh at these things? It is the concentration on the physical, as opposed to the spiritual.

Any individual is comic who individually goes his own way without troubling himself about getting in touch with the rest of his fellow human beings. It is the trifling results of our fellow men that makes us laugh. A comic can make us laugh, providing care be taken not to arouse our emotions. To view comedy is delightful, but to partake of its ingredients, might leave a bitter taste.

Systematic absentmindedness, like Don Quixote, is the most comical thing imaginable. The four greatest stimuli to laughter are rigidity, automatism, absentmindedness and unsociability.

John Bunyan said: "Some things are of that nature as to make his fancy chuckle while his heart doth ache."

One cannot give himself up to tears, yet there are few tragedies in which tragedy does not play its newly developed role. Comedy, at its best, has always pointed a moral. It has not set out to do so, but instead, has assumed seriousness as the foundation of laughter.[37]

It may be difficult to determine whether Langdon developed his philosophy based on what his team and reviewers were saying about his persona or based on what attributes he, as a veteran comedian, chose to give to his persona. It was, most likely, more of a mutual relationship rather than a cause-and-effect one. Langdon's "Johnny" struggling with a breakaway car onstage was never a sad clown—harried, frustrated, and exasperated, but not sad or tragic. By contrast, his cinematic stories were pulled from and dependent on Langdon's repertoire of physical reactions that resonated with audiences through an element of pathos hiding behind the laughable. Thus, this duality began to define and label who the Langdon character was and who he would remain.

Such "analytical spins" may have seemed premature, given that they were based on only a dozen comedy shorts and one feature. However, they were the foundation for Langdon's inclusion as the fourth face on the "Mount Rushmore" of silent film comedians. A clipping from the March 10, 1927, edition of the *Dothan Journal,* a small newspaper in Alabama, featured an item entitled "Harry Langdon Dubbed Saddest Movie Funster." This represented the broader perspective being delivered to and accepted by the public. Despite being a "comedy king," he was clearly one of the most "melancholy actors appearing before the camera today. . . . And according to film philosophers the mainspring of Langdon's irresistible comedy lies in his apparent sadness." Yet the trick that uplifts pathos into comedy requires a careful and ephemeral balance. The transformation from one to the other takes place in an instant; it is an exchange that involves stunning the emotions and then releasing them. "That whimsical little twist of the mouth and that slight, very slight, glimmer in his eyes. It is that moment of change that makes Harry Langdon funny. When you feel most sorry for him he lets you laugh. You are glad to laugh. So you do laugh." The article concludes by stating that "Harry is a great student of the human emotions. That is why he is a great comedian." The writer thought Harry would have made a great Hamlet if he had not been given such a magical "twisting mouth."

Langdon had now run the hardest race of his career, even though it was only two years long. His twenty-five years crossing the country with partners and props in vaudeville were trivial compared with the production of one film seen simultaneously by thousands of people who cast their ballots and decided whether he deserved their praise. For the moment, Langdon was selective in terms of what he chose to hear from reviews. Now familiar with the rugged terrain of filmmaking, he pronounced himself victorious and was convinced that the next lap would be easier.

The Strong Man became one of the most eagerly awaited and successful films of 1926. It was, in fact, a poignant comedy because Harry's love interest is revealed to be a blind girl, even though he does not realize it at first. Years later, Priscilla Bonner, who played that girl, captured the essence of Harry's profoundly real character in *The Strong Man*:

> Suddenly she is in the garden and the man appears and tells her that he is the one. She visualizes him as tall, dark, handsome-looking, glamorous and so forth, and she doesn't know that he's got the funny little hat on top of his head. Then she realizes that he's going to know that she's blind. He stands there looking at this dream girl and realizes that she can't see him. . . .
>
> It's an idyllic thing, it's a dream thing, it's a man's dream of an ideal woman. Which probably doesn't exist. But every man dreams. And every woman dreams of a knight in shining armor. It's a wonderful dream and they created the dream. Langdon and Capra created almost, you might say, every man's dream.[38]

Reviewers were likewise trying to capture Langdon's ephemeral nature with concrete imagery: "that little elf who floated to Hollywood on a moon beam," "a thistledown creation from Lewis Carroll," someone who gives "little half hearted gestures à la Lillian Gish."

Tramp, Tramp, Tramp might have garnered mixed reviews, but it seemed that with *The Strong Man*, all the elements converged to create a tour de force. Roscoe McGowen in the *New York Daily News* opined that dictionaries would not be complete "until Langdon leads the list of synonyms for laughter." Newspapers and fan magazines extolled the film's gradual emotion-building power: chuckles turn into howls, howls creep into tears. The *Los Angeles Record* advised audiences to stay away from the film if they did not want to laugh for three days after seeing it. Even Frank Capra acknowledged Langdon's "amazing scope." Exhibitors, whose box-office disappointments often led them to make testy comments about Langdon's weak films, cheered *The Strong Man*'s impact on their profits. One exhibitor claimed he had to shut off the picture three times so the audience could recover from laughing.

Hoping to nip unwelcome surprises in the bud, Langdon had for the first time invited newspaper critics to preview screenings of *The Strong Man*, and Tom Waller of *Moving Picture World* described how the Langdon team systematically measured the film's success during one preview: Jed Buell of the Deluxe Theatre in Los Angeles actually tabulated the number of laughs from the audience—293—while at another performance, the head of Langdon's company, William H. Jenner, counted 225. The difference was attributed to Jenner's admitted "inability to determine exactly where one laugh left off and another began."[39]

In retrospect, perhaps the most eye-opening review came from William Morris Houghton, writing for *Judge*. His words foreshadowed a landmark essay written twenty years *after* the end of the silent film period by James Agee, who paid homage to the golden age of comedy and set four particular clowns on a pedestal. Houghton unequivocally deemed the "big four" to be Chaplin, Langdon, Lloyd, and Keaton (in that order). He specifically connected the middle two: Lloyd may be funnier than Langdon, according to Houghton, but only Langdon had "the quality that robs laughter of its ruthlessness and brings it close to tears." It is interesting that Chaplin's ability to blend comedy and pathos did not strike Houghton as Langdon's competition. He may have been more impressed with Langdon's extremely subtle, ephemeral, and primarily innocent method of bridging the two emotions. With such careful preparation for a hit and glowing reviews rolling in, an ad for *Weekly Variety* could not keep from boasting: "Hercules of Hilarity—Samson of Smiles—truly the World's *greatest* comedian. . . . *Thousands* lined the sidewalks willing to pay any price to see *The Strong Man*." The fans responded so well that the first national Harry Langdon Fan Club was established, with Doris Rondeau as president. Dan Eddy, Langdon's publicity director, sanctioned the club through the Harry Langdon Corporation and supplied promotional materials such as autographed photos and "personal letters" from Langdon thanking members for their "interest in the Club and in my efforts to entertain you." At its height, this national fan club had 200 members.[40]

Langdon/Schweik revisited in *The Strong Man.*

What makes *The Strong Man* so special is that it starts with drama and then emphasizes Harry's comedy by contrast (the same approach also worked for Chaplin). The film begins in the most somber of settings: a battlefield. From the barrenness rises a late bloomer, Paul Bergot (Harry Langdon). This is a curious full name for a comic character who, up to this point, has been identified only by nickname or simply as Harry. The intent may have been partly to help localize the character to the French landscape during World War I and also to suggest the potential of a more dimensional creature at work. He has been abandoned in no-man's-land and futilely practices firing his machine gun at an empty can of beans; he fares better with a slingshot. Paul receives a letter from a girl back home and sighs over Mary Brown's photo, unaware that the enemy (Arthur Thalasso) is behind him. Paul is captured and is toted away with a quick hop out of the frame.

Another dramatic phase of history is illustrated as immigrants land at Ellis Island after the war.[41] Suspense builds as the camera focuses on the lettering on a well-traveled trunk: THE GREAT ZANDOW AND CO. Zandow is none other than the enemy soldier returning to his strongman act on an American vaudeville tour, and his company is Paul, his prize from the war.

Every sequence in the immigration office exhibits another Langdon characteristic familiar from his earlier films and now fitting sensibly into the story and personality of Paul. Once, Paul salutes the flag with one hand and gives an upturned-palm wave at it with the other. When Paul's cape is removed, the timorous ex-soldier happily exhibits the life belt he is still sporting. This sets off a fine routine in which Paul becomes entangled in the life belt while extracting something from his roomy trousers. Each time he moves, Zandow smacks Paul's pudgy hand like a child who cannot stand straight while his parent is dressing him. When Zandow spanks him, Paul moves into position like a chastened child, knowing he deserves the punishment. The routine contains an obvious, twisted love-hate, father-son relationship, with Paul trying to outsmart Zandow while pretending to obey him. In a stunning shot that not only climaxes the routine but also captures his total helplessness, Paul bumps into one bench, which falls against the next and the next, causing a cascade of benches to tip over in solemn progression toward the camera. He skips ahead and brakes on one foot to reverse the domino process. He never touches the benches; he only wishes they would stop falling. His fate is that they will not, and he leaves with Zandow, pretending nothing has happened.

As Zandow seeks work, Paul looks for Mary Brown, praying every time he passes a woman on the street that it will be her. As fate has it again, he encounters a con artist named Lily (Gertrude Astor), who stashes a wad of stolen bills in Paul's pocket. When she tries to retrieve the money, however, she finds it has inched deeply into his voluminous jacket. Overhearing Paul questioning a doorman about his lost love, Lily assumes Mary's identity and entices him to her apartment to reclaim the loot. Paul's routine with Lily is a full portrait of all that Langdon has suggested thus far about his toddler character confronting a real woman. Believing she is "Little Mary," he skips happily alongside her, swinging her arm, to her dismay. When a crowd separates them, he panics at losing his grown-up's grasp. In a cab on the way to her place, Lily uses her womanly charms to gain his confidence. Paul offers her popcorn and enjoys her cuddly arm around his shoulders, but he is horrified when her hand trespasses down his back. Frozen at the violation, he studies her, dumbfounded, as she lights a cigarette, gapes at her risqué leg, and puts his hand to his mouth in awe. He secretly compares her with the wrinkled photo of Mary and realizes his mistake. As Lily starts to unbutton his jacket, Paul's reflexes propel him from the cab.

Lobby card for *The Strong Man* with Gertrude Astor.

This routine flows into the next, prolonging his mortification. When Paul refuses to enter Lily's building with an indignant stamp of his foot, she fakes a faint. His uncertainty about this new reaction from a real woman prompts him to step-slide toward her inert body. The business that follows has become a classic that Langdon would repeat later in a sound film: He awkwardly totes Lily sideways across his chest to carry her up a flight of stairs, planting both feet on each step like a teetering tot. Exhausted, he sits down, with Lily lying across his lap, and then backs his way—seated—up the rest of the steps. The audience learns in a crucial cutaway that a ladder is aligned with the top step, providing another "flight" to nowhere. Paul cannot see the ladder, but he sit-climbs it until he tips over and falls off the top. He stands on rubbery legs, this time toting a nearby rolled-up carpet instead of Lily.

Once Paul enters Lily's room, his terror of intimacy explodes. When she whacks him with a bottle, he freezes, suspended in space, and then folds up instantly for a brief nap. A curious overhead perspective—jarring after the front-view perspective of the film thus far—provides a bird's-eye look at Paul's relentless assault by the vamp. He threatens her with a statue;

Langdon on the set at the height of his stardom. The top of the reflector bears a label that reads, "Harry Langdon Corp."

she threatens him with a knife. He painfully consents to her kiss, during which Lily retrieves the money. Having accomplished her task, she pretends to swoon. Paul, unnerved by the obvious power of his kiss, straightens his tie and backs away, saying, "Don't let this leak out!" for fear others will find him irresistible. In a bizarre after-gag, Paul runs into an art studio and encounters a nude female model, nearly suffering whiplash as he skids to a stop. He crashes through the door, leaving behind his cutout silhouette. Despite his imagined sex appeal, the sight of a woman in her full glory is far too terrifying.

With fate's occasionally kind intervention, Paul and Zandow perform in Cloverdale, where the real Mary Brown lives. The town is rent by controversy over bootleggers, whom Mary's father, Parson Brown, wants to oust. While Paul travels closer to his destiny by bus, Mary tells the local children the story of a plain girl who dared to love a brave, handsome soldier who won the war, but the girl never told him that she was blind. Through misty focus, the camera lingers on Mary's face, radiant yet saddened by a love she cannot have.

Priscilla Bonner, the pretty blonde actress who played Mary Brown, was best known for her work in the "tearjerker" category—her characters had given birth to illegitimate children and been dragged through rain and snow, caught in fires, and attacked by villains. She started her film career in 1920 and was soon typecast as the long-suffering heroine of such heart-rending vehicles as *Homer Comes Home* (1920), *Son of the Wallingford* (1921), *Little Church around the Corner* (1923), *Tarnish* (1924), *Drusilla with a Million* (1925), and her biggest film, *The Red Kimono* (1925). One of her special talents, well suited for the emotional role of Mary Brown, was the ability to cry spontaneously. She joined the league of other famous weepers such as Colleen Moore of *Flaming Youth* fame, who could cry separately out of each eye. Colleen once told Priscilla that she always asked the cameraman, "Which side do you want me to cry out of, this eye or this eye?"

When seeking an actress to play Mary Brown, Langdon wanted someone who could reflect his own character's thoughtfulness and sensitivity—the antithesis of Lily. When Priscilla was summoned for consideration, she was sent directly to the office where Capra and Langdon waited. The meeting was over as quickly as it began: they asked her if she wanted the part; she said yes and was paid $500, with no formal interview or screen test. Priscilla's background and appearance made her the perfect choice for what would be her first comedy.

When Paul enters the garden of Mary's residence, he is overjoyed at knowing that he has finally found her. Paul primps and struts back and forth, slaps his thighs in elation, and looks at her in the most debonair manner he can muster. Mary faces the crushing realization that he has not yet detected that she is blind. He asks with innocent irony, "Aren't you surprised to see me?" Moves and looks alone suddenly convey the depth of their mutual emotions—an exemplar of pantomime enhanced by the medium of film. Mary turns away from Paul, who stands alone and watches her from the background; the pride on his face wilts as he thinks he has disappointed her. She falters as she crosses to a bench under a tree; he

A moment of decision with Priscilla Bonner in *The Strong Man*.

studies her, wondering, slowly understanding. Though from different worlds, in this one delicate and dramatic shot, they are bonded. He follows her only with his eyes, holding his hands behind his back. The image fades at the intensity of their despair and hope.

When the scene fades in, there is no more pain. Paul and Mary are together under the tree, smiling. Paul tells her about his adventures while searching for her, replaying in boastful mime the "passion" of his date with

Lily. Paul's fear of women has evaporated; he has found someone who would never hurt him or destroy his innocence. He reaches out to touch *her* for a change, but draws back as he tries to overcome the vestiges of his fear. She looks toward him, sensing his need. He covers her hand protectively, hesitantly raises it, and quickly kisses it. He is more surprised than she is, but their love is sealed. For the first time, both Paul and Langdon are given free rein to express their purely romantic yet realistic adult feelings.

Bonner recognized that, despite being a comedy, the film—and her role in it—had layers, based on what both Capra and Langdon told her. There was no formal script for *The Strong Man,* or at least Bonner never saw one. Langdon helped her become comfortable with this new and difficult role for her:

> I told him very frankly, this was a new medium for me. And he taught me a great deal. He taught me about timing. . . . I said to him, "Well, just give me, you know, put a baby in my arms!" and he laughed so he thought it was funny. And then he told me I must time it and react more quickly, and so forth. And I listened attentively to everything he said. He could see that I was listening and he said, "That's fine, now, you've got it—you got it!" Then he would say, "Well, let's see how the little fellow will react." . . . He spoke of himself, the character of his in the third person. . . . Then we'd run through the scene and he'd always encourage me.[42]

Bonner was very shy with her costar at first and called him Mr. Langdon, until one day he asked her to call him Harry. He always appeared on the set fully made up, but when he was not working, Bonner marveled that the little fellow in the baggy clothes was very good looking behind his ever-present glasses: "He was well put together, he was well made. . . . That little coat that he wore made his shoulders look narrow. He wasn't like that at all. Every time I saw him on the set when he wasn't filming . . . he always had on a very handsome sweater. It was always sports clothes and sweater. He was a very attractive man." She was therefore flabbergasted when one day, out of the blue, he murmured to her between shootings: "How could anybody love such a funny face as mine?" She could only reply, "Oh, Mr. Langdon!" She found it unfortunate that such a kind, appealing man would think of himself that way. The question had popped out during a quiet moment, when Langdon might have been contemplating his wrecked marriage and his public adulation and finding himself at a loss to make sense of either. Or perhaps he was momentarily lost in the creation of his own persona now that the two—character and actor—were inextricably intertwined. For Bonner, however, this was a revelation of the insecurity that nudged the "little fellow" in every film.[43]

Langdon extended himself to help prepare Bonner for her part and to entertain her on breaks. He once asked her if she would like to hear him play music, and she shyly replied, "Oh yes, Mr. Langdon!" He transformed himself into a one-man band, alternating between violin, organ, banjo, saxophone—whatever instruments the set musicians, who accompanied the actors with mood music, had left lying around.

The blend of Bonner's emotional acting and Langdon's quiet, careful demeanor resulted in a garden scene that not only moved theater audiences but also moved the crew on the day it was filmed. The garden was built on a studio stage, yet it became an ethereal paradise through lighting, camera, and performance. The musicians played the piano, violin, and organ. Langdon limbered up for his little-boy eagerness and his dissolve into maturity. Bonner wore a pale blue chiffon dress and prepared to enter the world of blindness and newfound love. The workers on the set bustled around them, but for Harry and Priscilla, there were no other people, no other world. As Bonner recalled many years later with nostalgic detail:

> It was a dream garden, it was an out-of-this-world garden. It was a man's dream of an ideal girl. The garden was just perfectly beautiful. It was like a Utopia, it was a little Paradise. And the flowers and the roses, and they spent a great deal of time when the cameraman was working, and Langdon didn't say a word. Harry was very quiet and he didn't say "Hurry up" or "Get going" or anything. They just left him alone. And then they were turning on lights . . . and they took quite a long time when this scene started. . . . Stages . . . were very noisy places because they'd be working. When this scene started, the whole stage was absolutely quiet, and they were all watching. All of the workmen, the men who were building, all came over and stood in the back. Everything stopped. And everything was quiet. All we heard was "Love's Old Sweet Song" and "Lieberstrohm."
>
> After he learns that the girl is blind, and the shock, you see that on his face when he realizes it, and you see her turn away in

anguish. Then you see them sitting on the bench under the tree. Tenderness is the word that I would use in describing his manner toward the girl, the way he approaches her so gently, . . . so tenderly. . . . It was one of his most beautiful scenes.[44]

This sentimental dream-garden sequence is sandwiched between two prolonged comedy routines, an approach that was becoming an important component of Langdon's feature films. Critics and audiences howled over these comedy routines as much as they were touched by the dramatic interlude. Comedy contrasted vividly with the tone of the dream garden so that all reactions—humor and pathos—were intensified. *Variety* in particular commented on *The Strong Man*'s "light and shade" resulting from the sustained mix of sentiment and laughter.

The first of the two comedy routines contains much of Langdon's familiar, slow-paced reaction to a problem—in this case, dealing with a cold while riding a crowded bus. One critic lauded it as among the "masterpieces of modern cinema pantomime—the sequences where Harry, alas poor *Bebe,* is sniffling and sneezing in the toils of the heaviest but by all odds the most hilarious cold in the history of the movies." Langdon takes a mundane situation that has plagued human beings from time immemorial and makes it a pièce de résistance of self-recognition so that audiences can laugh at themselves the next time they catch a cold. A title explains that Paul has come down with a cold after taking a bath. His nose is darkened to show the effects of overblowing, and his cheeks blubber with sneezes and coughs. One advantage of silent film is being spared the physical sounds that exude from a person with such an ailment; instead, the accompanying music comically punctuates the sneezes and coughs while the comedian's physical choreography registers these reactions visually, with no sound to ground the reality. Case in point: an annoyed passenger asks if Paul has swallowed a fish horn; this potential sound, which the audience never hears, is "described" in this title, allowing moviegoers to imagine any variation of a "fish horn" Paul might have blown. Langdon dots the routine with small bits that intensify the overall comedy: Paul absurdly pours one cough drop from a Smith Brothers box into a spoon. He next uses two hands to force a spoonful of cough syrup toward his mouth, then flaps them in agony when he cannot bear to swallow it. He sneezes and sprays the medicine on his irate neighbor. When Paul finally swallows, he shivers in nervous flicks at the taste and stares for an inordinate amount of time as the alcohol in the medicine courses through his body, then swerves his large eyes to the other passenger, giving him a mock-fierce look. Paul suddenly flits a fist at the man, meaning to punch him, but stops short; in his mind, he has already knocked him flat. Paul continues to glare ferociously but subdues himself just as quickly. He practices punches from various angles, landing inches from his target. Obviously seeing Paul out of the corner of his eye, the annoyed passenger slaps him into stillness.

Next, Paul surreptitiously checks his mustard plaster, which he gingerly tries to pry off; the irritated passenger rips it off for him in one swoop. Dazed, Paul rubs camphor on his chest. The film cuts suddenly to the driver's cab outside, where Zandow is feasting on a Limburger cheese sandwich; the jar of cheese spread, which looks exactly like Paul's salve except for the label, rolls through a panel and lands beside the camphor. Paul obliviously spreads the malodorous cheese on his chest, his eyes widening at the sensation while the passengers turn away, aghast. Considering it a miracle cure, Paul announces: "My head's clear. I'm beginning to smell." Indeed—and the passengers eject Paul from the bus. The shots between Paul's downhill roll and the traveling bus are intercut until they unite, with Paul tumbling through the roof of the vehicle; he offers a friendly hand to the passengers, but no one will take it. Capra always acknowledged that Langdon alone was responsible for this routine, which became a comedy legend.

The next comic routine ends the film. Paul is forced to become the strongman on the town hall stage because Zandow is too drunk to perform. This routine symmetrically balances the leisure of the Limburger cheese ordeal as Langdon slowly builds entertainment through his character's mannerisms. Trapped within the oversized strongman costume of the Great Zandow, Paul repeats nervous moves and poses while wracking his brain, searching for ways to use the stage props. His physical frailty is never as evident as when he tries to lift 400 pounds. In fact, he is dumping bowling balls into a bottomless bucket set over a hole, then pretending to lift the bucket with great muscular exertion.

Simultaneously, the subplot of Parson Brown's crusade against the bootleggers is revived as he leads a march around town hall. Hearing an unruly crowd insulting Mary, Paul becomes a figurative strongman, determined to defend her with new force. He breaks bottles on heads while swinging from a trapeze; he destroys the walls with blasts from a prop can-

How to become a strong man.

non, even lying down beside the cannon for a quick nap after a job well done. During the shooting of this sequence, there was an accident as Langdon launched the final blast: "When the smoke cleared away, we found that one piece of the metal cannon had grazed the back of my head, struck a musician a glancing blow in the cheek, and buried itself in the wall of the stage. On the screen this scene was a scream."

This whole scene in which the walls of the town fall—like the walls of

Jericho, according to the pastor—elicited a piquant critique from Mordaunt Hall of the *New York Times*. Although he liked the film overall, he invited "Mr. Langdon" to study psychology so that he could construct narratives that would be "more than mere laugh-makers," especially because some of the "chapters" of the film tended to end abruptly before another sequence came along. He also questioned whether Scripture should have been included in a comedy and thought it was in bad taste to employ a "sightless heroine in a broad farce." In particular, Hall pointed out the exigencies facing the live musician who accompanied the film: "In this comedy the Mark Strand organist is kept continually on the alert watching his screen cues, for it would never do to play 'Onward, Christian Soldiers,' during a cabaret scene, and it would be equally disastrous if 'How Dry I Am' were rendered as the church people of Cloverdale march through the streets. Yet these two selections follow one another in the unfurling of this comedy."

Through his sheer will, little Paul has imposed peace on Cloverdale, and the finale of the film provides a clincher gag. Although short and simple, this gag is just as revealing of Langdon's character as the more extended Limburger cheese and strongman routines. Paul, clad in his baggy uniform as the town's new law enforcer, tells Mary sweetly, "Run along, honey. I don't need any help!" He then trips over an obvious stone in his path, and Mary leads him home safely. Clearly, not much is needed to present an obstacle for Paul; likewise, Langdon can convert the littlest gag into an important commentary on his persona and the comic world. This world is composed of details that the hero communicates visually by degrees—not by fully expressed intense feelings but by meaningful spurts. Yet the emotions bubbling below the surface emerge to create a dimensional figure unlike any Langdon had portrayed before. Richard Watts of the *New York Herald-Tribune* perceptively articulated the irony that the wistful and immature "Langdon mask" has maternal appeal—even, shockingly, sex appeal—but the latter is safely exhibited thanks to the love of a *blind* girl.

On some level, Capra had to acknowledge this new depth of character, and he admitted in his autobiography that Langdon indeed "had something extra special. There were things only he could do, and in his specialty he truly was a genius. No one was able to take a very simple situation, a passive one in which he is not initiating any action, and do more with it than Harry." Whether Harry was active and taking charge or passive and being acted upon, he was always reaching out to his audience with trademarks that now signified strength of character and emotional endurance.

Langdon's secret to success was working leisurely with these trademarks. It was necessary, according to Capra, to give Langdon enough time to construct a gag, even though it often felt like watching someone move in slow motion. However, Capra tempered his praise with the firm belief that Langdon ultimately failed to understand the importance of timing. In choosing between being too fast or too slow, Langdon would lose the character and the dynamism of the gag. Capra thus felt that, as a director, his responsibility was to keep Harry in character and moving at the best tempo for the task at hand. Capra's bitterness resulted in continual questioning of whether Langdon understood his own talents, despite his fame and philosophizing. Unfortunately, a shift in attitude had begun to affect Harry Langdon; it grew inside him as he lingered over his best routines, and it proved to be just as negatively forceful.

Priscilla Bonner did not notice any tension on the set of *The Strong Man*. For her, it was a dream of a film to make: "On *The Strong Man* everything just flowed beautifully. Capra was running everything, and everything was great. If there was anything wrong in *The Strong Man*, I wasn't aware of it. I don't think there was. There seemed to be a great rapport between Harry and Capra. But then . . . the scenes I was in were all emotional scenes and also touching, poignant ones, so everybody was very quiet. Everyone was concentrating on working very hard on that picture."[45]

Harry Edwards, however, had already noted a shift and acted on it: he split from the triumvirate when Langdon began telling him how to direct and he received no credit on *The Strong Man*. Meanwhile, Arthur Ripley sided with Langdon, especially because he had been invited back to collaborate on *The Strong Man* and received credit for revising the story. Ripley may have been the reason Paul's love interest was a blind girl, even though several team members, including Capra, had apparently argued against the idea.[46]

The shift in Langdon's attitude was recent, but given the nearly unanimous glow of his latest reviews, he thought he had proved himself to be a comedy genius of stage and screen. He felt entitled to make executive decisions about his work and the output of his corporation. Interestingly, the parallels between himself and both Lloyd and Chaplin had become less frequent because many Langdon fans believed he had caught up to his peers. Langdon had grown with each film, whereas some thought Chaplin seemed to be running in place, even though *The Gold Rush* was acclaimed as his greatest work. Chaplin continued unchallenged as number one, but the idea of Langdon surpassing the Little Tramp was no longer out of the question if he continued to dimensionalize his persona in these emotionally subtle comedies.

One key difference with Chaplin, who directed his own films, was that Langdon's magic was supported by a creative team. However, because most reviewers rarely mentioned the director or the writer, the spotlight was always full force on the star. This adulation may have caused Langdon to become myopic about his strengths and limitations. He continued to offer his analysis of the comedy formula, now planting its roots in sadness. For example, in an October 1926 article by Margaret Monks in *Cinema Art* entitled "Harry, Harry, Quite Contrary," Langdon states, "The absence of feeling which generally goes with laughter is what I find most interesting. In character I am an undying optimist.... No matter what awful predicaments I may find myself in, I must remain that optimist.... The greatest comedies of the future will be the saddest stories ever told."[47] These words shed light on Langdon's creative thinking behind his screen persona as well as events overtaking his personal life: the indignity of a failed marriage and an absence of feeling that led him to live only for the present. The line between personal beliefs molding one's destiny and destiny creating one's beliefs can blur, as it does when an artist's work consumes all aspects of his or her life.

When Edwards left the team, Capra willingly filled the void because it gave him his long-awaited chance to direct. He was sure he could handle Langdon, even when the star called on his writers to overrule Capra's directorial choices. But just as Harry's character became embroiled in a film routine that snowballed into a mountain of nuances, Langdon was rolling along a similarly perilous route, and Capra was troubled. Capra sensed Langdon's resentment even more acutely after *The Strong Man* was ranked "nineteenth in the *Film Daily* poll of 218 critics, a remarkable showing for a first-time featured director."[48] Instead of rallying together as part of the team, Langdon chose Ripley as a confidant and made his own publicity schedules that conflicted with shooting schedules. Capra perceived a pernicious malady in Langdon: "The virus of conceit—alias the 'fat head'—hit Langdon hard." It would become what Capra dubbed "a bad case of Langdonitis."[49] Although he recognized the tension, Capra was unprepared for the worst yet to come.

During the filming of *Long Pants* in the winter of 1926, Langdon attended a party given by Arthur Ripley. There he met Helen Walton, a striking bru-

Harry and Helen.

nette and former photographer's model.[50] Originally from Ohio, she was married to prominent businessman Thomas J. O'Brien, and they had a daughter named Virginia (Helen also had an older adopted daughter, Edith). Their marriage had been rocky for some time, and Helen had reverted to her maiden name, signaling that she was available. Harry, now legally separated from Rose, was residing in a bungalow on the United Studios lot, which was conveniently close to the First National compound. He was dating widely but found Helen strangely attractive and soon concentrated on her. Harry's penchant for a lavish lifestyle had not dissipated; he squired Helen to fancy restaurants and nightclubs, where they partied with Hollywood social climbers. Helen was strong willed, energetic, and ambitious—curiously reminiscent of Rose in terms of drive, but even more attractive. While the social scene was not Langdon's preference, he enjoyed the high life when a pretty woman was near.[51]

Helen had no problem juggling her marriage and attaching herself to a bona fide movie star. Her eagerness erupted into an intense interest in Harry's career, and he allowed her to visit the set of his next feature, *Long Pants*. Both Capra and Priscilla Bonner, who was again Harry's costar, recalled Helen's charming voice singing out, "Harry, dear!" or "Harry, darling!" for all to hear before she led him off for a private talk. Harry would soon return to the set and quarrel with Capra over how to direct a scene. Meanwhile, Ripley also confided his opinions to Langdon privately, rather than in front of the creative team, thus excluding Capra. A conference with Ripley, as the chief writer, was justifiable, but Langdon always seemed to be transformed after a conversation with him—a little more demanding, a little haughtier, and certain that his was the better approach to directing the scene. Langdon's idea may have been workable, but it too often clashed with Capra's plan. The discord was so thick that even Bonner noticed the difference in atmosphere compared with the set of *The Strong Man,* and she showed up for *Long Pants* only when it was absolutely necessary for a scene. She recalled:

> At that time it took me a while before I realized that there was something wrong. But believe me, I did realize it finally. Mr. Ripley . . . was a very dour, almost unpleasant individual. I didn't get along [with him] at all. He never spoke to me. . . . I can still see [him]. I would draw a cartoon of him with his mouth going down like this [demonstrating a frown]. . . . He was one of the dourest— just a man you'd turn away from. Of course, comedy is a serious business, and I understand that!
>
> Nevertheless, Frank Capra was so warm and so gentle with me, so understanding and sure of himself, and he was the director. I have a great respect for directors. Ripley was always on the side, calling to Mr. Langdon, talking to him. They'd go and stand in the

corner with their shoulders together, turned away from everyone else. Then Mr. Langdon would come back. There was never a blowup on the set when I was there. Never. But Capra became more tense and more tense and more tense.[52]

Capra was furious one day when he found Helen overseeing production while comfortably seated in his director's chair. The tension was beginning to make him ill. His nineteen-year-old nephew, Tony Finochio, worked on the set at the time and was responsible for bringing lunch each day. Finochio had to make sure that his uncle's sandwiches were toasted "because the situation was giving him an ulcer."[53]

Public interest in *Long Pants* and in the man behind its success (the star, not the director) had reached an unprecedented level. Ironically, the stamp of approval for Langdon's public face was bestowed by John Grierson, noted English publicist and critic, who considered him a "great exception" to stars who are "not often so much concerned with making the cinema great as with serving their own private interests." Grierson even included *Tramp, Tramp, Tramp* and *The Strong Man* on his list of great comedies for the year. It seemed only those closest to Langdon were seeing another "face" that served his private interests and would eventually impact his cinematic greatness.

On January 15, 1927, Langdon became a radio announcer for the day when he sponsored the national broadcast of the Catalina Island Channel Swim and inserted a plug for *Long Pants* on KNX, the "Voice of Hollywood." The broadcasting station was installed on the steamship *Avalon*, which conveyed the swimmers through the treacherous Catalina currents. Radio experts in charge of the stunt forecast that favorable atmospheric conditions would allow the announcer to be heard by steamers crossing the Atlantic. Langdon was clearly attaining a global sweep beyond his homeland.

Meanwhile, a flock of reporters repeatedly appeared on the set to interrogate and photograph Langdon. Capra tried to bar their interruptions, but Langdon relished the attention, which surpassed any notoriety he had achieved in vaudeville. Fame had come astonishingly quickly and with magnificent perks, and Langdon wanted to satisfy his staunch supporters and give them whatever they asked of him. He told the reporters he had spent $1,500 on head shots to mail to his fans but then received three letters in a row asking him to autograph his hat. His reaction: "If this keeps up I will have to start to make my own hats." Fans also sought his

Poster for *Long Pants*.

opinion on everything from comedy to women. He was asked to respond to controversial questions, such as: "Should a comedian have sex appeal, and if so, is an actor who can make love seriously a comedian?" Less earth-shattering concerns included Harry's favorite dish (sauerkraut and apples), his favorite sport (golf), and some of his pastimes (sculpting, painting, music). In one article Harry was described as "a student, very widely read. He finds pleasure in reading philosophy and works of historical romance. He is a natural musician, playing virtually every brass, reed, and string instrument, except the violin. He is excessively modest and reticent almost to the point of taciturnity." If he had taken time from his hectic schedule to reflect, Langdon likely would have admitted being caught between the hyperbole of film fandom and the strain of social expectations. He was having difficulty balancing his natural quiet with Helen's quest for the high life. He was abandoning intuition and becoming more deliberate in choosing what he thought he wanted rather than what he needed.

In his enthusiasm for publicizing *Long Pants*, Langdon penned a "lilting poem" for *Hollywood Vagabond* readers on the joys of "trousers wide and airy," a "gift from some kind fairy." He waxed nostalgic about his pants until, one fateful day:

The last time that I wore them
Was to a country dance . . .
It was there, alas, I tore them!
Farewell! my first long pants.

Langdon seemed more interested in these publicity opportunities than in the making of the film itself; instead, he left Ripley and Capra to clash with each other during production. When he returned to the set, Langdon sided with Ripley on almost all counts. Bolstered by the power granted him in his contract, Langdon believed (like Chaplin) that he had to oversee every detail of the film, even the dress worn by his leading lady, and he insisted on taking the extra time such choices necessitated. This reasoning made sense to Langdon, given that he had been lauded for his leisurely approach to routines and for his genius in working on a simple gesture until its nuances were revealed.

Langdon insisted on adding to *Long Pants* until it became nine reels, a challenging length for a comedy. Tom Waller's March 19, 1927, article in *Moving Picture World* entitled "Harry Langdon: A Serious Man Who

Makes the Whole World Laugh" reported on Langdon's obsession with working and reworking scenes. Waller devoted three pages to detailing the process of making *Long Pants*, from its conception to the editing of 325,000 feet of film to prepare the preview screening. Moreover, without consulting his writers, Langdon had set up a shoot for one of his own gags that lasted from 8:00 a.m. to 5:30 the next morning, producing eighty-five takes. According to the article, Langdon directed the scenes in which he appeared, given that he knew himself and his stories better than anyone else did. The conclusion, paraphrasing Langdon's own belief, was that a star who directs himself can create better pictures that capture and interpret the emotional content in its truest form.

After reactions to the first preview, Langdon decided to cut *Long Pants* from seventy minutes to sixty-one minutes and then held several more previews. A newspaper item described Harry's "yardstick" technique for measuring the audience response to a preview. A cable running from Langdon's seat in the projection room to the operator's booth was attached to an odometer-type device to measure the footage. Every time he heard a laugh, Langdon tugged the cable; the total number of tugs equaled the tally of favorable reactions. There are no records indicating the actual counts, but updates in the trade papers noted that much "alteration" was needed before *Long Pants* could be released. One witty writer even incorporated several "clothing" metaphors to drive home the point: the film has "been pressed and trimmed and generally fitted. . . . No hand-me-downs, these. They are custom made. . . . That the pockets of these same *Long Pants* will be lined with gold or greenbacks is a foregone conclusion. . . . They are guaranteed to last an indefinite time and never bag at the knees!" The writer also tellingly commented that such films usually started in the cutting room, but for Langdon the process was reversed: editing was a last-minute fix for an overworked product, rather than a deliberative process of assembling the film by shot and scene and sequence.

Despite desperate reediting and the tension between director and star, *Long Pants* features some of Langdon's best slow comedy. He perpetuates his youthful character by playing a small-town boy who finds thrills from romance and adventure books and is babied by his mother, who refuses to let him wear more appropriate long pants and act like a man. (This is the first film that refers to the origins of Langdon's persona as a helpless child, a mama's boy, offering a backstory for why he so frequently succumbs to timid waves, innocent stares, and the fetal position.) For this film, Langdon might have enjoyed the idea of playing a boy again instead of a soldier, another role that was frequently imposed on him. On some level, Langdon himself had barely lived his own childhood because he had started working at such a young age, although his occupations were certainly filled with adventure, if not romance.

One of Langdon's extravagant but sorely underused sets appears early in the film during a sequence composed of unusual shots: at first, the camera closes in on Harry's hand reaching for a book on a shelf, followed by shots of bodiless movements—the closing of a door, an ascent up a ladder, the shutting of an attic door. The flavor of someone indulging in a forbidden pleasure is intensified as the camera glides, seemingly on its own, along these key spots.[54] Finally, Harry appears, fully grown but still a kid at heart. He imagines himself an elegant officer wooing a lady on a balcony—a Romeo and his Juliet—and such a shot suddenly appears. Langdon spent a lot of time and money erecting a massive medieval castle set and selecting special costumes and colors. News items mentioned that once the set construction was completed, Langdon devoted ten days to color-scheme experiments to find those that would "be suitable for the environment, and yet which should not glare when transmitted to the sensitive technicolor film." Thirty-two sets were built especially for *Long Pants*, including a forest of fifty-foot-high sycamore trees and an orchard of peach trees in full bloom. Moreover, the sequence was filmed in Technicolor. By this time, some films had already included color sequences, notably, Keaton's *Seven Chances* (1925) and *The American Venus* (1926) with Louise Brooks; the color novelty added a degree of box-office insurance. Langdon boasted that he planned to make an all-color picture if the public welcomed his experiment. Unfortunately, there was an overblown quality to this scene in *Long Pants,* especially because of its brevity. Langdon had also discarded a lengthy introduction preceding the castle sequence with child star Frankie Darro because preview audiences had indicated (perhaps on the laugh-o-meter) that they preferred having Langdon play himself as both boy and adult. The upshot of this scene is that time has passed, and Harry stands on his terrace looking down at a girl who ignores him. Finally granted long pants by his mother, Harry heads off on a bicycle—another production extravagance, with a prop man spending more than a week to find a vintage 1908 bicycle that still worked. While rehearsing some bike tricks, Langdon tried to balance head down on the handlebars and fell, smashing his hat and getting a headache.

Harry, the would-be murderer, in *Long Pants*.

Through a series of miscommunications, Harry believes a gangster's moll wants to marry him, although Mother prefers the girl next door, Priscilla. Time elapses again, and Harry is about to marry Priscilla, as arranged by his parents. In another fantasy, he imagines shooting his bride in the woods—a rather shocking turn for Harry's character, who seems to have grown into a callous adult simply by donning long pants. However, his murderous efforts fail because of his bumbling. The comedy ventures down a dark path: Harry does not shoot Priscilla, but *only* because he is inept, not because he has changed his mind.

Reflecting on this daring theme, Marquis Busby of the *Los Angeles Times* credited Langdon with basing this sequence on the "jazz murders" being reported in newspapers at the time. He also noted that people had tried to dissuade Langdon from including such a bleak "gag," but he knew better—he had also been advised not to use a blind girl as the heroine in his highly successful *The Strong Man*. Busby concluded that the idea might even be "regarded as a clever satire of Dreiser's *An American Tragedy*." It is possible that *Long Pants* was inspired by the plot of this 1925 novel about an ambitious but immature youth who is infatuated with women and murder. The book might have appealed to Ripley's darker side as a satirical film, but if *Long Pants* drew from the novel, he clearly took great liberties in "adapting" it. Interestingly, pursuing this literary connection further, Monks also refers to *An American Tragedy*. In expounding on "the necessity for pathos in humor," Langdon had spoken of the importance of being indifferent to rather than emotionally involved with his comic situations, thereby triggering laughter. This indifference was necessary for "little Harry" to even consider killing a lovely girl like Priscilla. Monks concludes her article with the tragic-comic duality that was Langdon's emblem:

> When Harry says the funniest comedies are made from the greatest tragedies, we wonder whether he considers his own life a comedy or a tragedy, for of hard grinding work he has had his share. Certainly his admirers must hope that he will reserve for himself some of that joy which he gives to countless others.
>
> Yet, as I got up to leave him, he picked up a book. I glanced at the cover. It was "An American Tragedy," by Theodore Dreiser. How contrary, Harry.

It is worthwhile to dwell briefly on Langdon's reading habits, given these two references to such a dark work. Ironically, Dreiser's book was not on his reading list in February 1926, when *Photoplay* asked a number of celebrities, including Langdon, which authors they enjoyed. His response casts doubt on whether he ever read *An American Tragedy*:

> Perhaps it's strange for a comedian to pick humorists as favorite authors, but I can't claim to like philosophy and that deep stuff. I like the life that we see about us every day, chock-full of humor. I could chuckle over Nina Wilcox Putnam, Octavus Roy Cohen, Will Irwin, and Montague Glass by the hour.
>
> Sometimes I like my life dressed up a little with adventure. I devour detective stories. I've read Jules Verne's *Twenty Thousand Leagues under the Sea* many times. As a kid, when I traveled with medicine shows, I always had my eyes glued to an exciting detective tale.

Dickens, for his quaint characters and his charm of style, and
O. Henry for his vitality and ingenuity, are the most highbrow
authors I read.[55]

If Dreiser factored into Langdon's inspiration for *Long Pants,* it was likely
an acquired taste—or perhaps a good publicity prop.[56]

Despite the black humor of Harry's intended crime, *Long Pants* is still
a comedy, and Harry is still a naif. Thus, his evil intentions ultimately clash
with his innocence and are necessarily thwarted by his ineptitude. This is
all the more striking when Priscilla plays along with him, fully trusting his
affection. The sight gags—Harry's trembling, losing the gun in his oversized pants, getting dragged by a horse, walking into a bear trap—reinforce his ineptitude just as Priscilla, finding the gun on the ground, shoots
it like Annie Oakley directly into a "Wanted" poster of the gangster's girlfriend on a distant tree. Stuck between developmental stages, Harry next
tries to save the moll, and his anxiety spawns another classic Langdon
routine.

After an extended sequence of balletic moves and mimic reactions
with a dummy that he thinks is a policeman, Harry endures a violent confrontation with the moll. Although he sits with his back to the camera as
he watches her dispose of a victim, his disillusionment and disgust are evident in the subtle movements of his back, as plainly as if his face were registering those emotions. He becomes trapped in a grand shoot-out, sitting
on the floor like a lost child, immobile in a bustling crowd and able to see
only adult feet passing by. When the scene fades out and in, Harry is standing in the middle of a group of men pacing in a jail cell. When he is
released, he walks like one emerging from a paper shredder. There is a
throwback to the earlier disjointed shots creating mystery: Harry stumbles
toward the camera from the jail cell, through woods, up a lane, and into his
home. His parents and Priscilla are seated at the dinner table, heads bowed
as they say grace. He quietly slips into his chair and closes his eyes. They
are so pleased to discover that little Harry has returned that they spill food
on him in their haste to welcome him back.

The final film, despite its underused sets, creative clashes, and seemingly hurried editing, garnered generally favorable reviews, although a few
isolated critics found it less than adequate in terms of the chronology of
Langdon's development. Lui Venator called *Long Pants* "the most pitiful
comedy I ever saw—and I don't mean pitiful in a disparaging sense. . . .

Long Pants is a sad comedy, strange words, but true! . . . *Long Pants* has more wistfulness, more pity per foot than any comedy heretofore released." Joseph McElliott thought *Long Pants* would have worked better as an introductory film for audiences who did not know Langdon, but given his repertoire, it failed to meet expectations. *Film Spectator* worried that Langdon had missed his chance to fulfill his art with *Long Pants,* calling the film "crude" and citing "carelessness in a production that must depend on sheer cleverness for its entertainment value." At the same time, Harry's persona made revelations that forecast new potential in the character. The reviewer concluded that Harry did not have to worry about money on this one, but he hoped the comedian would focus on "his art" rather than props or eccentric makeup to remain a star. Interestingly, this reviewer also suggested that Langdon "should be surrounded by the cleverest brains in pictures. Some day he will be, for even in pictures ability ultimately comes into its own." This was a double-edged comment: clever "brains" *were* at work with Langdon, but there had been such a shift in the team that its coherence was shattered. As usual, Mordaunt Hall of the *New York Times* did not mince words: he pronounced that the film's flaws rested with Langdon's reliance on others instead of himself—an observation that obviously did not sit well with Capra or Ripley, who seemed to have an even greater influence on Langdon than the director did. Edwards too must have cringed when he heard from the sidelines what had become of the project he had left behind.

The comments of exhibitors from across the country were far more scathing: From South Dakota, "One big piece of cheese that patrons walked out on." From Illinois, "This star puts crepe on the box office. Might just as well hang a smallpox sign on the lobby." And shockingly, from his "home state" of California, "You can go back to two reelers any time you want to, Harry. You mean less than nothing here in features."

The reviews ran the gamut, which was not a good sign, but girlfriend Helen and crony Ripley continued to whisper into Langdon's ear, assuring him that he was still the sole executor of his film legacy, and the public response was overwhelmingly positive. With three independent features under his belt, Langdon felt he had broken the "three-time jinx" of the theater with *Long Pants,* proving that, because of his acting and his character, flaws in the film could be overlooked—and blamed on others. This new triumvirate of Langdon, Helen, and Ripley concluded that the fatal flaw was clearly attributable to the person in the director's chair. The solution would be to find the right director—possibly Langdon himself.

In February 1927, while finalizing the film, Capra needed to shoot some close-up inserts of Harry's hand removing a book from a shelf so the audience could focus on the title. Any hand would have sufficed, as long as it matched Harry's look and sleeve. But Capra wanted to use Harry's hand, believing that the audience should be given the real deal, even for such a trivial shot. He issued a call for Langdon to come from his dressing room for the close-up and expected no opposition, as Langdon was a professional and seldom objected to retakes. But when Langdon emerged, trailed by Helen and Ripley, he scolded Capra for bothering him and refused to do it. According to Capra, the incident became explosive before anyone realized what was happening:

> I had sent for him several times. Finally Harry arrived, wearing a gaudy dressing gown and a gaudier scarf, followed by a newly acquired retinue of leeches.
>
> "Why in hell do you keep sending for me? Don't you know I'm through in the picture?" He was as arrogant as Napoleon chewing up a menial officer.
>
> "Sorry, Harry. I need an insert of your hand reaching for this—"
>
> "Insert of my hand? You ain't learned nothing, have you? Directors don't use stars for stupid inserts. They use *doubles*."
>
> "Harry, there isn't another pair of hands like—"

Shouting an expletive, Langdon ranted about being interrupted during an interview with two important New York critics. As he stormed away, he muttered, "That's what I get for trying to make directors out of two-bit gag men."

Capra reflected on how to handle the situation: should he kowtow as Langdon's "yes man," or should he assert himself as the film's director and as someone who had been instrumental in creating Langdon's persona? Capra assumed that Langdon's arrogance was really a reaction to his sudden popularity—a sort of culture shock—and decided to confront him. He found Langdon lounging on a couch in his dressing room, staring at the ceiling. "Harry," he said, "I came to tell you what many of us have wanted to say to you for some time, to wit: that you've turned into an impossible, opinionated, conceited, strutting little jerk. The happy little guy we once knew and loved has become an ungrateful heel. . . . Comedians must be loved to get laughs—and right now the only one who loves you around here is you."[57] Capra felt relieved when he left, even though Langdon had offered him neither a word nor a glance. The young director felt he was being a professional as well as a friend, showing Langdon tough love. Unfortunately, soon after, Langdon's business manager arrived at Capra's home and handed him his last paycheck with the message that Langdon never wanted to see him again.

The stunning news leaked out, and it was soon followed by another story that echoed the Sennett split and its question of egos: Langdon would be assuming the director's chair from now on. *Variety* stated on March 2, 1927: "Harry Langdon has decided that he no longer needs a director to lead him through his paces. . . . The comedian feels no one can interpret his thoughts as well as himself, so he is going to hold the megaphone instead. Langdon is also said to feel that nobody can title his pictures like he can, so he is also going to title same. In the past, all ideas and gags used in the Langdon pictures were credited with having been conceived by the comedian, with the gagmen simply helping out in the construction."

Moving Picture World also reported that Langdon was planning to cut his "corps of gag men or comedy constructionists, as they have been called of late, down to one man." Studio executives hurriedly rebutted these stories, noting that Langdon was not a "high hat" and that these rumors were an "injustice" to him. It was more that Langdon's technique was so unique that it was impossible to find a "kindred mind" to direct him. They also erroneously pointed out that Langdon had been his own director since the Sennett days but was too modest to take directorial credit on his films; instead, he "selected one of his gag men to sit on the set during each picture and watch the action for ocular errors." There was also talk that if anyone were to assume the directorial chair, it would probably be Arthur Ripley.

Before this ultimate assault, Capra had already been badly burned by Langdon's executive control on *Long Pants*. The star had altered Capra's "vision," deleting a prologue because Ripley had opposed it, and reducing a ten-minute, two-strip Technicolor fantasy sequence with gorgeous costumes, a knightly duel, and a fairy princess to a mere fragment.[58] The experience made Capra feel like he no longer existed in Langdon's world. It must have been devastating to lose the support of a friendly team, and it shook his confidence as a director. However, Capra was determined to find his directorial niche and learn how to control a film. In the meantime, the

Top: New director Frank Capra. *Bottom:* Langdon and staff arriving in New York for *Tramp, Tramp, Tramp.* The caption identified the men as follows: "Tim Wehlen, gag man; Hugh McCullom of First National; William Jenner, business manager; Langdon; and Frank Capra, cutter."

focus on *Long Pants* had shifted from director to star on all levels: even a large ad in *Variety* screamed Langdon's name three times in type that was three times larger than that of the film's title. Capra's name was not included.

At one point, Capra wanted to attend a preview of *Long Pants,* and he asked his wife Helen, with whom he had a tumultuous relationship, to accompany him. She agreed, but when the time came, he found her unhappily drunk—a recurring pattern in their lives—and he apparently hit her so hard that she crumpled into a heap and lost some teeth. All Capra could remember afterward was feeling that she was lucky he had not killed her—a bitterly ironic statement, given the disturbing sequence in *Long Pants* in which Harry attempts to kill Priscilla.[59]

Capra moved on as a director—and temporarily away from Hollywood—when he accepted *Hell's Kitchen* (released as *For the Love of Mike*), which starred Ben Lyon, debuted Claudette Colbert, and was filmed in New York. Unfortunately, Capra had been persuaded to defer his salary until the end of production and was never paid. Despite many strong aspects, the film was considered a commercial failure (after generally bland reviews, Colbert vowed never to make another film, but clearly she changed her mind when she contracted with Paramount two years later). Capra persevered as well, but he had been scarred by so many experiences that, according to his biographer, he turned into "a gut-punching little man in order to survive."[60]

For many reasons, Capra believed Langdon would fail if he attempted to do everything himself. But Langdon now embraced the idea of taking full charge of the business: directing, acting, writing, and editing. If he was to be another Chaplin, this was Langdon's destiny. But life imitated art, and like his character in *Long Pants,* Langdon tried to wear a pair of trousers before he had matured enough to do so. He was drawn to the wrong fantasies, forgetting the simplicity in his own backyard.

At this volatile time, Mack Sennett was still watching the progress of his former protégé. He probably wondered about the merits of Langdon's latest independent film, which did not even benefit from a successful writing-directing team behind him. But Sennett no longer held a grudge, especially as he stood to profit by releasing the last two Langdon shorts and the feature he had shelved back in 1925 and 1926.

The first release was *Fiddlesticks,* a two-reeler from the fall of 1925. It was by far the most bizarre comedy from Langdon's Sennett period, with a touch of surrealism and the only Langdon film that lacked a love interest. Yet the film is all about unrequited love—love of music, or what Harry believes is music. According to the film, he has been in love with music ever since being run over by a piano truck. He is passionate about sawing away at his bass viol with his bow, which causes anyone within earshot to turn violent.

A second theme of the film is another kind of love—of money. Professor Von Tempo (Vernon Dent) is an unfortunate witness to Harry's music lessons, but he is willing to delude his student into believing he is a genius, as long as the professor is paid. Harry is so deafened by his need to belong and to use his hidden talent that he does not detect the discomfort his music produces. He is absorbed by his ambition, which only his mother can understand but cannot avert, and her baby must learn to endure the world's rejection. In the chronology of his persona's development, this becomes the deepest dimension of Langdon's child-man; it is not only ironic, given the theme of love and rejection that his character plays out in the film, but also surprising, in that this aspect of his persona was developed during the early Sennett period but did not carry over into features. In experiencing rejection, however, Harry finds that he can turn his lack of talent into a profitable venture: his musical screeching prompts people to pelt him with metal objects, and a junkman recognizes Harry's value. The poor lad never realizes that he is being used; he sees it only as an opportunity to play in public. This characteristic imbues new insight into the persona: to satisfy his heart's desire, Harry must withdraw or be wounded. He is protected by his passion, despite being used by others for personal gain. Eventually, Harry learns how not to be hurt; he joins the adult world and profits from it himself.

For the first and last time in a film, Langdon's character looks placid and resigned as his talents are misplaced in this harsh environment. His childlike reactions are abandoned early in the film once art and innocence yield to money. Harry's one "tee-hee" laugh behind his hand is the last trace of the babe, for once he has discovered a quick way to make money, he survives. By the last scene, Harry, well dressed and prosperous looking, informs his family that he has made his fortune by "fiddling around." The family is anxious to hear the secret of his success. Harry whips out his bow, but only after shutting the window, for he has finally learned that one must play a game with the world, just as it has played one with him.

In *Fiddlesticks,* Harry is not the vulnerable, enchanting persona of his middle shorts and his first feature; he is a cog in the mechanism of his environment. Visions of metal objects flying disjointedly into a shot, or images of Harry in a cage or a dismal hotel room waiting out his rejection, place him on strangely remote terrain, and he responds differently. No longer a little child caught in unusual straits, he is in a limbo of situations beyond emotional reality. His devotion to hitting the bass strings separates him from those who do not appreciate his desire to be talented. He is alone in this quest and ultimately decides to channel his passion into a money-making tool. Shrewdly, he uses his "art" as a vehicle to achieve new self-awareness, even without the impetus of a beautiful girl.

Fiddlesticks has an unnaturally sarcastic bite, which may be explained in part by Ripley's control over the script. He enjoyed digging at targets when given free rein and may have been commenting on the mercenary side of human nature. Ripley's brooding, introspective nature collaborated well with Langdon's at this time; the comedian was suffering from his sour and costly marriage with Rose and unsettled ambitions. One may also wonder whether Langdon's divorce settlement led him to question whether his talent was only a moneymaking tool. While the ear-piercing music Harry produces in the short is never "heard," it is rendered visually into a neatly drawn art title stating that Harry's favorite tune is "My Wild Irish Rose." A caricature of a cat (drawn by Harry) yowls the lyrics depicted in trembly letters to signify stridence. Perhaps Langdon was making an inside joke by selecting this song and this image just as he and Rose were separating.

Fiddlesticks is an unorthodox Sennett film but an oddly fitting one for Langdon's departure from the Old Man's laugh factory. It was the last film he made there before leaving for First National, where greater films and more money awaited him. The film's release at this time, when Langdon was oblivious to the limits of his talent as a consummate filmmaker, was a poignant coincidence. Unlike his character in *Fiddlesticks,* however, Langdon was certain that his art would not fail him and he would remain untarnished by purely mercenary ambitions. Money was just a natural reward for his boundless talent.

In the wake of *Fiddlesticks'* release, Pathé also released a three-reeler that Sennett had been holding since 1926. In *Soldier Man,* Langdon plays the familiar trusting boy guided by a sometimes kindly Providence and revisits the Soldier Schweik character, for Harry is in the armed forces but does not know the war has ended; he is caught in a mental no-man's-land. Langdon also plays a second character who fabricates untold complications for the little guy. Publicity for the film accentuated this special aspect, which was sure to appeal to audiences: "This is the first dual role Harry Langdon has attempted and to see him as the diffident doughboy and then as the dissolute king, reveals a new characterization and comedy angle. That will prove a surprise to Mr. Langdon's fast increasing number of fans and admirers."

As the film opens, Harry is visually and thematically abandoned as he stands on top of a small hill, calling, "Hey army!" While he encounters a variety of dynamite explosions and skirmishes with a Romanian peasant, the film introduces his "alter ego": King Strudel the Thirteenth, an absurdly arrogant monarch who is also a drunk. Langdon as King Strudel reveals an entertaining new dimension to his mime abilities in an inherently different persona: he registers disdain and haughtiness with the lift of an eyebrow or the flick of a hand. Harry's former fluttery hand signifying helplessness now gives way to a new and opposite gesture. Before too long, however, Harry the soldier is back, still chasing the peasant. Harry has an exquisite moment when he crawls around with his rifle and parks under the belly of a cow. He takes casual notice of the udders, then double-takes; he moves stealthily, as if to touch them, then withdraws, as if being indiscrete; finally, he pretends he has never seen them and smiles at the cow, embarrassed. Langdon proves once again that he can take the most insignificant element and milk it—pun intended—for laughs.

The purpose of the dual role is to ensure that Harry the soldier is forced by opponents of the monarchy to impersonate King Strudel when he is kidnapped. In a twist befitting comedy, the king's robes fit Harry admirably—baggy and oversized. He agrees to pretend to be the king as long as his captors will feed him, sparking visual banter with medieval armor. Harry spanks the metallic hand of the armor, which has fallen into a fruit bowl, as if to steal the contents. When the lieutenant (Vernon Dent) announces the king's arrival, the film cuts back to Harry, who is now throttling the armor to the ground. Other gags involving a crown and the introduction of the Queen (Natalie Kingston) flow organically from the royal plotline, with Harry at his bumbling best. Much like Harry's previous inexplicable allure, as evidenced by women who wilt at his kiss, the Queen swoons as he munches on a sandwich. His bites and chews punctuate her statements of passion. He daintily brushes crumbs from his lips before

Pretending to be King Strudel for the Queen (Natalie Kingston).

kissing her; he studies her lying in a heap as he takes another sandwich and then falls asleep. Harry a lady-killer? The catch is clear when the scene dissolves into one of Natalie in a housedress and Harry curled up asleep in a soldier's uniform. As before, Harry's romantic power lives only in a dream state, and his real attempts at lovemaking are ridiculous. Despite a long and passionate kiss, wife Natalie never swoons, even when he purposefully tries to tip her over. Confused, he wonders how the fantasy could have dissipated with his waking. More than ever, Langdon demonstrates in this short his large repertoire of expressions and his understanding of how to perfect a routine with the illusion of spontaneity. However often he repeats the same gestures, his variations keep them fresh.

The films Sennett released and profited from were well received, and the public overlooked or simply forgot any current gossip about behind-the-scenes arguments and resentments because they were being well entertained. Given his popularity, Langdon was asked to make a guest appearance in a First National farce called *Ella Cinders,* released in June 1926. It was a vehicle for Colleen Moore, the wife of John McCormick, who was head of production at First National. She was quickly gaining a reputation as a typical 1920s flapper. In this feature, Moore plays a small-town nobody whose photograph is entered in a Hollywood contest as a joke, but she wins a role in a film. After rushing to the film capital, she sneaks into a studio and disrupts production on several sets, including Langdon's. He is in the middle of a scene from *Tramp, Tramp, Tramp,* wearing the bulky Burton Shoes sweater and fending off the cyclone, when Colleen dashes in. She pleads with him not to betray her to the guard who is chasing her, and he agreeably covers her with a cloth and sets a table on her back. When the guard enters, Harry is calmly dipping into a bowl of soup. He chuckles into his hand at the clever ruse. A grateful Colleen rises to thank him but flips the bowl into Harry's lap. Langdon's quiet yet atten-tion-grabbing reaction to Colleen's intrusion adorns this cameo with the charisma that made him so popular. It is a film-within-a-film gig that fur-ther solidified his position as a star, using his first independent feature to enhance a rising star's movie.

By this time, Langdon had completed *Long Pants* under Capra's fully credited direction. The Sennett shorts had also been released, conveniently becoming successful "fillers" between his equally successful features, although the Old Man's intention was not to fuel Langdon's stardom as much as grab profits while he could. Beyond this lay new and uncharted territory for Langdon. Without the structured guidance of Sennett and Capra, he was wholly on his own. He was, as one press release observed, carefully putting laughs under a microscope to dissect their success. Lang-don's "philosophy" of comedy was simply to be what he was, as he described objectively and analytically in an interview: "In the first place, the laugh is the reflection of one's frailties—of everyone's weakness. We think that we are laughing at the screen character but it seems to me that we are laughing at ourselves. . . . To be successful in winning laughs, one must be sincere. I can't fool my audience and say, 'I am funny and I'm going to make you laugh at me.' I must feel my part. I must be wretched and consequently ridiculous."[61]

This philosophy had been epitomized in the character of Paul Bergot, the little soldier lost in a no-man's-land and inspired by a blind girl's love. If Langdon drew his characters and comedy from reality, then he himself must have been like a fragile child suspended in the middle of growing up, only occasionally fluttering into common sense to deal with adulthood. Besides naïveté, however, Harry's character and comedy possessed an indefinable strength, ensuring his survival whenever innocence attracted doom, as seen in the odd film *Fiddlesticks*. Capra and Ripley, in their own ways, had sensed this strength from the outset of their relationship; it was a strength that extended beyond a simple stage routine. Harry also knew that his persona's frailties were his strong points, and he expanded that view to include his filmmaking. What he could not see was that his view was in soft focus, blurred by greater ambitions.

Sennett avenged his injured ego with one last hurrah and closed the book on Langdon by releasing *His First Flame* in May 1927, just a month after *Long Pants* was released. The Sennett feature was eagerly received, but it paled in comparison to Langdon's three independent blockbusters. While one notice called it "great fun," another shrewd observer questioned the wisdom of "presenting a stellar comedian in an old picture." To observant reviewers, the clash between old and new was obvious. No doubt because of the Old Man's discomfort with features, the longer film struck some reviewers, such as Laurence Reid of *Exhibitor's Herald,* as a "typical two-reeler padded to five reels." Missing were Langdon's spontaneity, rhythm, and "sparkle," which his new pictures displayed more consistently.

His First Flame is a rehash of old slapstick routines, situated mostly in a fire department. One startling change, though, is that Harry plays a wealthy young man and recent college graduate—the valedictorian, in fact. However scholastically bright he might be, emotionally, he is still back in kindergarten. With his girlfriend (Natalie Kingston), Harry fumbles with various expressions of love (he loses an engagement ring, a truck runs over a box of chocolates, a car door decapitates his flowers). He is sent off to join his misogynistic uncle (Vernon Dent) in the firehouse but spends a lengthy, unfunny sequence dressed as a woman (shades of *The Sea Squawk*). He rescues Natalie from a fire while skittering aimlessly through smoke-filled rooms. The one genuine sparkle in this menu of slapstick fare is a brief scene in which Harry, carrying his girlfriend, confronts his uncle and tightens his hold on her, desperately turning to escape his bad influence. The mime is simple and sensible, but Langdon's expressive eyes and protective gesture reach into the gag for a sentiment that exaggeration would ruin. Harry is intuitively clinging to his greatest dream—simple romance, and the inner strength that comes with it—and no one will deprive him of that.

The release of *His First Flame* was Langdon's official break with the past. Now that Sennett and Capra were out of the picture, Langdon's only

Firefighting Keystone style.

support came from Helen, Ripley, his fans, and his inflated ego. Newspapers covered Langdon's plans for a new film and his search for the perfect story—one he touted as the greatest vehicle he had ever attempted. Langdon had rid himself of distractions that interfered with his ambition of full autonomy. Interestingly, despite his self-perception, some regarded Langdon as a bit of a conundrum, even back when he was making *His First Flame*. Although he relished fame and fortune, he sometimes gave signals that he considered interviews an invasion of his privacy. He was labeled a "modest clown" who found answering interview questions pointless; he perked up only when discussing the technical aspects of his work. Anyone seeking the man behind the comic persona found a curious mix of personalities: an intensely private man who was reticent when answering questions, an outspoken "academic" (informally educated through experience) who expounded on his craft, an avid filmmaker dreaming large visions that his character deserved, an artist defining himself before he understood his full potential.[62]

With *Long Pants*, Langdon crossed into a terrain lined with pitfalls. Frank Vreeland of the *New York Telegram* felt obligated to caution him:

> Harry Langdon has reached the stage where, as statesmen put it, there is need to Sound a Note of Warning. Sooner or later most movie stars who turn independent producers arrive at such a point, unless they have legal guardians appointed for them, like Jackie Coogan's parents. And Langdon's latest picture, *Long Pants*, shows that he is passing through this phase of growing pains pretty acutely.
>
> It is that critical period when a film actor who has attained stardom almost in one sweep begins to think his own presence in the foreground of a picture is of greater importance to success than a knockneed story lurking slyly somewhere in the background. Practically every film luminary has undergone this ordeal, and whether or not he has kept his head during the process has determined whether he has emerged a sweeter, grander star, a nature's nobleman of the screen or subsided eventually with only a few fleeting bubbles to mark his place on the surface.

Now, only Harry Langdon alone could make that choice.

3

Elusive Stardom

In the spring of 1927 Harry Langdon received fan letters from two boys from New York City's Lower East Side who wrote that they loved his work but were too poor to afford his next movie. Langdon sent them each a check to buy tickets. In no time, nearly a thousand fans from the Lower East Side had written to Langdon with similar requests. Whether the story is true or fabricated makes little difference: Langdon's celebrity was ensured and perpetuated by such stories. Coincidentally, his next feature was situated in a tenement much like those on the Lower East Side, and in his magnanimity as director and star, Langdon spared nothing in re-creating the ambience.

For ten weeks, Langdon ran a contest for studio employees offering a prize for the best title for his new vehicle. Technicians, artisans, and players all vied in the competition. More than a thousand names were suggested and rejected. For a while, the working title was *Gratitude*.[1] The winning title, *Three's a Crowd,* earned the ingenious contestant a cash prize and a paid vacation. In the meantime, Langdon had constructed a tenement set that was three or four blocks square, in which roughly 300 extras milled before the cameras.[2] More than fifty youngsters aged one to ten years and an organ grinder's monkey played throughout the opening street sequences.

When Langdon needed a blizzard for a number of scenes, he ordered an especially ferocious one, despite the ninety-degree temperatures in Southern California. Langdon arranged for steam to rise from a truck radiator and vapor from the nostrils of horses and pedestrians, even though the cast was sweltering in winter clothes. At least two carloads of "movie snow," concocted from gypsum, cornflakes, and salt, lined the streets in drifts.

Langdon even hired a new heroine for the production. Gladys McCon-

Hollywood blizzard à la Langdon for *Three's a Crowd*.

nell, a Portland, Oregon, girl, was a WAMPAS Baby Star—one of a league of promising young actresses[3]—and had been in the movies for two and a half years since graduating from high school. She had made a number of westerns, where her horse-riding skills proved handy, and she had worked for Hal Roach and Fox. Her contract had recently been taken over by First National, and Langdon chose her to be his leading lady.

Capra had prepared the script for *Three's a Crowd* during the final days of shooting *Long Pants*, but Langdon revamped it after their separation. Langdon bestowed the honor of story adapter on his brother Tully; he simultaneously shaved off excess jobs until he had a close-knit team working under him. Langdon was more cautious than usual about safeguarding his gags. He and his crew worked for several weeks behind high walls on the lot, with the door locked to anyone not working on the film. This precaution was a habit of Hollywood comedians who tried to prevent rival comedy companies from plagiarizing their gags, and Langdon was no exception.

Two hundred thousand feet of negative film for *Three's a Crowd*, twice the amount of footage shot for *Long Pants*, passed through the editor's hands before the final six reels were assembled.[4] At that point, Langdon began to test the quality of his picture through previews, prompting humorous quips in the papers that 6,000 fans were responsible for writing and directing Langdon's new film. Before settling on its finished form, Langdon screened the film for four theater audiences and totally revamped the film each time—until he finally heard enough laughter and applause. As a result, Langdon declared that all future productions would have no fewer than twelve previews and vowed that his audiences would choose and sanction the final film. The public would give him the last word, and he would heed it.

This extreme dependence on previews found one supporter in the press, who thought it was laudable that Langdon let audience reaction shape a film. Langdon must have been especially pleased that audiences seemed to demand his constant visibility in *Three's a Crowd*. While other characters had more prominence onscreen, Langdon's appearance was greeted with particularly effusive applause, which he took as a sign that he should intercut certain sequences with more shots of himself. The ego-stroking Langdon got from previews convinced him that he should be in command of his pictures. He was grateful for the audience's devotion and sincere feedback.

The end product was a work that indeed centered on Harry's character—but to the ultimate exclusion of cinematic coherence and continuity. It was Langdon dwelling on Langdon. Though audiences were engaged, critics' opinions were more mixed than ever, and Langdon was perplexed. He had boasted that this would be his greatest vehicle, but it was now suggested that he no longer rivaled Chaplin. Such a remark stung Langdon because he had followed Chaplin's lead in directing, writing, acting, and supervising the film's minutiae, from gags to costumes, from snowflakes to intertitles. Likewise, he had decided to film a story oozing with pathos, a story constructed from human situations rather than gags linked by slapstick glue. This formula had produced Chaplin's winner, *The Kid,* six years earlier.[5] What could be better than an emotional saga in the slums, where a babylike, Chaplinesque character struggles with love and dreams?

Langdon received a surprise answer to that question. *Three's a Crowd* was lopsided, despite his personal attention—or perhaps because of it. It verged on the pompous. It tipped toward self-indulgence, although Langdon had meant to indulge his fans. In enhancing his strongest assets, Langdon had exposed his greatest weaknesses.

Ironically, in *Three's a Crowd* Langdon plays a role that was ideal for him: the loner, the outsider. He yearns for a normal family life but is not destined to achieve it, even though a fake fortune-teller assures him that he will. Langdon tries to enter into Harry's head by controlling the camera. For example, to show how Harry feels when he wakes up early for another day of work as a mover for an unpleasant boss (Vernon Dent), Langdon includes several pans over the corners of Harry's cluttered room. The goal was to disorient the audience, just as Harry is disoriented upon waking, but Langdon does not construct the sequence with an organic attachment to the story. The sequence is stretched into a gratuitous tour of the room. Moreover, this waking sequence is peculiarly extended and lacks Harry's calibrated facial expressions that could visually suggest his drifting in and out of slumber. Instead, Harry stares blankly into space before lying down again. The alarm clock seems equally immobile: At the start of the sequence, it reads 5:00 a.m.—time for the streets to come to life. After Harry's endless waking-sleeping routine, the clock still reads 5:00 a.m. Langdon may have wanted to suggest that it is forever 5:00 a.m. at this ungodly hour, or he may have committed an editorial error. Forcing the audience to stretch its disbelief by this temporal impossibility only conflicts with the realism Langdon was trying to create with his tenement set.

The plot includes a love mix-up that endangers Harry's life, and the situation is ideal for exploiting his repertoire of "cornered" mannerisms. However, in reediting the film, the introductory scene with his love interest was omitted, and so the confusion with the other parties is never fully explained. The end result is the opposite of Langdon's intention: he has made Harry a masher instead of an innocent, and the audience is left to wonder at the dangling loose ends of confusing shots.

Despite Langdon's contention that he would not insert extraneous gags for their own sake but would concentrate on story development, there are some unnecessary routines in this film. For example, Harry waters a single posy on his windowsill in one sequence. He may have been still drowsy, but his actions come across as forced and deliberate as he drowns the flower, pushes it to the left and right, extracts it from the dirt to pour more water into the pot, and continues watering even when the pot breaks. In addition to having no plot relevance, the strained humor clashes with Langdon's goal of more emotional, even cerebral, continuity. The shower scene that follows is equally contrived, for Harry does not embellish the routine with his usual subtleties via eye expressions, gestures, and pauses. He instead becomes a small cog in an outrageous machine—too small to matter. The sequence is launched when a coworker hauls a brick at Harry's window to call him to work, instead dislodging a chimney that breaks a pipe in Harry's room and pours soot into his shower. The predictable and embarrassing outcome is Harry's appearance in blackface, with perfectly drawn circles around his lips and eyes. The ridiculous event is saved only by a tiny gag in which Harry is shown ready for work, with the clock now reading 10:00 a.m. Though this provides a small sense of unity in the scraggly edited sequence, linking it to the earlier scene of the clock at 5:00 a.m., it is a gag that takes too long in the making.

Langdon next introduces what was meant to be a running motif for the film: he finds a rag doll in a garbage can that bears a strange resemblance to him, with its wide eyes, baffled line of a mouth, and limp bagginess. It is a touching object symbolizing Harry's need for a family, but its treatment is intrusive and fragmented. For example, in one scene, Harry throws the doll into the air, mimicking his boss's action of throwing his son into the air. But the shots are awkwardly matched: Langdon cuts from a view of Harry's longing look to the sudden sharp fling of the boy and the doll into the air, breaking the wistful tone. After this, time is again blown out of proportion, for Harry has hardly been at work (presumably arriving after 10:00 a.m.) when the lunch whistle blows at noon. A sight gag of Harry's lunch box containing a perfectly filled cup of coffee (a gag Chaplin also used) adds another distraction to the film.

After an irrelevant, prolonged, and repetitive sequence in which Harry hangs by a carpet from a high window (perhaps intended as a nod to Lloyd's daredevil stunts), Harry finally meets his love interest during the great blizzard. In earlier expository footage that was cut from the film, Gladys has married an alcoholic (Cornelius Keefe). One stormy night she

A poignant encounter in *Three's a Crowd*.

leaves him, walking out into the snow. Harry finds her the next morning, nearly frozen. Like an omen of disaster, the rag doll has been carried on the wind and lands on the telephone wires. For a moment, though, Harry's discovery of love recalls his finer pantomime: awestruck, he flutters his hands to seek help, even though no one is near.

Despite the erratic construction of the film thus far, it is easy to be deeply affected by the emotional sensitivity conveyed by individual still images without word or movement. In one image, Gladys is in the foreground, huddled in a shawl and leaning against a brick wall with her back to the camera. Although larger than Harry from this perspective, her body serves as a directional arrow for viewers to follow the lines of brick, leading to our hero. He is crouched and tucked into his oversized jacket, a striped scarf wrapped around his waist and a battered hat perched on his head. But the darkness of his clothes almost illuminate the white paste of his face, which matches the snow. His pupils are like ink blots swerved as far as possible to the left, reaching out expressively to the woman whose face only he can see. The stance and expression convey childlike curiosity, but his fixed, magnetic eyes force us to examine his face more closely. The simple line of his mouth is curved a little to indicate multiple possibilities: a wish to speak, a loss for words, a sigh of compassion, a moment of concern, a recognition of the loneliness they share. Unfortunately, the power and artistic craft of such images are only flashes in a film that is diluted by prolonged, weak sequences that distort time and movement. It seems that Langdon's authoritative hand worked more expertly when his canvas was small.

As fate would have it, Gladys is about to have a child, and once he sees the booties in her possession, he yells for assistance: "Help—Storks!" In his jubilation at having a family at last, even if only by association, he shouts and dislodges a ledge of snow above him. When Harry enters the room after the birth, he stands stock still—for what is filmically a very long time—to contemplate mother and child. But such extravagantly lengthy shots jeopardize the very emotion Langdon seeks to wring, because the restless audience only wants to move on. Pacing is again unbalanced when Harry interacts with mother and baby: Gladys simply lies still, smiling monotonously, yielding her screen time to Harry the star.

The next sequence could have been an ideal comic contrast between a real baby and a man-child, but Harry's purposeful facial expressions as he tries to lull the baby to sleep only risk doing the same for the audience. The implication for Harry's comedy is clear: acting like a baby as a babysitter is not his forte; acting like a baby in the adult world is what he does best. His efforts manage to put both the baby and himself to sleep, and Harry's ensuing dream of fighting off Gladys's husband is poorly staged with an oversized boxing glove. The grosser movements of certain sequences contrast

Lobby card emphasizing Harry's doll alter ego.

sharply with more subtle executions in other sequences, leading to a lack of continuity in style and tone. It is hard to imagine that Langdon was still searching for his brand of humor at this point, so he was likely experimenting with different styles. However, mixing so much into one film clearly worked against his best directorial decisions.

The conclusion of the film shows that Harry's confrontation with the husband is not a dream, even though there is no transition from dream to waking. The husband has located his missing wife, and she happily leaves with him upon his promise of transformation. She thanks Harry, who sits like an abandoned child in the cradle as she departs with her baby. Pathos is revived in a simple gesture: Harry sadly touches her coat sleeve. Unfortunately, at the moment of emotional release, Harry reveals a dark side and goes to avenge his lonely destiny by revisiting the fortune-teller.

Like a misplaced punctuation mark, the rag doll appears on the wires for the last time. One critic felt that this prop could have been more delicately threaded throughout the film, instead of appearing as an afterthought. Also echoing Harry's dismal plight is an amusing but improbable gag: as he drifts through the snow with a lantern, he blows it out just as all the street lamps are extinguished. At the fortune-teller's window, Harry has second thoughts about hurling a brick; instead, he kicks the storefront and casts the brick aside, which lands in a truck and causes a huge drum to roll off and into the shop, reducing it to smithereens. Having enacted his intention by luck, but petrified at its enormity, Harry runs upstairs. According to Capra, he had done preproduction work for this drum gag before leaving Langdon's employ; this is Harry's hapless character again, as defined by the Capra-Ripley-Edwards team.

Three's a Crowd would have worked more admirably if it had been Langdon's first production as a newcomer. But at this late stage, with a strong body of work behind him, *Three's a Crowd* emerged as a technical "sore thumb" and an enigma for someone of his artistry. It released an onrush of mixed reviews citing bad editing, poor titling, heavy-handed pathos (referring to Chaplin's better balance of tragicomedy), average photography, overly long material, and an abundance of "doubtful sequences." Though an improvement on his two-reelers, Langdon had to reclaim his power to keep up with the Little Tramp. *Variety* noted: "Harry Langdon had previously threatened to direct his own pictures and in this one he's done it. *Three's a Crowd* is no sensation but neither is it a cluck. . . . Those who don't like Langdon aren't going to be won over by this release. It's too quiet and lacks the necessary explosive mirth to overcome that handicap. Those who do favor the comic, however, will be satisfied. There are spots in the picture where Langdon is brilliant, but on the other hand slow passages also creep in."

An astute reaction that properly represented the overall opinion of *Three's a Crowd* came from Baltimore reviewer Louis Azrael, who was simply stumped by the film. He lamented: "For some reason, Langdon has gone far afield from the usual full length comedy in this latest film of his. Too far, I'm afraid. He has taken a dramatic plot, a good plot for a dramatic actor, and he has put into its minor moments a lot of slapstick comedy. And what the result is you'll have to see for yourself." Azrael mentioned the possibility that Langdon was experimenting with a combination of drama and comedy, even suggesting that "he wanted to improve on Charlie Chaplin. And in this he failed." *Photoplay* warned, "A few more like this, and he'll be sent to that limbo of lost movie souls—vaudeville. Langdon reaches for the moon—and grasps a feeble glowworm." In a humorous but uncomplimentary metaphor, it announced that Langdon makes the audience "wade through thick layers of oleomargarine paths to get at the com-

"Reel" persuasive publicity for *Three's a Crowd.*

edy." At the same time, the reviewer was not ready to give up hope, and in a tongue-in-cheek manner, given that the film was silent, observed: "We like Harry Langdon and hate to hear the sound of his flops. May his next be louder and funnier."[6]

It is almost breathtaking how quickly the exhibitors' responses turned so hostile. Russell Armentrout from Pittsfield, Illinois, called *Three's a Crowd* "just three degrees worse than rotten," while W. H. Hardman from Frankfort, Kansas, based his comment on Armentrout's: "The fellow who said it was three degrees worse than rotten was too modest. Hope First National will condense the rest of his pictures into two reels and at that have somebody to direct it." A small-town exhibitor in Arizona gave a stern warning: "Oh! What a lemon! No plot, silly from start to finish. Don't do it again, Harry, or you will ruin yourself for life." Finally, R. C. Metager from the Cozy Theatre in Wagner, South Dakota, virtually shouted in print: "He ye! Exhibitors, hear ye! So lousy and contaminated with nothingness that it has no rival. There is no room in this industry for such talent. Because he is dumb looking, some think he should command a premium. Whether Langdon lives 100 years or dies tomorrow this picture bids him farewell."

Langdon had not produced the "laugh riot" everyone expected. His direction was rated "fair" by *Film Daily.* He also had to deal with a barrage of newspaper reports that called the film a comedown and "about as flat as a Victrola's record." There was fear that another work of this sort would lead to Langdon's being all but forgotten, and it would be his own doing. Even Carl Sandburg, poet, Lincoln biographer, and film critic for the *Chicago Daily News,* vividly concluded that "when the story has as little of humor and as much of tragedy as *Three's a Crowd,* the laugh stops in the throat." Caustic Mordaunt Hall of the *New York Times* disapproved with an excess of similes and metaphors:

As Harry Langdon toddles through his new film, "Three's a Crowd," one is impelled to observe that this screen clown has a mouth like the Mona Lisa and eyes like a Raphael angel or a Lorelei Lee. His current shadow adventure is a mixture of gentle pathos and Big Bertha exploits. In some respects it gives one a foggy notion of Chaplin's picture "The Kid," but it happens only too often in the present production that the bright bits are followed by a barrage of buffoonery that has about as much right in the narrative as a chimney sweep would have in a flour mill; the consequence is that these boisterous attempts to wring laughter from audiences have all the humor of Babe Ruth playing Peter Pan.

While imagining that he was creating a masterwork built on his style, Langdon had succeeded in presenting only a fractured version of his character. Audiences seemed willing to accept this transition because they were fans and remembered his best work. Critics were unafraid to hit the nerve and panned *Three's a Crowd*, drilling holes in Langdon's sinking ship of a reputation. Exhibitors claimed to be losing money and were quick to lambaste him. The mix of styles projected on the screen—which had evidently made sense to Langdon as he edited and reedited repeatedly— would have been acceptable only to someone who was already a study in contrasts. Both styles had worked for him in short films; perhaps he had expected the audience to provide the glue that bound the film together. His mistake was focusing on the pieces instead of the film as a whole. Langdon realized he now had an opportunity to prove himself again with the *next* film. He was, after all, still evolving as a filmmaker, but he believed he had what it took to go all the way.

Tom Waller, writing for *Moving Picture World*, seemed to be one of the few who looked past the flaws to consider the whole man and artist. Shortly before *Three's a Crowd* was released, he had written of Langdon's ability to be both reserved and relaxed, a devoted artist intensely bordering on the tragic, someone who could not articulate without a sympathetic listener:

Langdon's face is contradictory to his mind and his whole being. He isn't absent-minded. He is lonely only when he is not busy. Yet there surely seems to be something pathetic about the man. . . . Harry loves his trait because it is the backbone of his job. . . . The trait which can break off a laugh, almost bring a tear and wind up with a bigger laugh. . . .

Although a star and one of the biggest of his kind, Harry Langdon is not even an actor during an interview. To get him to talk the interviewer may often believe it necessary to do the acting. Then Langdon will detect it and close up like the proverbial clam. Loose limbs, plain language and plenty of cigar smoke seem to get the best replies from Langdon. Then his enthusiasm asserts itself and you see before you an entirely different face. It is the Langdon as he really is. Sheer animation because it's the job you're asking him about and not a lot of questions about himself which would cause many others to preen themselves for their best lingo.

Perhaps a few reviewers did take the time to probe the man behind the films, but others had no clue—nor did they seek one—to Langdon's inner turbulence. Admitting such turmoil in public—or even to himself—could incapacitate Langdon, causing him to lose all he valued. He was compelled to hold the work he loved with the tightest grasp possible—just as he had clung to the girl in *His First Flame* when he thought he would lose her. Now he would work to salvage his filmmaking, his reputation, and his independence. With his next film, Langdon would set right what *Three's a Crowd* had undone.

Langdon uttered the following words in a December 1927 interview for *Theatre* magazine as he was preparing *The Chaser*: "There are few more tragic businesses in the world than the making of funny pictures. There is the tragedy, for example, of working for weeks, sometimes months, on a sequence only to find that it fails to evolve even a ripple from the audience. The producer and the star often find that their most cherished material is not funny when transmitted to the screen, and the result is a tragedy not only for the audience, but for the makers of the picture." When the film was finally released, he might have recalled how prescient he had been.

Not every film earned "rave reviews," and fans and critics usually held each film to the standard of the last one, spotlighting its failings. However, few of Langdon's comedy peers experienced the insecurities, tensions, and extreme reactions he had suffered in less than three years. Eventually, every star undergoes significant transitions that dislodge him (or her, in the case of Mabel Normand) from the heights of success. Keaton, for example, experienced a terrible period of depression and alcoholism after losing his autonomy and moving to MGM. However, none paralleled Langdon's roller-coaster ride, shifts of attitude, bitter breakups, and swift descent.[7] A drastic situation required an equally drastic remedy.

Langdon's solution to the disappointment of *Three's a Crowd* would not arrive until February 1928 and the release of *The Chaser,* another self-directed, self-starring enterprise. This time, Tully's services as adapter were eliminated, and his absence caused no discernible difference in the final product. Until the film was ready, however, Langdon worked hard to resurface in the press and retrieve some respect. The rattle of critical doubt caused by *Three's a Crowd* temporarily subsided, especially when, in October 1927, English critic Roger Starbuck cast his "roseate estimate of Harry Langdon" upon visiting the set of *The Chaser.* He was certain that Langdon's human quality, articulated by "his stoical visage, his pathetic eyes, his immobile features, his unctuous movements," would prove him "the world's greatest tragedian if he should step across finally into the lachrymose land of lugubriousness."

Straddling the threshold of comedy and tragedy was not new for Langdon, but as a director, it seemed to provoke uncertainty about his abilities. Genuine pathos tended to infiltrate his life whenever he assumed the pedestal of "expert." "The ideal comedian is born and not made," he said at this time, defining the three inherent characteristics of a true comedian as personality, imagination, and a sense of humor. Curiously, he stressed the need for guided direction: "Direction even in a comedy is all important, no matter how big the star may be." The implication, however, was that for Langdon, such direction would be not external but internal; by this time, he was unwilling to be directed by another. Tom Waller gave Langdon the benefit of the doubt: "[Langdon] ventured the belief that a star, capable in these respects, directing himself would result in the motion picture industry probably turning out better pictures, or at least pictures more truly interpreting emotions as they really are."

Langdon could not even identify the self-sabotage in his own words. He offered an ideal theory but drifted from its application. In *Three's a Crowd,* the direction had fallen short of what Langdon needed. He seemed incapable of stepping out of character long enough to direct the three characteristics of every comedian. Even sublime individual gags lacked pacing and continuity when they were linked together in scenes and sequences. His immersion in his work was too deep and blinding.

Independence remained appealing to Langdon, who, after all, had been independent since childhood. But as much as he was a loner, setting off in new directions, Langdon was willing to collaborate with like minds. He had a "democratic way" about him on the set, as one newspaper reported, with a carefree smile and word of cheer when seeking solutions to problems. He seemed to genuinely want—or perhaps expected—harmony among his teammates. But clearly the disruptions that had driven Edwards and Capra away indicated the opposite—a clash of egos, personalities, and temperaments. Perhaps Langdon felt threatened by someone outside the spotlight, with differing views, wielding so much control over his work. Instead, he wanted to master the new medium of film, as he had mastered vaudeville. It would also be easier and more efficient to answer every question himself rather than share that responsibility with others. A democratic style no longer worked for Langdon when it came to executive decisions.

As a defense mechanism, Langdon shrugged off the negative reviews as bad luck, and he dominated the making of *The Chaser* even more rigidly. He tried another tactic, swerving from pathos to slapstick. It was a fatal decision. Slapstick had been languishing since Sennett's heyday—and Langdon himself had contributed to that change in style—but the star still had not found a way to blend his subtleties into broader comedy. It was an ill-fitting match, and *The Chaser* only added to the perception that Langdon had become a jack-of-all-trades instead of a master of directing while acting.

The Chaser suffered from star syndrome. Because his fans clamored for his screen presence, Langdon interpreted this as the secret to success, even at the expense of the film's structural and technical needs. The genesis of this film was Langdon's successful three-reeler *Saturday Afternoon,* and Harry again plays a henpecked husband with a shrewish wife and mother-in-law. *The Chaser* starts promisingly, with an unusual, subtle gag in which the wife screams at Harry on the phone; he drops the receiver in the waste-basket, and papers fly out, propelled by her hot air. He escapes his misery by visiting a speakeasy. Langdon had considered scrapping the speakeasy scene, but two previews encouraged him to keep it. He re-created a dance hall set, engaged more than fifty extras and a jazz orchestra, and spent three additional days to complete this "improvement." In the final analysis, the sequence adds little and fails to advance the plot. Instead, Langdon is simply present in an elaborate set.

Bits of creativity do shine through the chaotic direction. A dolly shot of a "chase" through three rooms of the house even received an honorable mention in some reviews. Langdon removed one wall of the set to create a "cross-section" of the rooms as his wife and mother-in-law chase Harry upon learning of his extramarital socializing. One reviewer quipped that this was a "literal cross-section of married life" played strictly for laughs. He also called Langdon the "common denominator" in the scene, hinting at the film's essential flaw writ large. That is, Langdon's subtlety works in the minuscule, but on a larger canvas, he hits and misses.

The henpecked husband theme was also distilled from an incident reported in the newspapers. Judge Theodor Ehler in the Chicago court of domestic relations had handed down a unique ruling in one case: he required a lazy husband to change places with his wife for ten days so she could earn the money he did not. In *The Chaser,* Harry's wife drags him to

Gender role switcheroo in *The Chaser.*

divorce court, and the judge imposes a similar order. A chagrined Harry resurfaces soon after in "drag," sporting a floor-length apron tied around his chest. The one indication of the man he used to be is his battered hat, which he wears indoors and out.

Three basic gags—or variations on a theme—result from Harry's humiliation: all the deliverymen make passes at him (as if an apron represents womanhood); Harry fumbles while making breakfast for his wife, forcing a chicken to lay an egg in a frying pan; and he contemplates suicide. Because Langdon had what he considered an effective sight gag—himself in woman's clothes—he lavished more time on his appearance than on pacing the scenes. Even this "vision" wore thin, however, as Langdon did not incorporate his unique mannerisms. The cumulative feeling is awkward self-consciousness. Langdon believed his mere presence was sufficient for comedy. His familiar gestures and expressions thus become conspicuous by their absence.

Moreover, forced symmetry weighs down the lightness of the comedy. For example, a pose of Harry holding a chicken alternates with a pose of Harry shaking the chicken. The chicken routine occupies an uncomfortably long span of inactivity within the frame. When the sequence is salvaged, it is only by a momentary reprieve: another chicken crawls under the crouching Harry and lays an egg. But the diversion is wasted because Harry finds the egg he wanted and illogically kicks it away.

Harry's run-ins with the deliverymen represent a peculiar treat-ment of a familiar theme. Langdon relies on humor based on gender stereotypes, a prominent theme in silent comedy: men become women, with all the inherent sexual and sexist implications. However, Harry's cherubic face is simply bizarre as he peers out from under his hat. His strength has always been playing a baby, or at best a child-man, but all his appearances as a member of the opposite sex have been awkward (as in *The Sea Squawk* and *His First Flame*). Even his approach here, when he yields to the deliverymen's advances, is ambiguous and listless, marred by forced gestures. For example, Harry chases one man with a broom and jumps up and down until he falls into an obviously precut hole in the porch. He throws a doorstop at the second man, who kisses Harry anyway. As the third man approaches, Harry simply offers his cheek for the unavoidable kiss. The basic premise—Harry's irresistibil-ity—strains the comedy because the child-man image overwhelms any feminine allure.

The actual suicide scene is filled with potential Langdonisms that turn into unsatisfying humor. He aims at vital parts of his body with a gun but at the climactic moment discovers that he is holding a water pistol. Intend-ing to drink poison, he accidentally picks up a glass of castor oil. Unlike *His Marriage Wow,* when Harry resigns himself to dying in a fetal posi-tion—a sight gag appropriate to his character—he now lies on his back and covers himself with a sheet. For forty-five seconds the audience is forced to stare at this motionless form, with only the insert of a medium shot of the same. The punch line to this static shot is Harry leaping upstairs, presum-ably to the bathroom, and the camera lingers on the empty staircase. After about thirty seconds, the scene fades. One might argue that this pacing allows the audience to imagine what is happening to Harry personally (under the sheet, presumably dead; upstairs, suffering the effects of castor oil). But the significance of these conditions is neither profound nor ironic. More poignantly, one might imagine Langdon sitting in the editing room, enjoying the shot of his body under a sheet, deliberately choosing to insert the medium shot and deciding that forty-five seconds of nothing is vital to build humor. Another cringe-worthy time gaffe occurs when the wife dis-covers Harry's suicide note and weeps dramatically into a handkerchief. The punch line to this scene is thirty seconds of staring at her convulsed face streaked with mascara.

After all these languishing scenes, Harry survives and goes off with his

Getting courage from Bud Jamison.

buddy (Bud Jamison) to enjoy his manhood. The production stories behind the golf sequence are more interesting than the actual sequence itself. Originally, the working title was *The 19th Hole* because the film was supposed to revolve around Langdon's famous vaudeville golf skit. But the final remnant of the golf routine is reduced to Bud missing shots on the tee, a long sequence with a dog burrowing into the ground for a bone and emerging from the other side to frighten Harry, and Bud sinking into the soggy earth while Harry threatens to punch him.

It is not clear whether Ripley, who was still on board, or Langdon decided to shift the focus from golf to gender. It is possible that another mysterious figure, Clarence Hennecke, came up with the idea; he was credited as cowriter and "comedy constructionist" on Langdon's independent films, including an uncredited spot as assistant director on *The Strong Man*. Given that Langdon had cut his staff, including brother Tully, it is puzzling that he retained someone in this position with an inflated title. Perhaps it reflected Langdon's self-importance. Hennecke died in 1969 at age seventy-four, after a lifetime of meager acting, writing, and directing jobs that were primarily uncredited.

While filming the golf scenes on the links of the Sunset Country Club in Sunset Canyon, a blaze broke out, causing $2 million worth of damage to the clubhouse and surrounding forest. In volunteering to battle the conflagration, Langdon was badly scorched on both hands, and his hair was singed; Ripley and Jamison, among others, suffered minor injuries. After the experience, Langdon apparently quipped that he was now more than ever in favor of fireless cookers and delicatessens.

At the end of the film, Harry reverses his gender identity dilemma and manages to melt some beautiful ladies with his kisses. Echoes of *Soldier Man* reverberate here, but this is not the protective cover of a dream. The audience is expected to believe that little Harry, in his baggy costume and with his daunting marital woes, can reassert his manhood because of golf. He is not a romantic lover enabled by a dream ex machina; here, Harry is meant to be a natural Lothario, and his out-of-character role unsettles and disappoints. Any possibility of sensible character development is abandoned as Harry yields to pure slapstick: he hides in a rumble seat to flee a jealous man and teeters on the edge of a cliff. For this risky scene, Langdon demolished six old cars, repeating the gag until it worked to his satisfaction. Once the car tips over, the painfully clear rear projection of the zooming landscape leads to a series of editorial mismatches: in one shot, the cliff is perpendicular; in the next, the cliff is a negotiable incline. When Harry returns home, his wife seems to be tamed enough to resume her proper spousal role. Langdon may have been at a loss for a punchier ending for this ill-fitting comedy without the right "tailor" to sew up the loose ends.

To add to Langdon's woes, the censors filed an unusually large number of complaints about offending scenes in *The Chaser*. Seeking a seal of approval from the Motion Picture Commission of the State of New York, First National instead received an "elimination list" of items that were sacrilegious (subtitles about God creating man and, a little later, woman), indecent (Harry in a woman's dress squatting on the ground as a hen walks under him), and tending to "incite to crime" (the gun and poison used for Harry's attempted suicide).[8]

If Langdon would not admit his weaknesses as a director, the critics did not hesitate to do so—and no one else could be blamed, since Langdon had announced that he was sole auteur. The *New York Sun* moaned: "The case of Harry Langdon is probably the saddest in the entire movie clinic. With the attributes of the finest comedian of all at his command, he, somehow or other, has been guided along paths that are gagged to monotony," with *The Chaser* being the worst of all. The *New York Evening Post* went so far as to call the film "a funeral that has its lighter points." According to other reviewers, audience members complained about Langdon's blank expressions or left the theater for fresh air. Katharine Zimmerman of the *New York Telegram,* noting that Langdon was a brilliant comedian, also opined that he had "abolished the institution popularly known as 'Director.' . . . We think it is time that some one explained to him, before he overacts and underdirects another feature picture for Broadway consumption, that while art suffereth long and is kind, cheapness and vulgarity are something else again." *Life* magazine's critic Robert E. Sherwood advised Langdon to return to Mack Sennett, and any comparisons with Chaplin were now made with deep embarrassment. Sherwood thought Langdon had developed a "Young Pretender complex." Similarly, Richard Watts of the *New York Herald-Tribune* declared that any critics who thought they had found Chaplin's equal now had to find alibis. Watts, however, pinpointed the root of the problem: "He has grown self-conscious, not as an actor, but as a director. Scorning imaginative comic business, he spends time and footage on lengthy close-ups that glorify little but his passion for being an exhibitionist and he delights in a slow paced movement that is probably intended as emphasizing his tragic side. Even though the star wants to be a tragic figure, he could never have imagined how really tragic he is in *The Chaser*."

Before its release, an optimistic ad for the film boasted that the biggest question in the industry was whether *The Chaser* was funnier than *The Strong Man,* and by "actual count—267 laughs," it was! Preview patrons were quoted as lauding *The Chaser* to the skies, but the actual returns were painful. Many critics who were now panning both the film and Langdon had once called him their favorite screen comedian. The secret to the success of consummate filmmaking, which Chaplin and Keaton had mastered, was eluding Langdon. In chasing that aspiration, he was only exposing his flaws and shortchanging his best qualities.

The definition of Langdon's famous persona was fading more rapidly than it had taken him to skate across the fragile surface of success. He did not realize how thin the ice was as he stood on the widening cracks. Try as he might to rid himself of excess weight, such as his ego, Langdon was reluctant to let it go, clinging to it as a lifeline. Moreover, he was too far from shore to call for help. When he fell through the ice, Langdon would have to rely on his own strength to survive.

Langdon was not willing to give up on audiences or critics, although they seemed to be abandoning him. He still thought he could satisfy them if he could just find the right formula. He and Ripley collaborated for one more effort and admitted, reluctantly, that perhaps Capra's characterization of Langdon as good Soldier Schweik had been right after all. They would revert to the past again, but not to either pathos or slapstick. Their focus would be Harry's gentle persona in a simple plot that drew on all the idiosyncrasies that had set Langdon's star in the firmament. Bravely pretending that business was running smoothly, the Langdon organization announced that its next project would be *The Volunteer,* an original story by Arthur Ripley about a patriotic boy who yearns to be sent to France during World War I but never makes it past the docks of Hoboken, New Jersey. The film was eventually released as *Heart Trouble* in August 1928.

Harry plays the son of German immigrants who tries to enlist, hoping to convince his sweetheart (Doris Dawson) that he is really American. But the recruiting officer rejects Harry because of nearsightedness and flat feet. Meanwhile, a German spy organization is using the harbor of Harry's town as a supply base for enemy submarines. Still smarting from his rejection, Harry blunders onto the base and innocently makes all the right mistakes to blow up the base and capture the spies. He also helps free an imprisoned American officer—the same one who had rejected Harry. His sweetheart now adores him, and his hometown holds a parade in his honor.

The reviews of *Heart Trouble* were encouraging, as anything even remotely positive would have been after two fiascos. *Variety* reported that "the comic does less of the emotion he gave way to in his last two. He abandons to a great extent his ambition to be the complex of tragedienne and a comedian." Also mentioned was Langdon's new attitude toward filmmaking, which had likely caused his flops: "That he is directing himself is less obvious." *Photoplay,* however, lambasted the film, suggesting it was a cure for insomnia and predicting it would "spell the exit of Harry Langdon."

Given Langdon's decision to find a more successful formula that blended his best styles into a balanced picture, *Heart Trouble* should have earned greater approval.[9] Its lukewarm reception, however, was linked to a new transition in film—the introduction of sound. Radio and Warner's Vitaphone short subjects in the mid-1920s, both of which "spoke" and played music with a startling reality, forecast the downfall of the silents, despite scoffers and skeptics. One by one, studios followed the trend of making films with dialogue to challenge the competition. More refined equipment and facilities were developed to accommodate this new dimension. Studio powers vied to control and outdo one another's systems and manipulate audience reaction to the novelty that promised to be more than a fad. For example, William Fox, a clothing examiner turned movie mogul, set up his sound-on-film Movietone system two weeks before Warner's Vitaphone premiered in July 1926. The Fox trend in newsreels yielded to the front-runner, Warner, which promoted the first full-length talking picture in May 1927. Although the film was not the first to experiment with sound, *The Jazz Singer* was the first major commercial release and success; its singing and speaking sequences captivated audiences with the phenomenon of voice accompanying image. Studios and theaters installed sound equipment and hired audio experts. As *The Jazz Singer* led to full speaking roles, actors' voices were exposed, and sometimes their romantic or heroic images clashed with the quality of their speech. Many stars were vulnerable because of their accents or vocal disorders, and they were reduced to character roles, bit parts, or unemployment. Those who adapted to the new conditions rushed to produce a steady output of films that excelled their silent predecessors.

By mid-1928, it was no longer fashionable to attend silent films. Chaplin, however, had persevered in the medium, producing the mostly silent *Modern Times* (1936). Chaplin believed his Little Tramp spoke a universal language through the visual and thrived in silence. When his character does speak briefly in *Modern Times,* his utterance is a mix of nonsense and foreign words. Given that the film is a satire on technology, it is not surprising that Chaplin pokes fun at the "sound" of the new film technology.

But his staunch opinion was that the visual, enhanced by music, was still the greatest medium for conveying emotion, and sound would only dilute its impact. In larger towns at the end of the 1920s, however, the majority of theaters had converted to sound and balked at silents.

Heart Trouble was one of the last wholly silent films, and it had only a fair run in rural areas; returns at the box office were not enough to save either it or Langdon financially. He now had to make the transition to talkies. This new challenge coincided with the prevalent view around Hollywood that Langdon was insufferable. He had tempted fate by wielding too much self-appointed power at First National, and Hollywood was not pleased. He could no longer pick his vehicles, and he had little option but to take whatever work a studio was willing to give him. Langdon's comfortable niche in silents had become a cage for which he no longer had the key.

First National dropped Langdon's contract.[10] The studio was being acquired by Warner in the fall of 1928, and all deadwood had to be trimmed. Under Warner, producer of *The Jazz Singer,* conversion to sound was the priority. Major silent films that had not yet been released, such as *Lilac Time,* were hurriedly adjusted, adding a few lines of dialogue, a musical score, and sound effects, and released expeditiously. But *Heart Trouble* was not considered salvageable with sound, and both it and Langdon were discarded.

Close observers of the revolution in the film industry were hardly surprised at Langdon's fate. In particular, a series of articles by syndicated columnist Dan Thomas chronicled Langdon's loss of fame, position, and ability to work. In one item published while *Heart Trouble* was still in production, Thomas expressed his hope that Langdon's latest film would be as good as promised, or else his tenure at First National would end. Langdon had not had a hit since *The Strong Man,* and Thomas lamented that it was indeed a shame to see such talent slip away, but in truth, Langdon had only himself to blame: "Harry's chief trouble is that he wants to be star, director, writer, and gagman. And he won't listen to criticism from his staff, some of whom realize his predicament and could pull him out of it." Thomas seemed to have a good "understanding" of Langdon's situation, based on what he had pieced together through observation, deduction, and hearsay from "informants" (possibly even Capra) whose criticism Langdon had rebuffed. Whoever his sources were, Thomas reported a few months later that his prediction had come true.[11]

Around the time of his "cinematic demise," Langdon made a curious statement to explain what had happened: "I had to turn out a feature in 10 weeks, where Chaplin and Harold Lloyd were spending up to two years on each of theirs. . . . It couldn't be done—the public quickly tired of the character, and there I was—out. I'm not the type who could make good as his own producer. The responsibility got me down."[12] Langdon's words have a core of honesty with regard to the time pressure. However, it is possible that he now found himself trapped: the consensus in the industry and in the media was that Langdon's ego had been his downfall. He had relished promoting his "study" of comedy and had expressed the belief that only he, as the director, could understand his character. Now he had to backtrack, eat his words, shake his head from a near-fatal blow, and admit he was simply "not the type" to be a consummate filmmaker.

Any hope that 1928 would be a zenith year for Langdon was destroyed by his dismissal from First National and the divorce suit initiated by his estranged wife Rose. She had hired private detectives to track him and obtain evidence of his indiscretions with Helen Walton to ensure that the judge would readily accept Rose's demands. Meanwhile, Helen's estranged husband, Thomas O'Brien, threatened to sue Langdon for alienating his wife's affections. Although Helen protested, saying he had never *had* her affections, Langdon's lawyer thought the resulting publicity would hurt him and advised Langdon to pay O'Brien $15,000 in hush money in return for dropping the suit.

Langdon appeared before Judge Sproul at the Los Angeles County courthouse on April 28, 1928, in between film flops. On May 2 the judge signed an interlocutory judgment ratifying the property settlement the couple had agreed on in December 1925. Rose was awarded $7,000 in alimony in addition to two-sevenths of the year's receipts from his First National films. Langdon may have wished that, like his character in *The Chaser,* he could have merely switched roles with his wife, rather than pay such a hefty penalty for divorce. His finances were depleted, and he had no immediate prospects. The divorce would not be final until July 3, 1929, and he hoped to marry Helen soon thereafter and adopt her daughter Virginia. But he could not marry an aspiring socialite like Helen, whom he had spoiled, nor provide for a growing child when he was unemployed.

Simultaneously, Langdon lost the support of his brother Claude. Claude's eyesight was failing, and he and his wife thought it best to return to Iowa, where she had a large family. Langdon was somewhat relieved that he did not have to bear the brunt of his brother's care, but he realized that this left him very much on his own, with only Tully to lean on. Unfortunately, Tully's personal struggle with alcohol only added to Harry's responsibilities, which he accepted out of familial devotion.

As he watched his career expire, Langdon may have felt that he was down but not out, as the saying goes. He shifted his attitude once again, contradicting a fervent declaration he had made in 1924, when the world had seemed rosier: "I am one stage actor who never expects to return to his old love." In fact, Langdon now returned to what was left of vaudeville, where his sketches had been successful and his rapport with live audiences had offered him immediate feedback. Joining a tour in Seattle under arrangements by Fanchon and Marco, Langdon created a new act called "The Messenger." The "Vaudeville Review" section of *Motion Picture Herald* printed a favorable albeit slightly sarcastic review, noting the star's backstory: "Harry Langdon is this week admitted by capacity audiences to be funnier on the stage than on the screen. His act is highly diverting."

His West Coast tour was a boost to Langdon's shaky ego as well as his wallet, as he earned $5,000 a week. Inevitably, he also received some negative reviews as his act wended its way east and back to the Palace in New York, the Mount Olympus of vaudevillians. But compared with the national assault on his last films, these smaller-scale local theater reviews were tolerable. The vaudeville bill starred Langdon's old friend Frank Fay as headliner, singing, "spoofing . . . his colleague, Benny Davis," and bantering with his wife Barbara Stanwyck. The *New York Times* noted that Langdon received "second honors of the program," but the show did not use his droll talents to their best advantage. Ironically, critical reaction now used Langdon's history as a top screen comedian as a touchstone for his return to the stage. It seemed that each phase of Langdon's career became the criterion for judging the next one: his films were compared with his old stage work, and now his new stage work was measured against his films. There was also the sense that Langdon was returning to the theater only because his films had failed, yet his best film work was supposed to guarantee that his stage act would be better than it used to be! Langdon never kept personal diaries, so one can only imagine his exhaustion in tracking the public's responses to his achievements. They ebbed and flowed like the tide; audiences exalted and criticized in rapid sequence. They wanted progress but advised a return to the past. A touching illustration of this perspective was *Variety*'s review of the Palace show, suggesting that Langdon would have been better off just returning to his "old and well-remembered auto skit."

Despite any reviews—good or bad—Langdon's spirit had rallied with his return to the stage, and at least he was still working. Like a chameleon, he reentered the theater environment and blended in as if he had never left. More important, he faced the enemy that had once been his friend: he stayed directly in the media's eye. What stamina and bravery were funneled into perseverance after such personal and professional upheavals only Langdon knew, and he did not describe them out loud. However, he made it possible for others to announce that he was very much alive and ready to work.

Leonard Hall of *Photoplay* was one such town crier. He met with Langdon at the Warwick Hotel in New York City to interview him for an article strategically titled "Hey! Hey! Harry's Come Back." It chronicled Langdon's return to the stage and his aspirations to make more pictures. Not surprisingly, it intimated that Langdon was still nonplussed by his decline and saw the world through the lens of a hapless victim—not unlike his character. The article began with a vivid announcement: "Harry Langdon, if God is good, is coming back to pictures! It's a new Langdon we'll see, too—a Harry with a well-deflated skull, a head full of smart ideas and a soul that bulges with pepper, hope and the old confy!" Although he boldly called Langdon's stage act "terrible," Hall proudly acknowledged that the pantomime used in his films—his "quaint, helpless mannerisms"—was still evident and "tremendous." Hall supported the many "yarns" that were circulating to explain Langdon's career collapse: "how he had tried to write, supervise, direct and act . . . how he suffered from night sweat, galloping ego, growing pains above the ears, and delusions of grandeur." He also allowed a moment for Langdon's take on the topic: it was all due to tough luck, much like his character's portrayal as "life's football, kicked around by fate." The article presented Langdon's life circumstances almost as a reflection of his screen persona, "the greatest living incarnation of harassed, frustrated humanity." These words were presented humorously to support the idea that it was still possible for Langdon to regain his former eminence and was, in fact, planning to do so. Anticipating great fanfare for such a day, Hall compassionately concluded: "And let yours sincerely be on hand to lead the cheering for the Happy Return of Dead-Pan Harry, whom we have loved long since, and just lost awhile!"[13]

With a few well-placed pieces of favorable publicity, Langdon was hopeful that all was retrievable. However, his announcement to the film industry that he was available for movies led to few overtures. When he had left Sennett four years earlier, the offers he received were rumored to be overwhelming. Now, his salability had evaporated with three consecutive failures and the emergence of sound. The one legitimate offer he received, from producer Hal Roach, included the proviso that Langdon could not be producer, director, or even star of any feature films; Roach wanted him only for a series of two-reel sound shorts. Langdon had once said, "Sometimes one has to go backwards in order to go forwards. You sort of step back and get a new running start at success, I guess." These words may have crossed his mind as he considered the offer.

Hal Roach was one of the three most famous producers in comedy. Mack Sennett, the best known, relied on a slapstick formula. Built on the absurdly visual, his scenarios did not transfer well to sound. Sennett's output of two-reel sound comedies with regulars Marjorie Beebe, Franklin Pangborn, Joyce Compton, and Walter Catlett contained many nostalgic moments of classic Sennett slapstick, but they marked the eclipse of his career as a comedy producer. The second comedy leader, Al Christie, was the most prolific, having started in the business in 1916. He specialized in inexpensive, simple-minded comedies with lesser stars, none of whom ever gained enough fame to reflect any long-lasting glory on his studio. Sennett unquestionably dominated the field of comedy in the 1910s, while Christie, in terms of sheer footage, at least, held the reins in the 1920s. Roach was the only serious contender for Sennett's throne. He moved rapidly into first place and led the short comedy field in the 1930s.

Since 1915, Roach's name had been linked with that of Harold Lloyd, a personal friend who became his first and most important star. Roach developed other comedy talent as well, including Snub Pollard, Will Rogers, Charley Chase, and Edgar Kennedy, all of whom made Roach's studio prosperous in the 1920s. He was also a pioneer in the use of children in comedy shorts, and Our Gang became the most celebrated group of child actors on the screen between 1922 and 1944. In 1927 Roach launched a comedy team that would become the most successful pair of clowns on film: Stan Laurel and Oliver Hardy. By the time the sound era arrived, Roach had parted with Lloyd, who went on to produce his own films, and Chase foundered in sound pictures because his style was more pantomimic. Laurel and Hardy transitioned to sound effortlessly—in fact, sound enhanced their characterization—and Our Gang was a comic staple for decades, even into the television era.

Roach always searched for new faces and new comedy formats. He tried musical shorts: a series called *The Boy Friends* starring Mickey Daniels, Grady Sutton, and David Sharpe; another called *The All-Stars*, with Don Barclay, Douglas Wakefield, and Billy Nelson; a delightful series of shorts featuring ZaSu Pitts and Thelma Todd, with Pitts later replaced by Patsy Kelly; and a number of solo comedians or teams that enjoyed varying degrees of success. Roach believed that Langdon was one comedy star who could make the transition to sound with the right vehicles. His hitherto unheard, slightly high-pitched voice, bashful and hesitant with a slight tremor, was well suited to his meek character.

With no other options to consider, Langdon accepted Roach's offer and signed a three-year contract in October 1928, effective January 1, 1929. With two months to idle away, Harry took Helen to New York and contacted old acquaintances in vaudeville booking offices. He managed to get billed at the Coliseum Theatre and earned enough money to pay for the trip. Langdon and Helen were openly living together, although marriage was not legally possible until his divorce from Rose became final. They returned to the West Coast in time for Christmas. Then Langdon reported for work.

Signing Langdon proved to be one of Roach's infrequent mistakes. There were foreboding delays, including technical problems with the sound equipment. Langdon's contract was renegotiated, and the amended version—for only one year—was signed in May 1929 and took effect in June, with options to renew for another two years. This committed Roach to pay Langdon $2,000 a week for the first six months and $2,500 a week for the remaining six months.

Despite the delay and Roach's underlying reservations, Langdon's voice was heard for the first time in a one-reeler that was part of the *Voice of Hollywood* series, released in the summer of 1929. This series was the idea of independent producer Louis Lewyn, husband of former screen star Marion Mack, who had played Buster Keaton's leading lady in *The General* in 1926. Lewyn had already made several series of shorts for various studios. He had approached one of the smaller outfits, Tiffany, with the idea of filming vignettes in sound for the many stars who were uncertain of their future with the microphone. Sound was innovative, financially promising, and the logical next step in filmmaking, but it created great tension in Hollywood. Some stars' voices did not fit their images; others did not register well on the equipment. Movie producers also imported stage-trained stars from New York, and singing and dancing became required attributes as musicals emerged as a popular genre in the 1930s. Thus, *Voice of Hollywood* permitted stars to record on a sound track and show prospective producers how well their voices registered.

The ten-minute *Voice of Hollywood* in which Langdon appears, teamed with Lew Cody, also crams in many other stars, including Taylor Holmes, leading man Montagu Love, Harry Jolson (brother of Al), Lola Lane, and songwriter Gus Edwards and his protégée, a Mexican starlet named Armida. Langdon and Cody trade quips about their first experience with sound film; Cody insists that Harry work solo. Langdon, when not purposefully stumbling over words in a tremulous voice and producing nervous baby sounds, pretends to be tongue-tied.

Once filming of the first Roach short started, the producer encountered a serious, though not unexpected, problem: Langdon was difficult to work with. He was used to directing himself (and his brief stage stint no doubt reinforced his independence), and he continued to be influenced by Helen and Ripley. Langdon was also somewhat resentful about his comedown, and he was bewildered by the adjustments required for sound recording, which involved camera techniques he was not accustomed to. His character in the Roach shorts is thus an ordinary nincompoop harassed by the spoken word, not the charming, sympathetic innocent that had served him so well in the silents.

Many of the eight Langdon-Roach shorts made that first year suffer from poor writing. This was typical of many early talking films, which were more concerned with capturing the novelty of the voice than with creating strong dialogue. Several shorts also reworked classic routines from Langdon's silent hits. In *Hotter than Hot,* Harry is trapped in a burning building with leading lady Thelma Todd (a vivacious and beautiful comedienne who, in just a few years, would be murdered in one of Hollywood's most infamous unsolved crimes). The film's connection to *His First Flame* seemed to have a positive effect on reviews. An exhibitor in *Motion Picture Herald* lauded it as the best Langdon film he had ever seen, and he thought more movies of this type would surely make Langdon popular in Iowa! Similarly, one of Harry's least successful routines—wearing women's clothing—is revamped in *Skirt Shy*. In that film, he works for a woman who cannot get a marriage proposal and dons a dress to help her get one—

Harry and
Thelma Todd
in *Hotter
than Hot.*

another illogical twist of gender roles that is as inexplicable here as it was in *Saturday Afternoon.*

Some reviewers found that Langdon's voice did not work as part of the comic business. With *Sky Boy,* in which Harry competes in an air exhibition with Eddie Dunn for Thelma Todd's hand, a reviewer for *Variety* admitted that Langdon had been "cute" in silent films, and "it may be to Langdon's credit that he adheres so closely to his old style in his new talk. They'll just have to pick his stories from a different angle." For an exhibitor reporting in *Motion Picture Herald,* Langdon had a "knockout voice."

The Head Guy, released in January 1930, clearly illustrates the risks of early talkies, but it is also the best example to date of Harry finding his place in the sound era—using his best visual childlike mannerisms to collaborate with his voice. Working at a small railroad station, Harry unloads the baggage of a group of vaudeville actors, and a duck escapes from a

The Head Guy with Nancy Dover and Edgar Kennedy.

crate. This establishes a running sound gag as Harry crawls after the duck, imitating its quack; but the noise Harry produces sounds like heckling, which insults the troupe. Later, when his girlfriend leaves him, Harry starts a prolonged weeping routine, funny in its mannerisms but also slightly disturbing, as the purpose of the skit seems to be to demonstrate the wonders of sound rather than advance the story. Nevertheless, when Harry contemplates suicide over this rejection, his speech is aptly child-like: "Nancy don't want me . . . I wanna die . . . I'll die like I never died before." He stares, crinkles his eyes and mouth, and squeaks his way into a crying fit, only to stop, sigh, and start again. He stammers, sputters, and performs a nonchalant manicure before putting his hand to his mouth as he ponders another option. With a slam of his hand on the table, which is meant to indicate resolution but startles him as well, Harry announces that he will get a prettier girl, a bigger girl, one who smokes even! His mock self-assurance translates into haughty laughter: "ho-ho-ho" and "ha-ha."

But his dejection is too strong, and he is again reduced to weeping. With nothing to live for, Harry pulls out a sandwich, then ends the routine by grabbing an apple, muttering, "I'll jump in the lake—I don't want no apple now, I'll have the apple later after now."

The timbre of his voice coupled with bad grammar, illogic, and child-man emotions were Langdon's way of building a subtle whirlwind of reactions to his problem. He seemed to be testing the best voice for his silent persona. Not coincidentally, Langdon echoed some mannerisms of Roach star Stan Laurel, who had mastered the slow spin into quiet frenzy and the quivering, pinched face and squeaky voice. Langdon was tracking new terrain, and comments in the trades seemed to acknowledge this trial and error. The general consensus, however, was that Langdon was still at his best in pantomime.

The last four Roach shorts made during his first contract year were variable, pulling now and then from Langdon's silent repertoire. *The Fighting Parson* harks back to *Horace Greeley Jr.* and *Boobs in the Woods,* with Harry as an eastern neophyte arriving in a western town and mistaken for a legendary two-fisted preacher.

In *The Big Kick,* Harry gets mixed up with bootleggers who are running from the cops. In *The Shrimp,* Harry comes to life in what may be his best short for Roach, reflecting the most helpless side of his character as he becomes the butt of practical jokes. Finally, *The King* finds Harry as the ruler of a mythical country—a throwback to *Soldier Man*—with Dorothy Granger as the queen trying to keep him from seductress Thelma Todd.

It was becoming common practice for studios to distribute their new talking pictures to foreign markets. Roach thus prepared several versions of his films with the actors speaking in the target languages, thus eliminating the tedious task of dubbing to sync with the actors' lips. This also gave overseas audiences the chance to hear the actors' real voices, instead of using unknown native speakers. Langdon redid several of his shorts while reading the translated lines phonetically from cards.[14] Roach also ran merchandise promotions, plastering Langdon's image on puzzles and games, as he did with the Our Gang kids and Laurel and Hardy.

Despite these efforts, Roach must have felt that Langdon was still groping for control and chose not to renew his contract.[15] No fewer than five directors had worked with Langdon in eight shorts; in one case, two directors made a joint effort. Roach himself took over on several occasions, relying on his tact and personal friendship with Langdon to produce

Harry and Nancy Dover in *The Fighting Parson*.

viable results. In later years, Roach reflected on the one key problem with Langdon that had likely hindered Sennett and Capra as well:

> Everybody ... did everything they could to get him to move faster. He would rehearse a scene exactly the way you wanted him to play it. Great! And as soon as you started the camera it was like slow

motion. He slowed right down to a walk in the thing. . . . I directed a picture myself because I thought it was the director's fault, and I couldn't move him any faster than they could. . . . The hell of it was you could argue and it didn't do him any good. No matter what you said, he agreed with everything you said and he'd go right back and do it over again.[16]

According to the directors and stars who served their apprenticeship there, the Roach studio had the most relaxed and friendly atmosphere in the film business, yet puzzlingly, Langdon did not share—or perhaps was incapable of sharing—that team spirit. Whether through obstinacy or helplessness, Langdon was unemployed and on the hunt for work again.

Despite the professional upheaval, Langdon may have felt that his personal life had finally stabilized, for during the filming of one of the eight Roach shorts, Harry and Helen were married on July 27, 1929. Langdon now had a family, although Helen's daughter Virginia was hardly the baby he had always wanted.[17] Langdon hoped this marriage would last, and he even filmed the event, courtesy of Roach's sound truck. Amid the festivities, however, there were some dire presentiments; for instance, in a perfect foreboding moment, the lights blew out during the wedding. Langdon quipped that this might be a sign not to continue the ceremony, or maybe Rose was lurking on the grounds and had blown the fuse. Nevertheless, the wedding proceeded by candlelight, and Langdon officially relinquished his carefree bachelorhood to settle down with Helen.

Langdon's business reputation had not regained a solid foothold, despite his work for Roach, so he began to freelance. He made his first sound feature for Warner Brothers, which had taken over First National at the end of 1928. Warner was cresting on the wave of *The Jazz Singer* and was committed to sound. During the transition period, while other studios were rushing the sound conversion, Warner supplied more talking films than anyone else. By 1930, the influx of profits from the first two years of sound had secured Warner's position among Hollywood's major studios, but it now had to compete on the merits of the product again. Because of the Great Depression, movie attendance, like all other businesses, had declined. Warner faced another serious disadvantage. Its original sound system, Vitaphone, consisted of a series of phonograph records synchronized with film. But the synchronization of two such distinct media was imperfect, and when other studios adopted the superior sound-on-film system, Warner switched as well, essentially undergoing two sound revolutions in a short time. Still, Warner maintained its edge in pioneering sound work.

Langdon premiered at Warner in a curiously uneven, episodic film called *A Soldier's Plaything*, set during World War I. It was directed by Michael Curtiz, the Hungarian maverick whom Harry Warner had brought to the United States in 1926. Curtiz, whose real name was Mihaly Kertesz, was known to be a dictator on the set, and both actors and technicians disliked him. He never learned to speak English well, but the words he knew best were graphic: the crew even nicknamed him "Goddamit Curtiz" because of his favorite expletive. Curtiz was destined to make more than a hundred movies for Warner, including *Casablanca* (1943) and *Mildred Pierce* (1943), but he was not exempt from producing routine programmers. *A Soldier's Plaything*, released in November 1930, was one of them.

Tim (Langdon) and Georgie (Ben Lyon) join the war effort, and their flirtations with various mademoiselles and fräuleins are punished with stable duty. The situation creates a running gag that permeates the film's wartime sequences and lets Langdon utilize his voice and mannerisms together to their best advantage. Whenever the boys are forced to shovel manure for their transgressions, Georgie feeds Tim the line, "How do we get out of this?" To which Tim, in a fine running sound joke, always replies, "Personality, my boy, personality." Tim's baby face belies the truth: there is no escape from the horse stables. In Germany, Tim falls in love with a pretty girl who is surprisingly reticent toward him; then her companion explains that she is deaf (reminiscent of the blind girl in *The Strong Man*). Thanks to sound, this sequence includes a Langdon rarity: he sings his first song onscreen, "If You Will *Oui Oui* Me, I Will *Oui Oui* You."

The date with the deaf girl supplies a thoughtful sequence promoting the story line while drawing on Langdon's silent mannerisms. He amuses her with his mime as he places two stones together and indicates in eloquent gestures that they should go off the same way. She vigorously shakes her head, so he sighs and sets the stones apart. He then shows her some French postcards; her voice unexpectedly returns, scolding him in harsh American vernacular before leaving him dazed. In the amusing epilogue to the film, Tim escorts his hometown sweetheart through Coney Island, where she wants to ride the merry-go-round, but at the sight of horses—

even wooden ones—Tim conjures up painful memories and leads her resolutely away.

The character of Tim is subordinate—the first time Langdon plays a second lead. Although he and Ben Lyon have approximately the same amount of screen time, Lyon's romantic escapade is the core of the picture, not Langdon's. In fact, all the other characters, including Tim, are undernourished in the film and fumble with plot twists and turns. Under Curtiz's restrictive direction, Langdon seems lost in the film, and he lacks opportunities to develop any meaningful routines in his leisurely way. Even the poignancy of his encounter with the deaf girl is played as a punch line when she reprimands him verbally—a full reversal of the sentiment sustained throughout *The Strong Man*. Another surefire gag receives perfunctory treatment as well: a reprise of Harry's memorable falling benches from *The Strong Man*. In the silent film, the stately progression of the heavy wooden benches, accompanied by Harry's fluttering futility, forms a perfect point and counterpoint. By contrast, in *A Soldier's Plaything*, the flimsy folding seats simply collapse all at once, with no chance for Harry to register his slow reactions. Langdon's best moments are simply scattered throughout the loose structure. A short scene that is nearly lost in the shuffle hints at Langdon's mix of pathos and laughter when he says goodbye to his friend and, with a subtle wave, underscores the imminent fatality of war: "If you don't hear from me, you'll know that I'm dead." After a pause, touched with regret and disappointment, Langdon's character brushes off the idea with a brave chuckle.

A final, more extended routine worthy of mention in this otherwise weak film illustrates Langdon's understanding of how his physicality could work with sound. Dangerous settings cause Harry to make childlike sounds of woe, usually emitted as agitated pulses: "Oh-oh, oh-oh." His expressive eyes dominate his face until the peril passes. He wants to assert himself against his nemesis but can do so only when the nemesis is not looking. For example, after ruining maneuvers, Harry stares at a comrade eye to eye because he is facing in the opposite direction from all the other soldiers. Although he has made a serious mistake, he is aware of it and even begins to enjoy it; like Soldier Schweik, his mistake undermines the established order of things. When the commanding officer shouts, Harry replies with small hand moves that the officer does not see. For each aggravated order by the officer, Harry's hands flip into a visual enactment of the order: "If I say fly, you fly!" and so the chubby hands flutter at his sides. "If

On the set of *A Soldier's Plaything,* directed by Michael Curtiz, with Ben Lyon and Fred Kohler. J. O. Taylor is operating the camera.

I say swim, you swim!" and so the pudgy hands paddle gently. "If I say stand on your head, you stand on your head!" His hands cannot follow suit, but when the officer spits for emphasis, Harry points at its landing spot in outrage, then wipes the leg of his pants. This sequence suggests Langdon's ability to do so much with so little, and to do so with grace. *Film Daily* recognized Langdon's magic in the small stuff by calling him the only bright spot in the whole film.

While filming *A Soldier's Plaything,* Langdon earned $2,500 per week for approximately three weeks of work. That same month, November 1930, Universal Pictures released a gangster film spoof, *See America Thirst,* with Langdon as costar. The gangster genre was a timely one, for America was in the midst of Prohibition (1920–1933), and gangsterism was rampant not only in the streets but also in show business. Starting roughly with Josef von Sternberg's *Underworld* (1927), which was also the last film for silent comedian Larry Semon in a supporting role, the gangster picture became standard fare. It also made a good target for spoofing, and in *See*

A debonair Harry and Slim Summerville in *See America Thirst*.

America Thirst, gangsters undergo some serious lampooning, especially with names such as "Tarface" Spumoni, "Insect" McGann, and "Shivering" Smith.

Langdon's former director Harry Edwards was instrumental in landing the comedian this job. At the time, Edwards was directing a series of shorts for Universal starring Slim Summerville, a fellow Sennett alumnus and an original Keystone Kop most easily recognized by his tall, lanky frame. When Summerville was selected to appear in this feature after his success in *All Quiet on the Western Front* (1930), Edwards suggested that Langdon would be a good partner for him. There might have been some notion of actually forming a team if the film proved successful. Unfortunately, this was the first full year of the Great Depression, theater attendance was low, and no hit materialized.

Langdon and Summerville complemented each other well, but Harry seemed to strain without an equal opportunity to improvise or relax with his character. He bounces off Slim's moves and lines like a random tennis ball. The two play hobos who arrive in town and are misidentified as out-of-town gunmen hired to rub out some rivals. They take their newfound fortune to a nightclub and fall in love with singer Ellen (Bessie Love), who is working with the district attorney to investigate the bootlegging operation and persuades the boys to help trap the gangs involved. Love, a versatile actress who had been appearing in films since 1916, was good in both comedy (with Douglas Fairbanks Sr. in *Reggie Mixes In* and *The Mystery of the Leaping Fish*) and drama (as the Bride of Cana in Griffith's *Intolerance*). She was the first to demonstrate the Charleston in *The King on Main Street* (1925). Undaunted by sound, she was such a hit in *The Broadway Melody* (1929) that she was nominated for one of the first Academy Awards.

See America Thirst is played purely for laughs, even if the routines are overstretched. There is mayhem involving hideaway weapons, sliding panels, hidden passages, trapdoors, and pop-up gadgets, and Harry and Slim engage in much physical repartee with cannons. Imminent danger again prompts Harry to chirp a few babylike cries for help, but his gestures are far from subtle in the havoc that resolves the gang warfare. One tongue-in-cheek gag that is typical Harry stands out: he incapacitates the gangsters with an oversized bug sprayer—appropriate, since he is up against "Insect" McGann.

The critics were not entirely complimentary, but they recognized Langdon's presence and even acknowledged that the material failed to highlight his true abilities. Thornton Delehanty for the *New York Evening Post* referred to Langdon's roller-coaster career by teasing his readers about a "one-time popular screen comedian who was temporarily abashed by the talkies, . . . [and] now comes forward in a full-length picture called *See America Thirst. . . .* Not to keep you in suspense any longer, the comedian's name is Harry Langdon, one of the best of the slapstick pantomimics." He made special note of the stultifying effects of the dialogue and observed that Langdon's brand of comedy was barely used in this film; in fact, the film handicapped him.

With his "potential" once again recognized in these films, Langdon was clearly doing his best. These roles kept him in the public eye. When a film received praise, it was usually because Harry had triggered a memory of his former greatness. It seemed that Langdon was still capable of sublime comedy, even in this new format in which his voice complemented his identity in novel ways. Without these efforts, Langdon would have been headed for obscurity. He would have to choose his steps carefully and wisely. He would also need the strength to continue.

Langdon had heard that Florenz Ziegfeld was planning to stage one more edition of his world-renowned *Follies* for 1931 and was auditioning acts. The press reported "negotiations" with Langdon, but when Ziegfeld heard of his supposed "offer" he denied it, adding a little abruptly, "I never heard of him until this minute." Ziegfeld was likely familiar with Langdon from both stage and screen, and perhaps his bold statement was merely a strategy to reduce Langdon's price or keep him away altogether. In any event, no offer was ever made.[18] When the *Follies* opened in 1931, Langdon was not in the cast. As it turned out, this edition was Ziegfeld's swan song, for he died the following year.

Langdon next signed with the R-K-O Vaudeville Exchange, one of the last circuits of this vanishing American entertainment. He toured a number of provincial towns, just as he had in his pre-Hollywood days, culminating in a three-day engagement at the Madison Theatre in New York in early August 1931. It was a tough grind for little money—only $650—but it was the high point of his employment as a returning vaudevillian.

To no one's surprise (except Harry's), Helen's tolerance for her husband's erratic career soon wore thin. Publicity during this time sent mixed messages. One photo showed Helen and her two daughters seeing Harry off on a trip to New York; Helen cooed to the press that she and her spouse were "happy as two turtledoves." But tabloids also reported on Helen's excessive spending and lawsuits from disgruntled landlords and vendors. The second Mrs. Langdon was accustomed to the luxuries of stardom and did not intend to share her husband's poor, peripatetic existence, as Rose had.

Meanwhile, Harry focused on performing in one city after another, enthusing publicly, "It's nice . . . getting your pay in applause and laughs" (no doubt meaning in lieu of an adequate salary). However, he also placed a notice in New York newspapers that he was not responsible for his wife's debts.[19] Both parties were irritating each other, or as Harry told his lawyer, she "crabs my acts and cramps my style by wisecracking." After enduring

Harry, Helen (behind him), and her daughters Edith (*left*) and Virginia (*right*).

more small-town hotels and uncomfortable train rides filled with arguments, Helen filed for a property settlement and returned to Los Angeles. A divorce action loomed, with unkind accusations that Langdon drank excessively (calling his liquor "Woof-Woof"), hit Helen repeatedly, and once even set some money on fire while he was drunk. At the last minute, Helen delayed the proceedings, just in case Langdon made a comeback. If not, she knew she could attract better prospects.

By filing for a property settlement, Helen ensured her security. She had observed with interest Rose's rather generous financial settlement, including real estate. For her five long years of devotion to Harry, Helen thought she deserved as much. But Langdon was no longer able to comply, even if he wanted to. He filed for bankruptcy as an "unemployed actor," claiming that the misfortune was due in part to the "advent of the talking pictures to which his particular type of humor was not suitable," according to an article in the *New York Herald-Tribune* on November 26, 1931. Citing his residence as the Hotel Warwick in New York, he claimed $62,637 in liabilities, $30,400 of which was back taxes. His assets amounted to $700 (an automobile valued at $200, props at $300, and $200 that his lawyer owed him). Finally, he valued his clothing, which was exempt in the bankruptcy, at $400. Specifically mentioned was a debt of $289 due to the Hollywood Athletic Club, as well as more than a hundred debts to various tradespeople in California. He was also contributing $50 a week to Helen's support in the interim. It was the third year of the Depression, and unemployment, stock prices, and businesses were at their worst. The FDR administration would work to turn the crisis around, but for millions of Americans, job prospects were bleak in 1932. A forty-seven-year-old out-of-work comedian was no exception.

At this time, an article appeared in *Photoplay* that placed the blame for "What Happened to Harry Langdon?" squarely on a mysterious letter composed by a "poorly paid gag constructor at Sennett's" who took over directorship on *The Strong Man*. No name was mentioned, although the "culprit" can be easily deduced: Capra. This person had allegedly circulated a hostile letter to movie columnists, calling Langdon "impossible" and "egotistical."[20] The letter, in short, had destroyed Langdon's reputation in Hollywood. Reporter Katherine Albert examined the impact of this letter on Langdon and concluded that it had deprived him of self-assurance: "He knows he's still a good comedian but every time anybody looks at him sideways he remembers the letter and its tragic results." She suggested that, if left to his own devices, and without reminders of his ego trips, Langdon would still be the best comedian in the talkies. Albert concluded with a definitive flourish: "And that's the story of how one man was beaten down at the height of a brilliant career, and licked by a letter!"[21]

The existence of a letter that sabotaged Langdon seems to offer an alternative explanation for his radically shifting career. Although Langdon's inflated ego was indisputable, the letter may have been instrumental in discouraging future offers and preventing others from employing Langdon. Hal Roach's insistence that Langdon not control his own work if he joined Roach's studio comes to mind. Langdon may have been his own worst enemy, but it seems he also received some anonymous help, compounding the problem.

The formal revelation in Albert's article may have helped disperse some of the negativity that shadowed Langdon, and colleagues who were willing to look beyond his "reputation" came to his aid. For example, comedian Robert Woolsey recommended Harry for a film being planned by Columbia, *So This Is Africa*. Woolsey had successfully paired with partner Bert Wheeler in the Broadway show *Rio Rita* in 1928 and in a number of shorts and features at RKO. But they were not yet a permanent team, and each had made a film without the other in 1931. Wheeler did not seem eager to be loaned out to Columbia for *So This Is Africa*, so Woolsey thought Harry could substitute. Unfortunately, Columbia insisted on the Woolsey-Wheeler team, and the film was completed in 1933. Langdon headed elsewhere.

Another project edged its way onto the list of possibilities. Royal Pictures signed Harry for a two-reel short tentatively titled *Show Goat*, for which he wrote the script. But no such picture was ever copyrighted, exhibited, or reviewed. Either it was never made, or it had such limited distribution that no trade paper acknowledged it. Langdon did, however, meet with the officers of Royal Pictures when he resided at the Cardinal Hotel at 243 West End Avenue in New York. The contract even provided for a generous $12,000 salary for his services and included a $10,000 budget for production costs covering seven and a half days of studio time and six supporting actors. But like many deals that seem too good to be true, it never materialized.

Yet cycles of misfortunate eventually rewind to better times. In May 1932 Hollywood producer Joseph M. Schenck approached Langdon with a legitimate deal: a character role in the upcoming United Artists film *Hallelujah, I'm a Bum*, starring Al Jolson. It promised to be a prestige production, and although nearly a year passed before its release, Harry's association with the project was enough to reestablish him in the movie capital. Before the year was out, Langdon had signed for another series of short films at Educational Pictures.

The stars were finally aligning themselves in Langdon's favor. While filming *Hallelujah, I'm a Bum*, Langdon was introduced to twenty-six-year-old Mabel Georgena Sheldon (née Watts). Born in Portsmouth, England, on February 3, 1906, Mabel had been brought to the States by her family when she was only four months old. William Gill, a newspaper reporter turned Hollywood agent, was representing Langdon at the time and had made the deal with Schenck. Hoping to give Harry some divertissement, since his personal life was in shambles, Gill asked his girlfriend, Louise Cianci, to find a date for Langdon. She suggested Mabel, who had been her classmate in high school and had ended a brief, unhappy marriage several years earlier.

Mabel initially resisted the idea of going on a blind date. She did not know of Harry Langdon, nor was she interested in show business. (In later years, however, she acknowledged that she must have caught him onscreen at some point when she went to the movies with her father.)[22] She had also gotten sunburned and did not want to attend a dinner party with what she called a "scaly-looking face." But Louise was insistent, so Mabel accompanied the trio to a Spanish restaurant, El Coyote. The next day she admitted to Louise that Harry was very nice—congenial, funny, and gentle—and she was touched when he called her that night to ask if she was interested in going out again sometime. Though it was not quite love at first sight, Mabel reflected years later that they might have had more in common than they realized:

My sister . . . Adeline—she was two years older than I was, she was keeping company with a gentleman [Surendra Guha] who was going to the university learning the motion picture business with intentions of going back to India and have his own producing company. . . . He taught me East Indian dancing [when] I was about fifteen years of age. Then, of course, so being connected also with the studios, he'd . . . do some of his work there. Nazimova was making a picture . . . I don't recall whether it was *Aphrodite* or if it was *Salome* that she was making, it was one of the two. They wanted East Indian dancers in the background, so I got the job of being one of the dancing girls and also teaching her some of the steps that I had been taught by an East Indian. They were authentic steps, you see. That was the only work I ever did in pictures. [Harry] also was working with the Sennett studios. . . . They were looking for a stand-in or a stunt girl . . . to replace Mabel Normand in some of her work. So, my being the same type as she, you know, dark and small, would I be interested in doing it? . . . I think it was my mother who turned them down. But I was trying to figure it out, if that could have been the same time as when Harry was working at the studio. Which would have been quite a coincidence to think I was working under the same roof, shall we say, that he was.[23]

This coincidence seemed like an illustration of destiny come to pass—a thought that would have pleased Mabel's mother, Georgena Watts, who was a noted astrologer in Hollywood. But Mabel did not ask for her mother's insight into the outcome of her dating Harry. A twice-divorced forty-eight-year-old man and a once-divorced twenty-six-year-old woman might find diversion in each other's company, but her mother doubted there could be anything more permanent. Still, unlike Rose and Helen, Mabel had no interest in Harry's fame or wealth—both of which he sorely lacked. At rock bottom, he could only ascend the cliff. Mabel enjoyed his kind manner and found in him a sympathetic, helpless child awaiting full expression. Harry found in Mabel a genuine companion. She recalled: "Of course, he didn't make [another] date right away . . . and so next morning I'm reading in the [Los Angeles] *Times* newspaper in one of the gossip columns that Harry Langdon had been seen at the Trocadero with Paulette Goddard. And I thought to myself, 'Well, heavens, who he goes out with! I'll never hear from him again!' But I did. . . . He came back."

Langdon had finally started to realize that success—however it is measured—can happen when one least expects it. When he purposely tried to control his work without understanding his capacity for it, he triggered his downfall. When he chased illusions, he trapped himself in a corner. But when the phases of his life dropped into perspective, he worked within his limitations. Langdon knew he was no longer the sensation he had been in his Sennett days, nor the haughty peacock of First National, nor the sullen fallen star of Hal Roach. If he was going to pursue the work he had loved since boyhood, he would have to be content with who he was, wherever he went. Langdon might be worn and tarnished, but he was still alive and ready for the next phase. He believed a promising career lay ahead of him, and now he had Mabel. His genius had not abandoned him either. It would surface again in different ways when he needed it.

4

The Stronger Man

Hallelujah, I'm a Bum turned Langdon's professional life around. In addition to the prestige of the project, Langdon later declared he had been paid $20,000 for his work on the film—a gift at this nadir of his life. Even so, Langdon was appearing in court more than he was onscreen, for each time he completed a feature, either Rose or Helen would demand back alimony, and each time he would explain he did not have enough money to comply. Despite his financial plight, Langdon was coming back with a run of steady work.

Made during the end of 1932 but released in January 1933, *Hallelujah, I'm a Bum* is a lighthearted musical in which Al Jolson plays a hobo who calls himself the "Mayor of Central Park." One day he finds a girl (Madge Evans) who has lost her memory, and he helps her regain it. In the end, she proves to be the girlfriend of the real mayor (Frank Morgan), a convivial type based on New York's bon vivant mayor Jimmy Walker of the late 1920s. Langdon has only a supporting role in the film, playing a rubbish picker named Egghead (his third role as a street cleaner), and he performs the character bit well. The film was a major hit, and many people were reintroduced to Langdon in one of his better moments. Jolson enlivens the film with a number of songs by Rodgers and Hart, both of whom appear in straight roles. Morgan is outstanding as the mayor who hates civic ceremonies. Langdon's role restricts him to expounding philosophical views to his fellow hobos, but even so, he fares well. The musical afforded Depression-era audiences a more entertaining view of life than they were experiencing. To Langdon, the film brought him more hope than he had known for some time. *Hollywood Filmograph* praised him as "the communistic park cleaner [who] gives his best performance since the memorable *Tramp, Tramp, Tramp.*" Jolson reportedly encouraged Langdon to look more deeply at his potential; he thought Langdon had "missed his calling by not

Harry in tight quarters with Madge Evans in *Hallelujah, I'm a Bum*.

going into more serious dramatic roles."[1] However, Langdon was a natural comedian, and despite a dramatic flair bordering on pathos, he felt he could not be anything else.

Though Langdon was not exactly a star reborn, he was working and had appeared in one good film. At the same time, he was churning out more shorts under his new contract with producer-director Arvid E. Gill-strom, who was releasing two-reel comedies through Educational Pictures. Gillstrom, a director for Mack Sennett at one time, knew that any graduate of that madhouse had been well trained in comedy. A native of Sweden, Gillstrom had worked for Sennett while Chaplin was there, and although he was not directly involved in Chaplin's films, this association helped him obtain a job with King Bee Comedies, which was producing a series of Chaplin imitations featuring Billy West. Gillstrom later went to Fox and became an independent producer, directing his own films and selling them through an established releasing organization. For the Langdon series, Gillstrom assembled some other Sennett alumni—Langdon's sidekick Vernon Dent and leading lady Ruth Hiatt. Harry Edwards sometimes assumed the director's chair, and Arthur Ripley contributed as scenario writer. Some routines from the silents were also resurrected for this reunion.

Langdon's contract with Gillstrom's Mermaid Unit at Educational required the completion of one short per month for twelve months at $2,500 per picture. The formula of incorporating new bits into strong Sennett material and relying on the dependable interplay between Langdon and Dent proved successful. For Langdon, the combination must have been a source of comfort and security, like returning home. However humble the vehicles, Langdon felt the ground was fertile enough for his character to grow. He even hoped the pairing with his close friend Vernon would launch a new team, as they had the "opposites" quality that characterized the best comedy duos. Unfortunately, they were too similar to the successful team of Laurel and Hardy, who overshadowed them at this point and made them redundant.[2] After the first six shorts were completed, Gillstrom moved to a more prestigious releasing setup through Paramount.

The first of the shorts for Educational, *The Big Flash,* was released in November 1932. These shorts opted for action and simple basic laughs; they were less strained than all the Roach shorts put together. Without artistic pretense, each short allowed Langdon to either reactivate some of his virtuoso silent solos or dream up fresh routines that modeled the brisk pacing of the old days. These silent triumphs refurbished with sound gave Langdon confidence that the public would easily accept him. These were the routines that had pleased his devoted fans—many of whom were still in the audience.

In *The Big Flash,* Harry and Vernon are janitors in a newspaper office and rivals for a girl. When they are recruited as reporters to catch a jewel thief, Langdon's character once again demonstrates a wonderful awkwardness with weaponry, calling a machine gun a pistol and quivering with fright when using it. In his best pantomime since the silent features, Langdon uses little expressions to embellish his actions and give continuity and comic sense to the routines. His repartee with a policeman is constructed of small gags showing the futility of anything he does. For example, Harry tries to distract the cop by reporting that his watch has been stolen, but when someone bumps into Harry, his watch falls from his pocket, ruining his strategy. Though his ideas seldom work according to plan, thanks to fate, his wistful thinking manages to claim the final reward in mysterious ways—probably also thanks to fate. This was the essence of his character in the silents, and the Gillstrom shorts were rekindling this essence.

"Comeback" was now the word being bandied about by Langdon's critics. *Motion Picture Herald* called this comedy "an excursion into the technique of the silent days." Heralded as a former king of two-reel comedies, Langdon had reentered his métier. The series of reviews published since Langdon's glory days provide clues to his emotions as he endured the vagaries of stardom: from frustration and despair at misplaced genius, to mockery and shame at self-sabotage, to regret and hope that all was not lost. Langdon did not openly articulate his feelings about reviews, but he must have experienced a sense of whiplash, reading a rave one month and a brutal pan the next month, or sometimes both simultaneously. In assembling his albums of clippings, Langdon may have selected only the best, but he had to weed through the worst to find them, and they no doubt formed a part of his mental "album." He might have found the most comforting—and helpful—reviews the ones that acknowledged the extreme journey he had taken in just a short time to reach his current destination. In reviewing *The Big Flash, Hollywood Filmograph* articulated a compassionate view of this journey: "Who ever said Harry Langdon is to make a comeback in pictures is absolutely wrong. As far as the public is concerned he never went away. He is more welcome than ever."

Langdon's January 1933 short, *Tired Feet,* derives many gags from the notion that fate's "motherly instinct" determines what her children need to grow up. Here, Harry and Vernon go camping with their respective love interests, and Harry's car slides to the bottom of a gully (perhaps a nod to Langdon's vaudeville car). Harry whines in protest to his girlfriend, who wants him to push it uphill: "Why don't you—why don't you—all right." He knows only too well he is subservient to man, woman, nature, and auto—and accepts it as his destiny.

Harry also provides a vivid contrast to his disastrous waking-up routine in *Three's a Crowd*. Harry, who is a mailman, is asleep but dressed for work, with the mail beside him. As he ambulates in his drowsiness, he inserts his whistle backward in his mouth and delivers mail to the furniture. There are no overly extended views of Harry just *staring*. Here, he acts out his sleepy condition with sharp pacing, ready to tackle another fateful day no matter how tired he is. Even though his voice crackles with infantile edginess, Langdon's best moments remain silent ones, such as when he tries to extract water from a recalcitrant hose that gushes merrily only when his back is turned. Unlike the "dishonest," manipulated, mechanical tricks of Sennett's films, here the trick is explained by showing that Vernon, hiding from Harry, is controlling the faucet. Thus, the situation is believable because it is organic to the narrative. It is also a showcase for Harry to submit to his child-man behavior, believing that the hose really hates him. Harry coaxes the water from it, pretending he does not care, sneaking up on the hose, challenging it to behave, and walking on it like a tightrope—all to retrieve his hat, which has fallen on the other side of it. The expression of his eyes balances his body language, both moving in a symbolic dance with the temperamental hose.

As a welcome distraction to all his hard work during the week's shooting of *Tired Feet* on location in Arrowhead, Harry continued to pursue his relationship with Mabel. Now working as an insurance agent, Mabel drove up to Arrowhead after work each day and back the next morning so she and Harry would not be apart too long. After each day's filming they socialized with the crew and walked along the lake. Their relationship seemed easy, with both Mabel and Harry involved in their own careers. There were no demands except to share time together while Harry continued his nonstop output of short films.

The Hitch Hiker, released in February 1933, revived the Limburger cheese routine of *The Strong Man,* with spoken dialogue instead of titles and the same exasperated passenger (Vernon Dent). Interestingly, the reenactment demonstrates that the classic routine is actually *not* enhanced by sound effects and dialogue; they almost seem like intrusions on the silent skit. Harry's succession of coughs, wheezes, and sputters is both comical and irritating, while the protests around him are superfluous

Knight Duty.

questions and remarks. The situation is resolved when the passengers eject Harry from the plane—mercifully, with a parachute. Those involved in making *The Hitch Hiker* likely banked on the expectation that this routine from *The Strong Man,* revised for sound, would be favorably received. Despite the differences, it had endured.

From *The Hitch Hiker* on, Langdon's output was relentless. In May 1933 *Knight Duty* finds Harry in a game of cops and robbers, which makes up for in hilarity what it lacks in logic. Harry, again playing a hobo, falls for the daughter of a wax museum curator; the setting provides a fitting location for Harry's innocent confusion about reality. He does wonders with a fake pretzel, a rubber sandwich, and solid beer in a mug. When he dodges the wax cops and gangsters on display, the scene works best in silence. His hand flutters at nearly being guillotined, and his run-ins with mirrors speak more loudly than any voice.

Langdon and Dent also worked together in the July 1933 release *Tied for Life*, in which Harry wins the girl but Vernon spoils the honeymoon. However repetitious the Gillstrom shorts were—based on Langdon's earlier silent routines or rivals-for-the-girl plots—they highlight an important aspect of the comedian's development that he was acknowledging through his actions. He had found a formula that made his little character fully human, giving voice to his conundrums as well as miming them masterfully. By developing his character, Langdon could retrieve a modicum of his former eminence—and even a small bit was enough, since he had lost so much. There is no monetary equivalent for this kind of fulfillment.

Fate was funny: it had played with Langdon as much as it had made his career. Fate made Harry fail when he was too sure of himself. It encouraged him when he was humbled. Like the temperamental hose, fate made Harry dance for his hat, and Langdon responded in the way he knew best—taking the long road and getting drenched. But that hat was *his*, and he *would* get it. Langdon was beginning to see that his fall from the heights was not the end of his career. It was fate's way of reinventing and reappreciating it.

About the time *Tied for Life* was released, Paramount decided to control the distribution of the Langdon shorts from Educational Pictures, which meant that he would receive the same publicity as Paramount's other contract players. Paramount kept its stars in the public eye by having them appear in the *Hollywood on Parade* compilation films that Louis Lewyn was making for the studio. Langdon's next appearance onscreen was in one of these shorts.

Hollywood on Parade for 1933 consists of informal footage of Paramount stars in their homes, at public functions, or clowning in front of Lewyn's camera as they rest on the set. The bits resemble newsreels, with a narrator identifying the stars, and they are structured much like the *Voice of Hollywood* shorts that Lewyn made in 1929 and 1930. Now, however, the stars had no need to dread the microphone, and these shorts depict a relaxed atmosphere. The reel in which Langdon appears is his briefest film appearance—less than a minute of screen time. But for the first and only time in a publicly released film, Harry and Mabel are shown together at the Agua Caliente racetrack in Mexico, just a short drive from Los Angeles. It was a popular vacation spot for celebrities to go to gamble or enjoy the excellent hotels and restaurants. Langdon relished his time away from work and frequently drove there or up to San Francisco with Mabel.

Langdon's next short was *Marriage Humor,* released by Paramount in August 1933. Harry and Vernon are two buddies who make a night of it but are afraid to face the wrath of their wives. The film was directed by Harry Edwards, who had proved his mettle with *His First Flame* and *Tramp, Tramp, Tramp* but, like Langdon, had returned to shorts. Edwards had developed a drinking problem, and studios did not trust him to work on features. Yet he was a sensitive artist who had always appreciated Langdon's humor and style, and he had the patience to obtain the best results from the comedian, despite their earlier falling out.

A week after Paramount released its first Langdon short, Educational put *Hooks and Jabs* (1933) on the market, one of two shorts that were in the can but not yet distributed. Vernon plays a saloon owner, and Harry plays a freeloader and a thorn in Vernon's side. At one point, Harry unwittingly gets involved in sparring with a punch-drunk boxer. His encounters with real he-men provide a great contrast to his childlike quality. In one scene, the boxer poses with his thumb at his mouth as he flexes his muscles; Harry tries blowing into his thumb, but only his hat flies up. An added treat in *Hooks and Jabs* is when Vernon joins his barroom buddies in singing "When You and I Were Young, Maggie," a perennial favorite from 1866. Vernon had started out as a member of a singing trio, but he hardly ever used his fine baritone voice onscreen.

Gillstrom gave Langdon the opportunity to do some screenwriting at this time, but his efforts were surprisingly weak. *The Stage Hand* (1933), the last of the Educational shorts, suffers from the same flaws that plagued Langdon's self-directed features. Here, Harry's character bungles the sound effects for a play being staged as part of a fund drive to build a new firehouse in town. An unexpected but not unfamiliar side of Langdon is evident here: from a structural and technical perspective, Langdon still misunderstood his screen character when working in capacities other than acting. He made Harry an irresistible lady-killer—an aspect of his character that had never been convincing in his silent films. Having two matronly women turn into romantic fools over Harry is merely ridiculous.

The climactic chase results in Harry falling off a fire engine and into a romantic clinch with a pretty girl. All this unmotivated and baffling feminine attention works against the story line and character. Even though it is mildly amusing to see Harry attacked by a lovesick spinster, it would have been more persuasive to see him woo the right girl with childlike awkwardness. Harry is more successful in a routine that enhances his otherworldly persona under the influence of drink. He employs many of his blushingly naïve traits in fending off an evil brew that a friend foists on him. Once he submits to a drunken stupor, he can only throw his hands into the air and call out "Yippee!" For once, sound, expression, and gesture merge into a coherent skit utilizing Langdon's childlike attributes.

Langdon's next venture was a musical version of George Bernard Shaw's *Pygmalion* called *My Weakness,* which premiered at New York's Radio City Music Hall in September 1933. Shaw's play would be filmed in 1938 as a British production starring Leslie Howard as Professor Henry Higgins, who transforms a street flower girl, played by Wendy Hiller, into an "aristocrat." And in 1956 *Pygmalion* would become the classic musical *My Fair Lady,* with book and lyrics by Alan Jay Lerner and music by Frederick Lowe. In 1933, however, the plot of *Pygmalion* was the basis for this Langdon film, although the adapter, Buddy DeSylva, did not credit Shaw for his inspiration and, in fact, took great pains to disguise the origin of his idea. Still, the plot elements are unmistakable. A lowly servant (Lilian Harvey) becomes a lady after Ronnie (Lew Ayres) bets his uncle that all she needs is the proper coaching. The ruse works, and the girl fools Uncle Gerald (Charles Butterworth) into falling in love with her. Meanwhile, as in the original play, the tutor finds that he cannot live without the girl and eventually marries her. DeSylva further disguised the piece by staging the musical as a whimsical fable with the cast speaking in verse, while dogs, cats, and even inanimate objects join in song. Romance is helped along by Cupid: enter Harry. He pops up throughout the film, always in miniature through trick photography, promoting love in his clumsy fashion.

An ad for *My Weakness* called it a "sparkling romance of melody, beauty and fun" that boasted three big songs—"How Do I Look," "Be Careful," and "Gather Lip Rouge while You May"—none of which ever made the hit parade. The film was also the first feature for Irene Bentley, who received favorable reviews for her work as second lead. She made only three movies in her career: *My Weakness, Smoky* (the most successful western up to that time), and *Frontier Marshal.* After her last film in 1934, she dropped out of the Hollywood scene, married three times, and died in 1965. Although she was the subject of the book *Ginger, Loretta, and Irene Who?* author George Eells could find little information on her whereabouts or activities after she left Hollywood.

Lew Ayres remembered *My Weakness* as "a very remote picture. It wasn't a great success." As small as his role was, Langdon caught the eye of *New York Times* reviewer Mordaunt Hall, obviously jarring his memory: "A familiar countenance pops up here and there as a mature Cupid. After thinking it over, one decides that this person who is shooting darts now and again is none other than Harry Langdon." Despite being cast in a lighthearted fantasy, Langdon may have been frustrated by such a small and silly role, full of corny couplets. Fortunately, Cupid was an appropriate character for Langdon to play at this time, and one of his arrows may well have pierced his own heart.

Langdon's two-year courtship of Mabel Sheldon finally blossomed into marriage. He found Mabel refreshingly different from Rose and Helen, given her self-imposed lack of involvement in the Hollywood social whirl. She was not even interested in filmmaking, and Langdon felt no need to construct a glittering façade to please her. Mabel had met Harry at one of his lowest points. He had even turned to alcohol to forget his losses and the seemingly irreparable mistakes made in his private and professional lives. Even so, Mabel cared for his whole being and neither expected nor asked for the high life. Of course, with Langdon now welcome in celebrity circles again, he and Mabel occasionally visited the fashionable nightclubs—Trocadero, Macombo, Sebastian's. But after their marriage, the tinsel yielded to a simple home life, which they both craved. Harry gave up his bohemian lifestyle at the Garden of Allah, the mecca of artists, actors, and writers owned by silent screen star Nazimova.[3] Nor did he ever again live in the house on the hill owned by Rose and for which she had demanded rent. Mabel wanted Harry to pick himself up for his own sake, but she gave him the incentive to quit drinking and to work. Although Langdon had never actually stopped working, he sometimes felt unsure about his path and what the effort was worth. Mabel provided him with a logical and necessary goal, even if she never said as much.

Harry and Mabel got married on February 10, 1934. Mabel recalled that the decision had been as simple as, "Well, why don't we get married?" With their friends William Gill and Jeanette Snowden—she had been

Harry and Mabel Georgena Sheldon.

married to an Italian prince, when marrying princes was all the rage in Hollywood—they first holidayed in Mexico so that Harry could obtain his divorce from Helen. Cows ambled on the roads they traveled, and a "gas station" consisted of a man standing under a tree with a fifty-gallon tank. When the engaged couple arrived to pick up Harry's divorce papers, one stenographer gasped, "You're Harry Langdon." She brandished a fan magazine with his photograph in it, which he signed with pleasure. Then they drove to Tucson, Arizona—their chosen wedding site. During breakfast the day after the ceremony, reporters spotted the newlyweds and cornered Harry, asking where he had met Mabel. "Oh, out in the desert," he answered. "She crawled out barefooted from under a rock." That response was printed in the next day's papers, along with an item describing Mabel as Harry's "fourth wife." This would not be the last time the tabloids misreported Langdon's tangled marital life. Upon the couple's return home, Mabel's mother expressed her disappointment at not being invited to the wedding. Guilt ridden, they promised to make it up to her one day.

The papers enjoyed contrasting Langdon's miserable financial condition with his happy new marriage. They chronicled his ongoing money woes in detail—including a curious claim by cheese salesman Frank Monguso, who was suing for $150,110 for injuries suffered in a car accident. An article in the *New York Sun* dated February 13, 1934, advised the new Mrs. Langdon that she might want to check whether Harry had resumed his old habit of pinning thousand-dollar bills under hotel chairs to prevent their theft—a reference to a complaint Helen had made in their divorce proceedings. In short, the press duly warned Mabel that Harry's debts were considerable—in case she had not noticed already. She also accompanied her husband to innumerable court appearances to work through these settlements; newspaper reports sometimes included photos of Mabel and Harry looking haggard as they slumped in hallway chairs while awaiting a hearing.

Fortunately, Langdon had a steady stream of work to compensate for his personal challenges. Two more Paramount shorts were released in 1933. *On Ice* finds Harry and Vernon once again playing buddies who are dating two pretty girls and get caught by their wives, a plot reminiscent of *Saturday Afternoon*. In *A Roaming Romeo*, Harry and his girlfriend inspect a model house that holds numerous surprises for them. The year 1934 started with Harry appearing in another compilation of the *Hollywood on Parade* series (this one labeled B6). He and Bing Crosby discuss their favorite hobby—golf—and Langdon stages a pantomime routine for the camera, reminiscent of his golf-themed vaudeville skit: he tips his hat and golf balls cascade from it. In Paramount's next release, *A Circus Hoodoo*, Harry and Vernon escape a bunch of crooks by joining a circus. Finally, in *Petting Preferred*, the last of the Paramount films released in April, married couple Dorothy Granger and Vernon Dent quarrel over keeping a dog and visit Harry's pet shop to settle the fight.

After *Petting Preferred*, Langdon found himself out of work again. The situation suddenly became crucial when he learned that he was about to become a father. Mabel recalled that when she told Harry the news, "He could hardly wait till we got to all the nightspots so he could tell everyone I was pregnant. Oh, that was a very happy day. I can almost hear him now: 'I'm gonna be a father! She's pregnant!'" For the first time, at the age of fifty, Langdon felt a thrill greater than any he had ever known. He would have an heir to carry on his name. The prospect of becoming a father motivated him to overcome the obstacles placed in his path when his fame and fortune had collapsed. He was not shy about expressing his enthusiasm in a September 14, 1934, interview for the *Los Angeles Examiner,* in which he acknowledged the many changes he had undergone:

> All this business of being a big shot—I've found it really doesn't mean much after all. It wasn't many years ago that my name was in lights emblazoned on billboards in huge letters. Certainly, it was pretty swell and all that. I can't deny that I enjoyed it. But Fate or whatever it is played tricks with me. I sat around relaxing and writing and sculpting for quite a while. That became tiresome, so I decided to go back into pictures.
>
> They're not feature length any more, but that's nothing. And they've taken away the sloppy clothes that were so much a part of my character and are dressing me up like a fashion plate. That's not so bad. I rather like it.
>
> And last but not least, if I didn't have anything else to be ridiculously happy about it wouldn't matter at all, for I'm going to be a father pretty soon! That's enough to take care of any amount of unhappiness that might come along.

The article also featured a photo of Langdon sculpting a bust of his mother in her Salvation Army bonnet—revealing another of his many talents. Her head is larger than his, her face beatific, her eyes wide (much like his could be). Langdon's choice of subject was important. Lavinia had died in 1929, having witnessed her son's rise and fall. It was perhaps symbolic, and a tribute to his mother's fervent belief, that he brought her back to life with his own hands at this time.

Langdon's optimism, which he managed to maintain for the rest of his life, persisted through the setbacks and disappointments that inevitably followed him. These included hopscotching from one job opportunity to

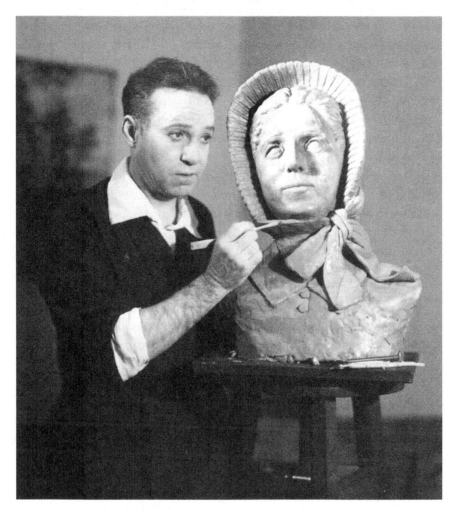

Son and mother.

another as they arose and grappling with the nasty residue of his divorces. Somewhere, there was always a solution. In one moment of financial despair, for example, Mabel suggested that Harry apply for a loan. After informing her mother Georgena of their destination, she and Harry drove down to the Seaboard Finance Company, but just as Harry was about to sign for the loan, the telephone rang at Seaboard. It was Georgena, calling with the news that Jules White had phoned and Harry needed to return the call immediately. Langdon leaped up, telling anyone within earshot at Seaboard to forget the loan—he was back to work in the movies. He and

Mabel raced out to take advantage of this promising offer, presented in the typical cliff-hanging tradition of movie serials.

Jules White was one of four brothers, three of whom had entered the motion picture business (Ben White, a pioneer in aerial photography, was not involved in movies). Jack White started working as an extra in 1917, and two years later, at age twenty-six, he was in charge of a comedy unit at the new Educational Film Corporation of America. Earl Hammons had established Educational in 1919 to make educational films for schools and churches, but he quickly discovered that the real money was in entertainment and transitioned to comedies with Jack's help. Educational never returned to making educational films, but it kept the name. Meanwhile, Jack taught his brothers Jules and Sam the mechanics of the business, and both wholeheartedly embraced it. Sam worked as a cameraman, still man, writer, and film editor before directing at RKO in the 1930s. He made a number of pictures with Edgar Kennedy and Leon Errol, as well as musicals with big bands such as Ted Florito's orchestra, featuring Betty Grable as singer.

Jules, the unexpected savior in Langdon's moment of need, had been a child extra for D. W. Griffith around 1912, and he can be glimpsed in the original 1914 version of *The Spoilers*. He directed his first film at age twenty-four and moved to MGM in the 1920s. His break came in 1934 when Harry Cohn, the head of Columbia Pictures, decided to place his studio on a par with the majors. Until then, Columbia had been considered a "poverty row" outfit: starting on a shoestring, it had neither the stars nor the facilities to produce large-scale work. Its original name, C. B. C. Film Sales Company—the initials stood for the two Cohn brothers (Harry and Jack) and their partner, Joe Brandt—was mocked as standing for "corned beef and cabbage." Harry Cohn headed Hollywood operations, while brother Jack and Brandt ran the New York branch. Harry gained a reputation for being stingy because he used a set painted on both sides to cut his lumber bills and liked to employ directors and actors who could do scenes in one take. Instead of having his own stable of actors under contract, Cohn borrowed the specific actors he needed from the major studios for individual pictures.

After a wobbly start in the early 1920s, Columbia (as it was renamed in 1924) built a solid reputation, thanks to Cohn's frugal strategies. In 1928 Columbia triumphed when it hired Frank Capra, whose films removed the stigma of poverty attached to the studio. He directed *The Matinee Idol*

(1928) with Bessie Love, *The Power of the Press* (1928) with Douglas Fair-banks Jr., *Platinum Blonde* (1931) with Jean Harlow, and *The Bitter Tea of General Yen* (1933) with Barbara Stanwyck and Nils Asther. Capra's other 1933 release, *Lady for a Day,* adapted from a Damon Runyon story and starring May Robson and Guy Kibbee, received four Academy Award nominations. Although it did not win any awards that year, Columbia had shed its shabby image, which was victory enough. Then, in early 1934, Columbia borrowed Clark Gable from MGM and persuaded Claudette Colbert to give the studio four weeks of her time to film *It Happened One Night.* The film premiered at Radio City Music Hall in New York but received lukewarm reviews and was withdrawn after a week. When it played neighborhood theaters, however, Columbia found that it had an unprecedented hit. The picture played for months and won five Oscars (best picture, actor, actress, director, and screenplay).

Cohn finally thought Columbia was ready to expand, and he loosened his grip on the purse strings so that the studio could increase its physical facilities and diversify. First, he established a short subjects department and hired Jules White to head it. White searched for creative minds to produce inexpensive but sharp comedy shorts. At MGM, he had directed a couple of comedies with Ted Healy, a vaudeville headliner, and his three assistants. Healy was too expensive, but White made a deal with the three assistants and launched one of the most popular comedy teams of all time: the Three Stooges. He also brought on board a number of experienced directors and writers, including Arthur Ripley, to build his comedy series.

Jules invited other stars, including Andy Clyde and Leon Errol, to make shorts for his new department, and brother Jack directed. To avoid charges of nepotism, Jack initially worked under the pseudonym Preston Black. Jack had just released the Arvid Gillstrom series of Mermaid comedies with Harry Langdon, which proved to be moneymakers, so he suggested that Langdon be put under contract. Ripley also made a case for Langdon, citing his hard luck and need for a job, especially as Gillstrom had died suddenly of pneumonia in May 1935 at age forty-five. More important, Ripley vouched for Langdon's comedic talent. As Jules remembered years later, he met "this little guy"—Langdon—at the Lakeside Country Club:

> I knew he was going to put on a front for me and I had to put one
> on for him. "Glad to meet you, Harry," I said. "I've always been
> one of your greatest fans." Well, his face brightened. And I had to

Harry with Leon Errol (*center*) and Arvid Gillstrom (*right*).

lead him to talk, he wouldn't say much. So I finally said, "How would you like to make some pictures for me?"

"I'd like it," he said.

"Well, great," I said. "How about coming to the office tomorrow and we'll sit down and talk turkey?"

He said, "Fine."

He was elated. I left Ripley with him to talk it over. Ripley came to the studio later. Arthur said, "Geez, he's all enthused. He's really high. He hasn't worked for some time. He has no transportation. But I'll pick him up and bring him to the studio in the a.m." I made a deal with Harry and he drew up a contract with options.[4]

By mid-1934, Langdon had made what was to be his most permanent move, and a comparatively lucrative one: $1,000 per picture to start. He was not obligated to work for more than a week on each short, but according to Jules, "Because it behooved [Harry] to give everything he had to offer for his own comeback, I didn't count the hours."

Langdon's arrangement with Columbia was flexible; it allowed him to take on other work, which he accepted at every chance. No specific unit produced his shorts because writing and directing duties were rotated, sometimes resulting in films of uneven quality. But Columbia seemed willing to give Harry a break and allowed many of his old associates to join him. Both Harry Edwards and Alf Goulding, who had directed Langdon in his first two Principal shorts in 1923, returned. Ripley wrote story lines and directed some of the shorts. Jules White, Harold Godsoe, and Del Lord alternated in the director's chair as well. Vernon Dent stayed on, although his talents were often wasted in third-rate supporting roles that limited his interactions with Langdon in his greatest capacity—as the little man's chief antagonist.

The first Columbia short, *Counsel on De Fence,* was released in October 1934 and is one of the funniest of the lot. Langdon, sporting a rare mustache, plays a shyster lawyer defending a woman accused of poisoning her husband. Since Ripley directed this film, it is not surprising to see a re-creation of the *Long Pants* routine, with Harry trying to stuff the woman into a crate, just as he had manhandled a dummy in the feature. Another routine parodies a scene from a popular contemporary film, *The Mouthpiece* (1932). Harry swallows some of the alleged poison from a bottle exhibited as evidence, thinking that his assistant has substituted iced tea for it; the assistant, however, failed to make the switch in time, and by the end of the film, Harry has suffered three stomach pumpings in his best fretful manner.

By the time Langdon's next film was released at the end of 1934, he had received a special Christmas present. On December 16 Mabel gave birth to a ten-pound son. Newspapers related uncanny stories of the comedian's "father fixation": "Several months ago Langdon . . . painted his impression of how his baby would look after birth. This might sound all very mad if it weren't for the fact that both picture and offspring tally in every detail, even to the existence of a dimple." The infant was also reported to be an "astrology baby." For instance, "[Georgena] Watts said that if the baby was born before 5 o'clock on a December morning, he would have great qualities of leadership and strength of character. Young Langdon was born at 4:49 a.m. on a December day. . . . His future still rests with the stars. Papa wants him to be many things, but not an actor."[5] Dubbing the occasion the happiest New Year he had ever known, Langdon announced that he was building his own monument, and its name was Harry Philmore Langdon Jr.

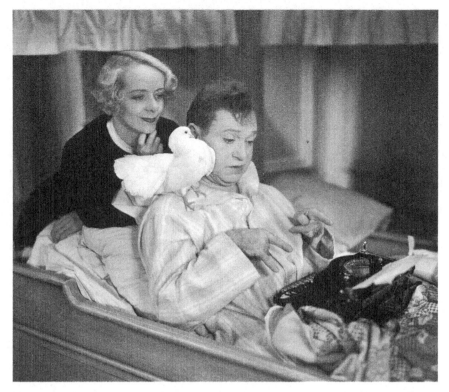

Settled in for inspiration with his typewriter in *Shivers*.

Two of Harry's former costars, Joan Crawford and Thelma Todd, gave the new parents layettes for Junior. Mabel remembered that whenever he was not at work, Harry spent all his time with the baby. He carried him in a diaper tied around his neck like a hammock, even when playing the piano. She recalled, "Once we had a nurse and she didn't want Harry to handle the baby so much. Harry said, 'Well, you can just leave.' He fired her. That child just meant so much to him."[6]

Langdon's next short, *Shivers,* was released just after the baby's birth. It features Harry as a mystery writer who moves to a haunted house for the atmosphere. Again directed by Ripley, the film reprises some of the material from the early Langdon short *The First Hundred Years*.

Langdon pursued his work on the Columbia shorts with greater motivation than ever throughout 1935. In the first release of that year, *His Bridal Sweet,* newlywed Harry escorts his wife to a model home. The humor here comes from the unlikely premise that several house-hunting

Harry and Billy Gilbert in *His Bridal Sweet*.

couples are examining the model home at the moment one of them is struck by smallpox and must be quarantined. The first half of the short plays with their reactions to the troublesome gadgets in the house; the second half is a comic duet between Harry and Billy Gilbert, who is both his roommate and a homicidal lunatic. Despite the potential hilarity of seeing Harry juxtaposed with his opposite, the execution lacks timing and punch. The dialogue is ridiculous ("If I try to kill you, quack to remind me who you are"), and the visuals rely on cheap tricks (Gilbert imagines Harry to be a bottle of liquor).

Nearly halfway through 1935 came another Ripley-directed short called *The Leather Necker*. This film does not simply borrow from one of Langdon's previous endeavors; it is a complete remake of 1924's *All Night Long* (its original title had been *The Leather Necker*). The action, however, is moved from France to the Philippines, where Harry is in the Marine Corps, still peeling potatoes. Assuming Dent's old role as the sergeant is

Looking glazed in *The Leather Necker*.

Wade Boteler, who is looking for someone to accompany him to his girl-friend's house. There is the same welcome kiss between Harry and the girl and his stunned reaction of falling backward out the window. Then come the battle scenes. Here, Ripley thought he was improving the action: instead of having the sergeant send Harry on suicide missions, he tries to shoot Harry himself. This, however, paints the sergeant as a vicious brute rather than a mildly sneaky adversary. *The Leather Necker* has no post-script that shows Harry married to the girl; the film ends with a car chase. Although this film was a dud, Langdon's youthful charisma was lauded as the chief reason anyone found the film amusing. Yet it had a wartime set-ting with a dark edge (likely Ripley's influence) and indulged in slapstick to push the images and sounds. Harry reacts with pronounced rather than subtle facial gesticulations, although his eyes retain an unusual glaze as he moves through the listless gags.

On the home front, Langdon's financial stresses led him to reach out for help from people he could trust. One particularly touching note illustrates Langdon's determination to pretend his heart was light, despite his problems. Harry's letter to W. C. Fields, a comrade on the golf course as well as a fellow vaudevillian, resonates with the typical humor Langdon infused in his public persona, even in tough times. He tried to downplay his dire situation while asking for help. Those who understood this aspect of his personality gave without hesitation, as did Fields. Langdon wrote:

Dear Billy,

I am not really as nervie as this letter may sound to you. But desperate circumstances forces me to ask for help. The X wives and the income tax authorities accomplished their purpose, and left me temporarily flat, financially.

Two hundred dollars will pull me through until I start my new Columbia contract, which starts in July.

This amount will save my furniture, automobile, and supply kid Jr. with milk, etc. My credit is good for other necessities, until I start to work.

Can you? . . . and confidentially?

Ye Gods, has it come to this.

Very gratefully yours,

Harry Langdon

Around this time, Langdon was hired for a film sponsored by the B. F. Goodrich Company to promote safe driving. What makes *Love, Honor and Obey (the Law)* (1935) such a surprise is not that it is very funny but that a private company, sponsoring a twenty-minute commercial, allowed Langdon to present a simple, entertaining story without hawking its product or sermonizing to the buying public. No deadening voice-over extols the sponsor's point. If the cars in the film were equipped with the sponsor's tires, they were not prominent in the shots. Whatever B. F. Goodrich had in mind when it hired Langdon, hard sell was not the goal. Stanley Rau was credited as producer, but whether he was the one who approached Langdon is unknown. The film was made by Audio Productions Inc. at the studios of the General Services Corporation, and Rau could have been connected with either of them. Columbia readily agreed to let Langdon do the project. Because Columbia borrowed stars from other studios, it was willing to loan out its players in return. There is no account of the remuneration paid to either Columbia or Langdon, and although he is not credited, Langdon may have been the writer. It is a sweet and well-paced story about Harry, a reckless driver engaged to a police chief's daughter. His vain efforts to avoid traffic infractions only seem to ensure that they happen, especially because his best man (a rival) is ensuring the pitfalls. In a fine characterization, Harry's child-man is oblivious to his circumstances, yet he marries the girl and gets a new car while turning the tables on his rival. The company's message about safe driving is delivered subliminally under the film's more comically urgent message that one should not trust one's best man.

Langdon's palette was diversifying as he took whatever work was offered. In 1935 he appeared in the feature-length Columbia programmer *Atlantic Adventure,* starring Lloyd Nolan and Nancy Carroll. Harry plays news photographer "Snapper" McGillicuddy, a friend of reporter Nolan who is tracking a murderer on an ocean liner bound for Europe. They meet an assortment of unsavory characters and eventually expose the murderer in a happy ending. The part of "Snapper" was neither juicy nor fitting for Langdon's persona. The character is supposed to be imperturbable, as evidenced by his incessant chewing on snacks, but such a trait is not inherent to little Harry, nor is the breezy casualness that marked hardboiled newspapermen in the journalism movies of the 1930s. Harry is reduced to a tangential figure, almost like a prop that complicates Nolan's task by, for example, getting himself captured. Nevertheless, he got some good reviews for supplying "the intentional farcical aspects entertainingly" (*Brooklyn Daily Eagle*) and succeeding as a "splendid foil" (*Variety*). There is one telling studio shot of Langdon resting between takes on *Atlantic Adventure:* He is caught in the shadows and framed by the straight angles of the equipment around him. His rubbery face contrasts with the reflected glare of the metal; his hunched shoulders, faraway eyes, and curved cartoon-line mouth almost preface a sigh waiting to emerge. His face is puerile, his expression weary. He simply waits for his cue to continue the film and then meet whatever life has in store for him.

Langdon's portfolio of films at this time fluctuated in their texture and comedic quality. Success is always the intention, but the reality can fall

Reflective moments onscreen and off in *Atlantic Adventure*.

short. Langdon may have felt that he was just along for the ride—stardom was no longer pressuring him to create and prove himself, but his veteran star reputation did precede him. And if the duds had any saving grace, it was that Langdon stood out from the mediocrity. Either the material was so weak that his comic strengths were wasted, or Langdon alone gave the audience its money's worth. At least with a string of short films in quick succession, each one provided a new opportunity to improve on the last.

His Marriage Mix-up was the first of Harry's films to be directed by Jack White, using the name Preston Black. Black was also the brand of humor in this comedy, in which the beautiful Dorothy Granger plays the unlikely role of an axe murderess with whom Harry unwittingly becomes involved, while Vernon Dent contributes to his woes. Critics seemed to like this short for its original gags and fast pace, but the *Exhibitor* called it "not very funny, except when Harry Langdon looks extremely dumb"—a dubious compliment.

The last short of the year, *I Don't Remember* (December 1935), is a tale of financial woe and fateful choices. When his furniture is repossessed, Harry paints the furniture on the walls—a trick that worked for him in *Plain Clothes*—but his wife is not amused. He buys a winning lottery ticket, but it blows away in the wind. Langdon is on familiar ground in this short, for he essentially plays an odd little amnesiac whose helplessness cuts a pathetic figure reminiscent of his silent persona. For example, he wears an oversized nightgown with his ever-present hat and stares at his mother-in-law before asking, "Who's that?" He absentmindedly cracks eggs into his coffee and eats the shells. Whenever he cannot remember, he lifts his pudgy hand to his mouth and ponders. When Harry tries to lie down on his painted couch, he wonders what happened, nervously twittering, "Oh my goodness!" and projecting a wary look.

Ending the year with such a docile character was a good sign for Harry at this point in his life. He himself had become docile, at least on the surface, though perhaps unrest and frustration still stirred in his core. On the set, however, he displayed none of the ego that had challenged others to confront him or had driven them away. Jules White found the comedian surprisingly agreeable:

> Harry Langdon was *not* the man of the reputation that I had heard. He was a very nice guy. He was a very subdued, quiet fellow and all he wanted to do was make a comeback. He worked like a Trojan. He did everything and anything—sat in with us on story conferences, helped work on the gags. Any time we wanted him he was Johnny-on-the-spot. . . . As with all people, time had taken a toll, his baby face had wrinkles. He now had to play a more mature type of Langdon, but Harry rose to the occasion. . . . Unfortunately, towards the end, the short subjects business went to hell.

Columbia had been planning to give Langdon more work, but toward the end of 1935 he made a surprising, but not totally unexpected, choice. He decided to take his family on a vacation—an escape from their volatile life in Hollywood. The break would last for two productive and personally rewarding years.

Langdon had received an offer from booking agency J. C. Williamson Ltd. to tour with a road company of the Cole Porter musical *Anything Goes* in Australia. Although the last time Langdon had appeared regularly onstage in a musical revue had been in 1920 with *Jim Jam Jems*, he thought this would be a welcome diversion for himself, Mabel, and little Harry, so he took a leave of absence from Columbia. The Langdon family sailed from Los Angeles on the Maritime Line steamship *Mariposa*, with journalists in tow to report his adventures to their readers.[7]

Anything Goes was a smash hit on Broadway, thanks to Cole Porter's snappy tunes and a fine cast that included Victor Moore, Ethel Merman,

Father and son on board the SS *Mariposa*.

William Gaxton, and Bettina Hall. Moore portrayed a gangster who "disappears" for a while, disguised as the Reverend Dr. Moon; he packs his machine gun and sails for Shanghai. Moore, a droll comedian and fine dramatic actor (*Make Way for Tomorrow*, 1937), relished the role as the sham clergyman and added another definitive characterization to his acting résumé. The play opened on November 21, 1934, and was a hit that season, running for 420 performances. For the young Ethel Merman, it was a major step to stardom. In addition to the title tune, her powerful voice launched two songs that became show business evergreens: "You're the Top" and "I Get a Kick Out of You." Paramount retained Merman for the 1936 film version of *Anything Goes* but replaced the other leads with Bing Crosby, Charlie Ruggles, and Ida Lupino.

It was only natural for road companies to take such a successful play and perform it across America and overseas. In the Australian company, Langdon played the role of "Moonface," the gangster-clergyman, Lillian Pertka assumed the Ethel Merman role, and Robert Coote was the leading man. The company arrived in Sydney in February 1936, prepared to spend a few weeks there; instead, they stayed for more than a year, playing big towns and smaller communities in the Outback—wherever there was a theater. Local reviews uniformly praised the show and Langdon's performance. In fact, the response was heartening for Langdon, who was recognized for the many gestures and subtleties that had characterized his silent work. He was "as one remembers him," according to the *Morning Herald*, but this time with an appropriate "mournful little voice" to complement his physical and visual vocabulary of "helpless gestures" emanating from his skillful pantomime. The *Sydney Sun* called him a "familiar friend," and an advertisement for the forthcoming performance in a theater program welcomed him warmly, saying, "His reputation as a screen player speaks for itself, but when you see him in the flesh, you'll fully realise you are seeing a real star."

Audiences were equally receptive and supportive, and they seemed to be having as good a time in their seats as Langdon was having onstage. In particular, the *Labor Daily* remarked that Langdon held the audience from his first entrance, especially when he indulged in a "refreshing 'not-in-the-script' monologue," mostly at the expense of his good-natured fellow actors. An important observation in the favorable reviews was that Langdon was a master of the theater, balancing his eccentric character with teamwork. Even when he was the center of the action, he avoided overshadowing the others—a lesson Langdon had learned from the days he had been eager to inundate scenes with his own presence. However, it seemed that even without any exertion, Langdon stood out from the crowd. As one critic observed: "The eye will always wander from the spot of romance in the centre of the stage to the effortless, almost immobile form of 'Moonface' sitting in the background." Langdon automatically controlled the stage just by being himself.

Mabel's support of her husband's decision to work on the other side of the world was generous, especially as it meant uprooting her family. Members of the press frequently and graciously followed her activities as well. They extolled how, back in the States, she had helped Harry count the laughs during film screenings or assisted when he wrote stories. For her, this adventure was both an exhilarating opportunity to see the world and a trip that promised a more secure future. It was, in essence, the honeymoon the Langdons never had. Although Harry received a number of congratulatory telegrams from his colleagues on opening night in Sydney, perhaps the most special was the one from "May and Harry" (wife and son), expressing their optimism for a better life together in the future.

Top left: Harry in his dressing room for *Anything Goes,* with a photo of Junior on his table. *Top right:* Scene from *Anything Goes* (Harry in clerical garb). *Bottom left:* Langdon clowning around with costar Lillian Pertka. *Bottom right:* "Conducted by Ken Slessor" in *Smith's Weekly,* February 12, 1936, drawn by Jim Russell and captioned "ANYTHING GOES, a J. C. W. Stage-show at Sydney Theatre Royal, with Harry Langdon."

During his Australian tour, Mabel worked backstage as Harry's dresser and prompter, which gave them many opportunities to discuss important ideas. In fact, one of these "conversations" was published in the *Morning Herald,* and the topic was what spouses argue about—something familiar

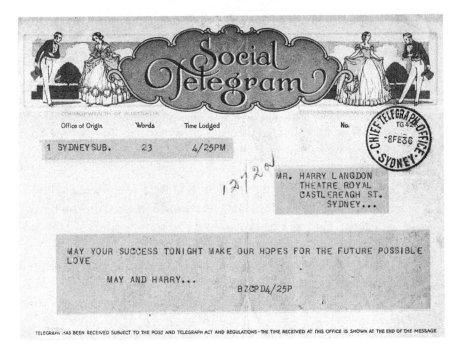

Special delivery.

to Langdon from his two prior marital debacles. It is not clear whether this was an actual conversation or simply a humorous fabrication, but it was printed in the paper's Sunday supplement. The upbeat banter between Harry and Mabel reveals a playful camaraderie as they teased each other about their respective roles in the marriage. Responding to Harry's question about whether she had read a piece about husbands and wives nagging each other, Mabel pondered why spouses would waste time quarreling when they could simply enjoy each other's company. Harry suggested that perhaps they were not "suitably mated" to begin with, and Mabel logically answered: "But, why don't they find that out before they get married?" They discussed how engaged couples could measure their compatibility before tying the knot and then moved on to more "personal" matters:

> Mrs. L: This article says men grumble about their food. Now you never complain about the food I serve you—eggs, for instance. I give you eggs every morning. Why don't you squeal about it?
> Mr. L: I guess I like eggs. Besides, you always serve them different

styles, and I know by the way you dish them up that you are endeavoring to please me, and I feel I appreciate your efforts.

Mrs. L: Of course, mothers-in-law usually are supposed to cause a lot of trouble.

Mr. L: That's where we are lucky. I like your mother around because she takes such darn good care of Harry Junior. Anyhow, if a mother and daughter get along well, a man shouldn't worry. You can't say we haven't had [a] single row yet, though.

Mrs. L: Oh, Harry!

Mr. L: Oh yes we have. You remember that time you wanted to buy six pairs of silk stockings all at once, and I insisted on you having a dozen? That was a real row—and I won it—easily.[8]

The press followed the Langdons around Australia as Harry appeared at various events for both publicity and pleasure. The *Brisbane Telegraph*, for example, captured this American celebrity's view of the country's cities and citizens:

After his arrival by train from Sydney yesterday [Langdon] was reclining on the balcony of the Hotel Cecil, and finding the "placid traffic" in George Street restful. . . .

He had seen some modern buildings in Brisbane, and fine examples of concrete construction with effective decorativeness, but it was the old type of structure, as in George Street, that made him feel at home; not as in New York, but in Pittsburgh, Boston, or Philadelphia, which had many resemblances with Brisbane, except size . . .

He found Australians more like Americans than the English in their ways and habits, though they had more reserve or, perhaps, less aggressiveness would be more correct. The big difference between Australian cities and American was the right-hand drive . . . The traffic was similar, "going like heck," and Australian taxidrivers "scared him to death," but as he had not seen one hit anything it "must be O.K."

Between performances and sightseeing, Langdon also drew a popular series of cartoons for the Sydney newspapers and entertained children in hospitals and orphanages with his ventriloquist dummies—another skill

Langdon sharing his comedy with a young audience in New South Wales.

learned in vaudeville. The *Sun* used the opportunity to tell a story from Harry's younger days: Stranded in a "backwoods town," Harry had been forced to part with the doll from his ventriloquist act, handing it over to the hotel proprietor to pay his bill. As luck would have it, Harry met the proprietor years later in Chicago and was thrilled to learn he still had the doll. Unfortunately, it was rather worn, with broken limbs and tattered clothes, but a visit to the doll hospital revived his "girlfriend." Harry eventually gave the doll to the daughter of Hollywood director Victor Schurtzinger. Another photo of Harry clowning among a group of enthralled children is particularly poignant, as they were students at the New South Wales Deaf, Dumb, and Blind Institute. It shows one little blonde girl smiling radiantly as she turns toward Langdon, who is making some corny gesture, even though she cannot see him.

Junior's popularity in the Australian press: the *Sydney Telegraph*, December 31, 1935 (*left*), and the *Brisbane Telegraph*, March 24, 1936 (*right*).

Junior also became a sought-after figure during the Langdon interviews, stealing the limelight from both his parents. The *Brisbane Courier Mail* noted that fifteen-month-old Junior had traveled 8,000 miles and "knows neither seasickness nor railway nerves." He made news when he took his first walk across the stage of the Theatre Royal, causing people to wonder whether he was destined to follow in his father's footsteps—although both his parents insisted that they had already decided he would be a lawyer. Langdon, however, was always quick to concede that Junior was a "born comic . . . he could do all my routines as well as I ever could. No, he does 'em even better."

Junior made a lasting impression on one Sydney reporter for the *Truth*, who was interviewing Mabel about her experiences as a mother in Hollywood and her secrets for a happy marriage. The conversation was easily sidetracked by Junior's bright blue eyes and precocious yet gentle manner; he had determined that the reporter was a friend and extended a small hand to her, which relieved her no end. When Mabel talked about the States, she admitted that her greatest concern was one shared by all celebrity parents: kidnapping. The reporter thoughtfully wondered whether Junior—despite being only a "fortnight" old—should not be exposed to this frightening conversation, so she arranged for him to play in the next room while his mother continued: "We were thankful to reach Australia. . . . Everyone at Hollywood who has a child is in constant terror lest it will be stolen. They have a night watchmen's corps of their own, all armed, and every half-hour the watchman goes to the nursery and flashes his torch to make sure everything is right." Mabel also gave her view of why her marriage seemed to be working so well: she was not in show business and never wanted to be. She thought this prevented jealousy and resentment between two professionals vying against each other. "Harry and I never discuss his work at home. We can do all the talking we want to about 'shop' when we go for a walk." At that point, the *Truth* reporter heard an insistent bump on the door:

> It was Harry, Jnr., on one of the cutest aids to early walking I have ever seen. We opened the door. Junior deposited in my lap one of the Three Little Pigs—the one with the violin. It had on it a small notice. "Sorry you've got to go!"
>
> As I stared at it, Junior next produced a large wooden elephant with enormous ears. Elephants never forget! I took the hint and left him to monopolise his mother's time.
>
> I hear that he is going to take both his parents (if they are good) over to Taronga soon. He wants to show them the Koala bears.

Langdon himself found that the trip gave him the freedom to speak his mind in the press, through his usual quaint and quippy humor, without fear of censorship. As he mused in one article, "Eighteen years of the quick-fire life of Hollywood, and now this quiet contrast—it will do me, your Brisbane. . . . My wife and I are not the right kind for the popular conception of Hollywood life." Given the "high-speed work, the competition, and the struggle to excel the highest standards of previous achievement," Langdon was, if only wistfully, thinking of settling for a few years in Australia, just to relax and watch his son grow up safely.

Almost in playful retaliation for the cutthroat treatment he had received in the States, Langdon penned a zany article in the May 1936 issue of the Australian publication *Table Talk* titled "I Squeal on Hollywood." It included cute caricatures of moviemaking and of Greta Garbo

Mabel and Harry strolling in Australia.

and Marlene Dietrich "looking hamburgers instead of daggers" at each other, and it proffered Langdon's colorful ideas on "NOTORIOUS HOLLY-WOOD! WI-I-I-LD HOLLYWOOD! WICKED HOLLYWOOD!" by ribbing the tinsel and gossip of the celluloid city:

> When one reads of Chicago, one immediately visualizes a montage of scattering people, bullets, machine guns, and blood. Flip a page to Hollywood, and I'll be a cream-puff if one's imaginate cells don't focus on Clark Gable's dimples, Shirley Temple's curls, or Mickey Mouse.
>
> My, my tuff Hollywood. If those cinemaites do not reverse their behavior, you and your brothers and sisters will forever be reading, via hot, sizzling press wires from Hollywood, such pansy news as . . . "Helen 12 trees divorces herself from a little Woody, asserting she had too much timber in her family. . . . Vernon Dent, three hundred pound Columbia Studio comedian, slapped Jack Oakie on account of Jack Oakie acting like a Jack Oakie at the former's party. . . . Jean Harlow's hair returns to its natural color, with a round trip ticket, we've been told. . . . Al Jolson and wife adopt child; mother and father choosing well. . . . Harry Langdon in court again for non-payments of alimony; he has been before the Judge so often, it is rumored, he gets his fan-mail at the courthouse."

Underlying the jesting, however, were sardonic jabs at how grim reality was handled in the superficial town:

> It is near time the cinema village come out from behind Max Factor's cosmetics, wipe that carmine lip-rouge off its face and counterpoise itself with the hoodlum reputation it has. . . .
>
> Shame on you Warnermayerfox, and the cop at Hollywood and Vine, for your persistent interferences of outlawery, illicitness, and rowdyism. . . .
>
> Occasionally Hollywood exerts herself in courageous attempts to compete, in crime, with other cities, including Los Angeles at her elbow. Recently she endeavored to establish a murder case in the death of our dear Thelma Todd. After local detectives warped their backs and magnifying glasses, and kept the public in sus-

pense for two months, they sheepishly announced that she had died of natural causes. Money, time, and rubber heels wasted.

For a man whose life was full of extremes, Langdon acknowledged that Hollywood was equally guilty of mixed messages: "Eleven minutes from Hollywood's most sophisticated cocktail rendezvous lies a cornfield . . . a hop-skip-and-a-jump from a wedding chapel is a STOP signal . . . one flight of stairs from a marriage licence bureau is a divorce court."

The change of scenery gave Langdon an opportunity to reflect on his career. Joking about his two failed marriages was easier in light of his stable third marriage. He was also willing at this point to reminisce about another, more disastrous phase of his career that, in hindsight, he saw as a series of dire mistakes. His silent film career had involved a number of heady executive decisions that, given his inability to recognize his limitations, were admittedly not the best. In addition, for perhaps the only time ever, he penned a reflection on his Capra days. Whether the product of a reporter's inquiry or the fulfillment of a private need to respond to an item Capra had written, Langdon composed an easygoing answer. But between the lines were regret, sarcasm, and nostalgia for the old days:

> I noticed an article by a very old friend and co-worker of mine: Frank Capra, one of the finest directors in the film business.
>
> Quite apart from its contents, that story of Frank's made me think.
>
> "Why, say!" I said to myself, first thing. "Here's Frank busting into print. Why, it's only the other day. . . ."
>
> Well, I pulled myself up in time. That other day was quite a few years ago. Things move so fast in Hollywood that time seems to jump by you. The eighteen years I spent there were in a flash; it is only yesterday, to me, that I was working on the old Mack Sennett lot, turning out comedies that the public of those days went into fits about. . . .
>
> . . . Good old Frank—a fine guy if ever there was one. Wonder if he has time these days to remember the way the two of us worked together when he was starting off in the business as a gagman, and I was everything from director to cutter and emergency scenario writer for the small producing company that paid both of us our dough.

Langdon's bitterness, bubbling up toward the end of the article, seems to melt into resignation about the choices only *he* made:

> I've been asked since I arrived in Australia just why I quit films after spending so much time in the business and learning so much about it. Actually, I haven't quit. I'm still under contract to Columbia. But I figure it was time I took a holiday.
>
> Eighteen years is a goodish time, and—the pace in Hollywood is hot. It's go for the lick of your life all the time, and take care that the man on the next rung doesn't step on your face. They say the theatre is a hard game. Believe me, at the moment I'm enjoying myself. After what I've been doing, getting back into the role of comedian is like coming home after a long term in gaol.
>
> At any rate, that's how it seems now. Maybe I won't be able to keep away from celluloid, but I should worry—yet.

The statement about "getting back into the role of comedian" is telling: perhaps Langdon wondered at what point he'd stopped being considered a comedian or his films had stopped being considered comedies.

He purposefully strove to meld Chaplinesque pathos into his films—what might be termed "dramedy" today—but his comedy was still the thread holding the serious aspects together. Some of the Columbia shorts seemed to fall short of Langdon's best comedy because they failed to merge sentiment into the story. Langdon may have been worn out by the struggle to produce the "best" film each time, instead channeling his creativity into cartooning, ventriloquism, music, painting, and sculpture. His drive was to keep working in the arts, if only to support his family and to satisfy his need to create. The frequency with which many of his new short films replayed his successful silent routines suggests that Langdon believed this return to the past would work—and it seemed that neither he nor his gag writers could concoct anything better.

This need to cling to the past was cited in an Australian paper reporting a peculiar bit of news about a symbol of Langdon's past—his character's hat: "There is a hat in Sydney, money could not buy! Just a battered piece of felt worth thousands—in sentiment." Unfortunately, despite Mabel's scrupulous attention to Harry's property during the show's run, the famous chapeau had been stolen. Concerned fans sent replacements to Langdon at the theater, but none of them could match its sentimental

Enjoying himself as Junior waits to hitch a ride.

value. He had had that hat for twenty years, he claimed, and had mastered the technique of "indenting" it by pinning the four inner corners together. He had reportedly bought it in Newark, New Jersey, for $4.50, although another version of its provenance was that he had designed the hat himself, tailoring his wardrobe to his own brand of comedy. Once before it had been lost in the ocean during a shoot at Santa Monica, but a prop boy had dived in to retrieve it. According to another report, "Mr. Langdon has had his hat souvenired on 11 occasions and has lost it five times," with big rewards offered for its return. This time, however, it had definitely been stolen—and it was almost fitting that this symbol of his fame went "missing" on this life-changing trip. After his eventual return to Hollywood, Langdon would seldom wear this trademark part of his wardrobe and would be offered an assortment of characters—and hats—to redefine himself.

At the conclusion of the Australian tour, Langdon received an invitation to make a film in England. Mabel was delighted at the prospect of returning to the country of her birth and showing Junior another part of the world. He had already celebrated his first birthday in Honolulu en

234

route to Australia, and she wanted his second to be celebrated in London. Harry made certain of this, as well as planning a rather big shopping spree for toys on the special day. The Langdons sailed from Adelaide through the Suez Canal and made stops in Ceylon, Bombay, Tangier, Malta, and Gibraltar before arriving in London. The little vessel, the *Narkunda,* was caught in a monsoon on the way to Bombay and tossed around like a cork, but Junior enjoyed the adventure. Before setting off for Tangier, however, Langdon picked up a bug in a marketplace in India that caused his leg to swell. "They had told us not to go down in the marketplace, in the bazaars, because it was unclean," Mabel recalled. "And we found it out when we got there. All open sewage and dead bodies and everything." Langdon recuperated on the *Narkunda,* and the family disembarked in London in time for King Edward's coronation on May 12, 1937.

While in England, Langdon worked in front of the cameras in one film and was asked by Fox British to direct another comedy feature starring Charlie Naughton and Jimmy Gold. While in London, Langdon also made sketches for an intimate Hollywood-style nightclub featuring a small stage and audience boxes, as well as "bas-relief plaques" depicting celebrities. An investor had expressed interest, but the plan never materialized.[9] All in all, for the Langdon family, the trip was replenishing.

Mad about Money, the musical project that had brought Langdon to England, was not released in the States until April 1938, under the title *He Loved an Actress.* Though made in London, the film had an American producer, American director, and American choreographer. The four stars were from Hollywood, and Elstree Studio, where the picture was shot, had been built by another American, Joe Rock. All this Americanism was the result of the quota system in effect at that time. The British film industry had gotten off to a slow start, and native products could not compete with either Hollywood's output or the best European films. After the first few pioneers rushed into the business, there had been slow attrition, and by 1925, the British film industry was in shambles; fully 90 percent of the films shown in British cinemas were Hollywood products. To remedy the problem, in 1927 Parliament enacted the Cinematograph Film Act, designed to revive interest in British film production. It imposed restrictions and duties on imported films, encouraged the construction of local studios, and established a quota for exhibitors, who were obliged to show a minimum percentage of British-made films or face heavy fines. This attracted many producers to England to make "quota quickies." As a result, numerous fly-by-night enterprises sprang up, cashed in by producing poor-quality films, and disappeared.

By the mid-1930s, however, the situation had stabilized. Filmmakers like Michael Balcon, Anthony Asquith, and Alfred Hitchcock ensured that British pictures had a place in the world market. Alexander Korda, a Hungarian who had learned about films in Hollywood, was a major motivator, giving his company London Films a polish that, ironically, became identified as "typically British." As a by-product of the quota system, some American entrepreneurs opened branch production facilities in England, bringing personnel from the States and making American films that exhibitors could show as part of the British quota because they had been made in England.

Elstree Studio, which had just opened in London, was the largest and best-equipped facility in England at this time, and producer Henry Barnes and director Melville Brown thought it well suited for a glittering Hollywood-type musical. Busby Berkeley was not available, but they secured the services of Larry Ceballos, who had staged lavish musical numbers for Warner Brothers. Brown chose Ben Lyon for the lead. Lyon and his wife, Bebe Daniels, had recently moved to England because they felt their Hollywood careers were in decline. They played the Palladium in London in 1936 with great success and stayed in England during World War II to entertain American troops. Later, they had a popular situation comedy on British radio called *Life with the Lyons*.

Langdon was the next star recruited by Brown, who also brought in Lupe Vélez and Wallace Ford. Fresh from his success in Australia, Langdon had no desire to rush back to Hollywood and welcomed the London detour. Vélez was happy to leave America because her marriage to Johnny Weissmuller (whom she had wed on the rebound after a passionate fling with Gary Cooper) was ending. Ford, a lead and character actor in a score of American films, had been invited to his native England to act in several films, including *O.H.M.S.* (shown in the States as *You're in the Army Now*) and the Paul Robeson vehicle *Jericho* (shown in the States as *Dark Sands*), both released in 1937.

The plot of *He Loved an Actress* was strangely complex for a musical, and it had all the earmarks of being too ambitious for its own good. Two poor promoters hurry to finish a shoestring-budget film before the creditors foreclose—a plot unintentionally close to the reality of the filmmaking process. Even the film's title had a troubled development: in addition to

Mad about Money, it was called *Star Dust* during shooting; then it opened as *He Loved an Actress*. Several years later, when promoter J. H. Hoffberg acquired and reissued it, he gave it the less satisfactory title *Hollywood Racketeers*. *Mad about Money* may have been the most suitable one, given that money was the crux of the matter both on and offscreen. The film was originally supposed to be shot in color, but Barnes and Brown could not afford color stock. The stunningly choreographed production numbers rank among the best of their kind, but because they were shot first, at high expense, the budget for the rest of the film was inadequate, and many scenes had to be omitted. As a result, the plot is spasmodic, and promising subplots are abandoned. Langdon's part was among the casualties. Based on the buildup he received when first introduced to the others involved in the project, it was clear that Langdon was meant to be a key character, but he was reduced to a minor hanger-on. One bright spot is his "dream" as he falls asleep at a nightclub table and becomes part of the most elaborate musical number of the picture. The set was designed by experimental artist Len Lye, who had won recognition for his "direct film" technique—painting or scratching an image directly on film—and other innovations. In this sequence, a rocket flies to the moon (the face of which Langdon designed), and chorus girls dance amid the stars. People sit on Saturn's rings, and drinks are served on the planet, which is oddly shaped to form an umbrella. Langdon even sings a chorus of "We'll Go Dance in the Stars."

Midway through shooting, those working on the project sensed that the financial situation had become dubious. Joe Rock had rented the studio to Brown, whom he knew from Hollywood, and Rock had agreed to guarantee the lab bills, but he became suspicious and instructed the lab not to release any materials until all the bills had been settled. His mistrust was confirmed when Brown tried to take the negative to France after filming was completed. But as Rock had instructed, the lab refused. Apparently, Brown had made an arrangement with J. H. Hoffberg, a marginal film dealer who was adept at finding enough distribution to allow a foundering project to turn a profit, but at the expense of not paying the participants. Rock was paid in full because his agent had insisted on getting his money in escrow up front, but Langdon received only a fraction of his salary. By this time, he took such disappointments in stride. He had, after all, plummeted from the mountain of success without a parachute. Now that he was on level ground again, these bumps in the road were comparatively mild. Lupe Vélez received virtually nothing. But as Rock recalled, Vélez was

He Loved an Actress.

probably more interested in having a good time than in making money: "She had money and she was having a ball. She always kidded around on the set until my wife's sister-in-law, a French girl married to cameraman Freddie Granville, saw Lupe one time showing me that she was nude under her coat, and went to report to my wife that we were indulging in some hanky-panky."[10] Adding to its checkered history, *He Loved an Actress* earned dismal reviews. One particularly biting critique from *Variety* lambasted its color as "brutal to the faces and [it] thins the photography until players can hardly be recognized except in close-ups."

Langdon had better luck directing the Fox British comedy, which was released in August 1937. The working title was *Yours in Confidence*, but it was eventually released as *Wise Guys*. Why Langdon was asked to direct is a mystery, considering his dismal directorial track record—three critical failures in a row. It may have been that Langdon was the only one willing to work for the lowly amount of 500 pounds being offered by producer Ivor McLaren.[11] The picture was a vehicle for music hall duo Charlie Naughton and Jimmy Gold, who had already made a short and three feature comedies. The plot of *Wise Guys* follows their efforts to become respectable businessmen. Langdon received fair reviews for his megaphone work: "Episodic but understanding direction of mainly slapstick material with plenty of laughs aroused by stellar foolery and ingenious gags." This was fairly positive for Langdon, considering that his efforts directing himself had been skewered. Because Langdon was not acting in the film, his concentration may have been more focused. It was a lesson for him—one that was imposed rather than sought. He learned to set his actors in the best light for the script at hand. In an interview, Jules White summed up what Langdon may have come to understand: "[He] bit off more than he could chew. Writing is one man's job, directing another, producing another, and being the star, still another. Some few supermen have done all this. But they are few and far between. Often one who wants to be the whole schmear ends up on a cracker and is eaten and forgotten. I guess for Harry it was better to have been a star and lost than never to have been a star at all."

Harry Langdon was no longer a megastar. If he had the lead role in a production, he might be its "star," but he was spinning in a humbler orbit and reflecting the light of his past. He was no longer trying to be a super- man—nor could he be if he had wanted to. He accepted smaller chances— every chance—to show that he was still capable of working. One step at a time, onscreen and off, Langdon worked cautiously and carefully, with all the strength he could muster, to stay on an even keel.

Only at the end of 1937 did Langdon return to Hollywood, where he reported to Columbia to make more shorts. His first work back in the States was *A Doggone Mixup*, released in February 1938. A mustachioed Harry is an incurable bargain hunter who cannot resist a "good deal," which of course, it never is. Someone sells him a doghouse and a "genuine imitation dog collar," and he must buy the only dog that will fit it—a St. Bernard. For the rest of the film, Harry is the one in the "doghouse," as his pet runs amok. This is, in fact, one of Langdon's better shorts echoing his silent persona. He scampers helplessly after the dog, apologizing meekly for the chaos it causes. One particularly touching moment is a tribute to his talent for measured pathos: the dog has been driven from the house, and Harry kneels to pray that his dog comes back. He opens his eyes to find the dog kneeling beside him. Harry hugs his pal, but not before send- ing a small grateful wave heavenward.

Langdon sold Columbia an original story in the summer of 1938. He called it "The Ambulance Chaser," but it was filmed under the title *Sue My*

Harry's best friend in *A Doggone Mixup,* with Ann Doran (*right*).

Lawyer. Harry plays a small-time lawyer determined to work in the district attorney's office. Langdon's scenario included the classic routine from *The Strong Man,* in which he carries a woman up a staircase that turns into a ladder. Another flawlessly paced pantomime has Harry rocking in a chair as a cat flicks its tail back and forth until the inevitable yowl happens, causing Harry to leap to his feet and step into a bucket. The act of removing his foot is a testament to his comic virtuosity.

For all his apparent ease in executing lengthy silent routines, Langdon the actor required a firm but compassionate directorial hand to rein in his excessive slowness—a criticism made by previous directors, including Capra. In an odd twist, while Langdon was filming the staircase scene, Capra was working next door on *You Can't Take It with You.* Capra recalled in his autobiography that he visited the set and heard director Jules White yelling at Harry to speed up, while Harry silently reconciled that command with his own instincts about playing the scene. Capra was both shocked and sorry to see Langdon essentially being reprimanded, and he left the set before Harry could see him.[12] Capra's memory of this incident is both startling for his compassion and suspect for its context, and his eyewitness account has an undercurrent of "I told you so." It is also possible

Lobby card for *Sue My Lawyer*.

that he made up the whole episode to exonerate himself for sending the letter that had ruined Langdon's reputation. It was a bit of irony that one reviewer for *Box Office* said of *Sue My Lawyer:* "Not one of Harry Langdon's best, but he works hard and takes a lot of punishment before convincing the district attorney he has what it takes to make an able assistant." The reviewer likely did not know the backstory of Langdon's "punishment" on the set, but in retrospect, it highlights the ongoing conflicts over Langdon's acting style, even as a veteran performer.

Despite these challenges, Langdon considered 1938 the start of his happiest years. As one article reported, Harry and his "dream girl" finally made amends to her mother for eloping. On June 23, 1938, they consecrated their marriage a second time in a more formal ceremony in Ventura, California, with Georgena, Junior, and a few friends in attendance. Harry said he did it because he "got a kick out of it." But for Mabel, the second ceremony fulfilled a vow she had made to her sister, Adeline. Several years before she met Langdon, Mabel had been a bridesmaid at Adeline's wedding to Indian film producer Surendra Guha in Ventura, and Mabel

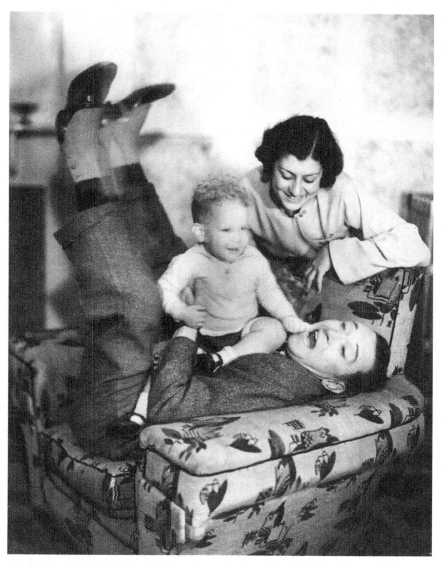

The Langdon family.

had promised to hold her own wedding there one day. Even though Adeline had later moved to India and died in Calcutta, Mabel had finally kept her word.

According to Mabel, Harry was always bringing her surprises, and at Christmas he would hide gifts throughout the house for her to find. But as giving as he was, he also withheld his deeper feelings, particularly feelings of failure. Langdon tried to keep professional conflicts and financial concerns from affecting his home life; he seldom spoke of them. Harry was never moody around her, but Mabel could always tell when he was preoccupied. She recalled:

> I could tell when he was depressed, he would become very quiet. He never bemoaned the fact to me if things weren't going good. He never unloaded that on me. He just went to work in the morning, did what they wanted him to, and came home that night. Not enthused at all. The only time he would get excited was when they would renew his option.
>
> I would see a difference in him . . . when he was writing in his own little area, and he'd be writing until the wee small hours of the morning. We would all retire and maybe we would wake up and hear the piano playing, and this was one of the ways in which he would relax. He wrote a lot of songs. . . . One was "She Was a Black Sheep of Angels." But he wrote all these songs after we were married, so they were more or less about me, I guess.

When he was not working on a film, Langdon drew, sculpted, or wrote treatments for scripts. Some of his stories, including "Stop that Corpse," "The Wizard of Main Street," and "Let Her Go Gallagher," were not timely or were better suited for feature-length films rather than shorts and were rejected by the studios. Despite the rebuffs, Langdon held on to his sense of humor, and when he could not enact his baby persona onscreen, he did so at home. Feeding Junior, for example, became a reenactment of the scene from *Three's a Crowd*, with Harry pouting, fluffing his cheeks, and goofing around to encourage his son to eat. When happy, Harry liked to kick into his "Shuffle Off to Buffalo" dance-step-run routine.

When Junior got older, the family moved to a ranch house in Canoga Park. Decades later, memories of that time were still vivid to Harry Jr.:

> It was really a lot of fun for a young kid because of the turkeys, and we had a lot of dogs, and I used to watch my dad working in the wood shop. He had a large carpentry shop and always liked to work with redwood as it was easy to work with, almost like balsa wood. He knew that I was fond of airplanes, and one day he said to me, "Wait and see what I'm going to fix for you." We had break-

When inspiration hit . . . or didn't.

fast and afterwards my dad went outside and I followed, and he had a model airplane which he had carved and which was all in pieces ready to be assembled by myself. This was the first thing that I ever became involved in as far as my dad and his hobbies were concerned. This grew and grew, and after a while we began to work together in his garage. This was the way in which he used to spend a lot of his time while he was thinking and writing; to keep his hands busy he would work an awful lot with wood. I think he instinctively was trying to teach me certain trades at a young age to fall back on. . . . He taught me to draw and to paint, and carpentry and everything to do with crafts. I even won first place at school for a model airplane! Before I was ten years old, he gave me a crash course in all sorts of trades.[13]

Langdon built a tree house among the walnut trees in the yard at Canoga Park, which Junior became adept at climbing. During the war, Mabel planted a Victory garden, and the family ate so much homegrown produce that they became vegetarians for a while. As he lay in bed at night or early in the morning, Junior often heard the soft tones of his father's piano playing; he had some sense that his father was lost in his own world, even if Junior had no idea why. When Junior joined the Boy Scouts, Langdon pitched in by organizing a vaudeville show, teaching the lads how to paint backgrounds and often singing and dancing for the troop; for one show, he even built cannons that fired projectiles, which the boys must have enjoyed, if not their leaders. Harry Jr. was extremely shy, and his father's involvement at his school gave him a little more confidence, allowing him to break out of his introversion.

Langdon's in-laws also lived at the ranch house. Mabel's father was a carpenter, and he and Langdon created beautiful woodwork for the home. Harry Jr. recalled that whenever his East Indian grandmother made dinner, the aroma of curry prevailed, especially on Wednesday, which was curried shrimp and chicken night. However, when the perfume of sandalwood incense permeated the air, Langdon retreated to another room. After a while, the sound of piano music filtered in, and Junior knew his father was immersed in his own imagination.

Langdon also painted and drew cartoons. His watercolors were mostly depictions of life and current events as he saw them. When there was talk about midwesterners moving to California, Langdon drew a series titled "Okies West," filled with crazy cars and human caricatures. Before the United States entered World War II in 1941, Langdon drew a series he called "Rosie the Riveter," featuring a doll-like little girl working in a plant and using a riveting gun to assemble planes. Langdon's watercolors—whether of seductive women or idyllic landscapes—vibrate with a simplicity of line and space, capturing the essence of the images. One painting of a sultry woman in pastel, reminiscent of Marlene Dietrich, is particularly evocative; it captures a wispy curl on her forehead, a spark in her eyes, an almost-sneer with her dangling cigarette, and a tilt and twist of the head that both beckons and dares one to come closer. Looking at her eyes, one can see both a girl pretending to be a grown-up and a woman's gaze reflecting her lost innocence. It is no coincidence that Langdon gave his boy-man persona some of the same expressions.

Feeling more settled in his family life, and not burdened by the responsibilities of stardom—he was basically just an employed actor fulfilling his contractual obligations—Langdon indulged his artistic talents. Years earlier, in Jean North's June 1925 article for *Photoplay* entitled "It's No Joke to Be Funny," Langdon had compared the various arts that filled his life—clowning, circus tumbling, cartooning, and acting on a vaudeville stage—all for the purpose of creating comedy:

Each [artistic medium] is hard in its own way. Newspaper comics are hard because you have four or five frames in which to tell your comedy. You don't have the elbow room of the circus, the stage, or the screen.

Vaudeville is sometimes harder and sometimes easier than the newspaper or screen ways of cracking jokes. If you get a cold

Harry's artwork.

Left: Harry relaxing with friends, including Stan Laurel, his wife Vera, and Oliver Hardy. *Right:* Mabel and Harry witnessing the wedding of Eunice and Vernon Dent.

> house, it's harder than anything else on earth. The oddest thing about this whole funny business is that the public really wants to laugh, but it's the hardest thing to make them do it. They don't want to cry, yet they will cry at the slightest provocation. Maybe that's why many comedians want to play tragedy—they want a sort of vacation.[14]

Langdon had entered a stage where, perhaps for the first time in his life, the arts were coalescing into a source of rejuvenation and self-expression. Challenges on the film set would take care of themselves, and Langdon could trust himself to do whatever was needed.

Although Langdon's other wives had been social whirlers, Mabel preferred entertaining at home, and the press regarded her as one of Hollywood's best hostesses. Friends such as Dent, Ripley, Edwards, Laurel, and Hardy visited frequently and showered Junior with toys when they came. He recalled:

> One set of toys that I acquired was toy pieces from an orchestra, like a toy saxophone, toy trumpet, toy kazoo. These guys used to get together, Dad, Stan Laurel, Vernon Dent, Arthur Ripley—who in fact played the saxophone . . . I seem to remember he looked like Howard Hughes. One day at Canoga Park . . . all these grown men would go into my toy closet and then got together in the

backyard to fly airplanes and play on my toy instruments. . . . They were so serious about it all and playing like crazy. Life around our place was really quite a ball because my dad was always clowning.

Usually when he first got up in the morning he would wear a robe. He was usually up very early doing his sketching or drawing and . . . he was quite a musician and would be playing the piano in the middle of the night and just had to keep his mind going. We would always have breakfast together, and he was always clowning or mimicking public characters such as Winston Churchill, Mahatma Gandhi, and so on, and wore a robe like a Hindu would wear. He always had me in stitches around the house. I guess he enjoyed seeing me happy and cheerful because at that time, world conditions were pretty serious. . . . A few times he was very serious and looked very preoccupied with his work. That was when he was doing films. After a day's shooting he was usually pretty bushed. My dad would come home from work wearing Max Factor greasepaint and wash it off with cold cream in the family wash basin. As a kid, I was taken aback by the oily orange stuff that was sticking to the basin. I thought all fathers came home like that! I imagine on the lot he would move from one set to another, still made up and in character, perhaps not wanting to "lose" that role he had worked many years to develop. It was such a unique makeup, it had become Harry Langdon. Not many knew what was underneath.

Always the funnyman, Langdon would throw paper into his typewriter and peck out jokes until he had accumulated a hefty sheaf. These came in handy when he went back to work for Hal Roach, principally as a gagman. Langdon brought Junior to the Roach lot, which contained a large colonial hall by a lake and several one-story buildings; for a little boy, this was a fantasyland where he met famous stars, including Alice Faye and Billie Burke. The propmen gave Junior objects they had built, and he rode carriages around the lot or watched behind the scenes as films were shot.

Although the initial collaboration between Langdon and Roach nearly ten years earlier had been tense and short-lived, and the eight shorts they produced were among Langdon's weakest, this new venture proceeded smoothly. Langdon most often wrote for Roach's top moneymakers, the

Laurel and Hardy features, and devised their gags. But he also joined several productions as an actor. He had a whimsical bit as a minister in *There Goes My Heart* (1938), a part that Mabel described as "an earth-bound angel," befitting Harry's gentle personality. His fleeting appearance prompted a *News-Sentinel* reviewer's amazed observation of the audience's reaction to Langdon, who had not received any prescreen billing for his part in the film: "When a shy dough-faced little bundle of frustration stepped on to the screen in those final reels, the audience burst into one round of applause. Yes, Harry was back. They hadn't forgotten him." The reviewer astutely connected Langdon's newfound popularity with the idea that he was in a better place and enjoying another kind of wealth: "He has found a wife who stayed by him, uncomplainingly through the bitter years. He has become the proud papa of a curly-headed son who thinks his dad a world beater. He has found the real way to contented living even on almost nothing a week, and has been given the chance to learn a precious lesson few of us are ever given. And he isn't going to toss it over lightly. He hopes he'll never become a big star again in pictures."

Upon his return to Roach, Langdon received telegrams from friends and colleagues conveying good wishes, along with words of wisdom: "Keep your feet on the ground" and "Take care of your dough this time." His friends knew he was a trouper in every circumstance, and his charisma always managed to dispel the clouds that threatened to gather. Langdon's was a veritable case of mind over matter, and he forged forward with a new attitude.

As a result, Langdon's working environment at Roach was a congenial one. He shared much in common with Stan Laurel—not rivalry, but friendship—which facilitated their collaboration on scripts. Oliver Hardy did not spend as much time on the mechanics of filmmaking, as he was more focused on performing, but he shared Langdon's enthusiasm for golf, and they played many a game together. Langdon worked on four Laurel and Hardy films. For *Blockheads* (1938), he worked out the opening sequence in which Laurel is a World War I soldier who has been forgotten in the front lines for twenty years—shades of *Soldier Man*. Langdon's work was singled out in *Showmen's Trade Review*: "Best laughs of the film must be credited to Harry Langdon . . . since they are adaptations of gags from his old vaudeville acts." The *New York Herald-Tribune* praised "the fine Italian hand of Harry Langdon" and added that, in his day, his comedy skills had surpassed those of both Laurel and Hardy. The next year Langdon worked on *Flying Deuces,* with the boys joining the French Foreign Legion to forget their troubles. This was followed by *A Chump at Oxford* (1940), in which Laurel plays an amnesiac, and *Saps at Sea* (1940), in which Hardy suffers a nervous breakdown and recuperates on a sea voyage. It must have given Langdon a strange sensation to regenerate his old routines for other comedians, but he was willing to share with those he trusted—geniuses in their own right—confident that his material would work for them as it had for him.

Langdon also contributed gags to a Roach musical called *Road Show* (1941), starring Adolphe Menjou and Carole Landis, with songs by Hoagy Carmichael and others. It was a routine light production, and the emphasis was on the music. But behind Langdon's scripting jobs and the bit part in *There Goes My Heart* lay Roach's ulterior motive: he wanted to see if the moviegoing public would accept Langdon as a star again. When it seemed that they would, Roach tried to convince the public to accept Langdon as a substitute for Laurel in the 1939 film *Zenobia,* in which Hardy had a featured role. This seemed sensible, as Laurel and Langdon had similar mannerisms and a similar style of humor. Ironically, although Laurel and Hardy were Roach's top-drawing team, they were never officially a team during their tenure at his studio. Their contracts expired at different times and were negotiated individually; Laurel had a multiple-picture contract, while Hardy had a multiple-year contract.[15] This left Roach in control; the two men could continue as a team only if they agreed to Roach's terms at each negotiation. But this arrangement proved troublesome. Laurel, a dedicated filmmaker and a sharp businessman, was generally paid more than his partner; this irked Hardy, who felt he was doing equal work and deserved equal pay. By 1937, when his contract expired, Laurel was tired of dealing with Roach and let his contract lapse.

As a quick fix, Roach made Langdon Hardy's new partner in *Zenobia,* hoping the team would click, but it did not. Langdon and Hardy play antagonists, and neither is a comedy role. Hardy is Dr. Henry Tibbett, a benevolent country doctor in the mid-nineteenth-century Deep South who quotes patriotic adages and gives inspiring speeches. Langdon is a disagreeable traveling medicine quack named Professor McCrackle who has a pet elephant called Zenobia. McCrackle engages Tibbett's services when the pachyderm becomes sick, then sues him in court for alienating her affections because the elephant prefers to be with the doctor. The only scene in which Langdon and Hardy play off each other well is when they

Langdon and Hardy contemplating a problem script.

examine the elephant. They trade lines easily, but the dialogue consists of labored joking about the animal's size. Even a publicity release focused more on "Queenie" the elephant than on the human stars.[16] In fact, titles for the film played up the animal's prominence over her costars, including *Zenobia's Infidelity* and *An Elephant Never Forgets* (in England).

The film was based on the novel *Zenobia's Infidelity* by H. C. Bunner, which Roach had purchased as a vehicle for Roland Young. It features Billie Burke (as Hardy's wife), Alice Brady, Hattie McDaniel, and Stepin Fetchit. The music was composed by Marvin Hatley, who had also written the beloved theme song associated with Laurel and Hardy: "Cuckoo Song." Roach invested in the production by hiring top-notch cinematographer Karl Struss (*Sunrise* and *Dr. Jekyll and Mr. Hyde,* among other eminent films) and art director Charles D. Hall (who had designed for Chaplin's silent films and Universal's horror films *Dracula* and *Frankenstein*).

In its review, the *New York Times* drolly remarked that this southern story was "a rough idea of what would happen to *Gone with the Wind* if Hal Roach had produced it . . . an antebellum, costume romance in slapstick." Although the same reviewer opined that Langdon's "pale and beautifully blank countenance" would excite the "professional jealousy of Mr. Laurel," the consensus was that the new team was a disappointment. Contrary to expectations, Hardy did not display his usual comic mannerisms; he was more of a straight comic lead in period costume, and Langdon was simply his costar, following an awkward script. It was, in fact, Hardy's one and only chance to carry a feature film on his own. Roach may have used *Zenobia* to punish Laurel and Hardy for not staying together, and although the tactic worked, Roach's victory was only temporary. Laurel waited until Hardy's contract came up for renewal, and then they signed with Roach as a team. A year later, they switched to 20th Century Fox, but none of those films equaled the comic masterpieces they had made with Roach.

Though intended to be a comedy, *Zenobia* presents an uncomfortable view of racial inequality through the presence of the servant characters. In a small speech, Dr. Tibbett draws a well-meaning but embarrassing parallel between the two races and the black and white pills in a medicine cabinet: each is good for something, in its own way. He then proceeds to offer a quarter to his servants' young son if he can learn the Declaration of Independence by heart, and the boy eventually recites it to the white townspeople. The critical line "all men are created equal," however, falls on deaf ears. As a current review of the film notes, "The larger message of the inequality of the race was not even intended for consideration in 1939, although it is clearly the elephant in the room."[17] This became even more apparent when McDaniel won the Oscar for her role in *Gone with the Wind* the following year but was banned from attending the movie's Atlanta premiere because of segregation laws.

Langdon with June Lang and Jean Parker.

During the filming of *Zenobia*, Langdon participated in preparations for the upcoming Golden Gate International Exposition, which ran from February to October 1939 and from May to September 1940; it was San Francisco's third and final world's fair. Publicity stills show Langdon immersing his hands and feet in trays of plaster for display at the exposition. It was the typical grand exhibition of pavilions celebrating the engineering marvels and artistic grandeur of the world's various states and nations—in short, a symbol of human spirit and enterprise. Diego Rivera painted a mural live before spectators; a flower show covered 6,000 square feet in the Hall of Flowers, with botanical specimens from around the world; buildings were illuminated with hundreds of thousands of lights (the official guide boasted that 40 million kilowatt hours would be consumed during the exposition's run). There was a "fun zone" dubbed "Gayway," which used light and color as a "stimulant to fun and frolic" and depicted thrilling pastimes: a western town with eighty-two "little people" in cowboy costumes, live babies in an incubator from a modern hospital,

Langdon "cementing" his hands and feet for the San Francisco Exposition.

an auto racetrack for monkeys, breathtaking rides such as the Cyclone roller coaster, and "Sally Rand's Nude Ranch," which allowed a glimpse (through windows) of cowgirls in G-strings tossing horseshoes and whirling lassos. Hollywood Boulevard was re-created, and the Lux, a modern miniature movie theater, showed cartoons. The Hollywood Building, located near the exposition's lofty symbol, the Tower of the Sun, offered a huge free museum with displays of movie stars' wardrobes, a sideshow, more than 50,000 stills of stars on exhibit, and a special Hollywood show, "Stage 9," which presented "screen stars, writers and directors in action . . . to show you how movies are made and produced . . . educational as well as entertaining."[18] When the fair closed toward the end of 1940, it was, in hindsight, the symbolic end of a joyous celebration of international harmony and ingenuity and the beginning of a time of global fear and war.

For Langdon, *Zenobia* offered little in terms of artistry, but it was a paid role that involved ongoing public appearances. Mediocre material no longer threatened him. He focused on the finer things of life: "I made a divan for our house this summer—got more of a kick out of it than if I'd

On the elephant, *left to right:* Alice Brady, June Lang, Jimmy Ellis, Jean Parker, and Billie Burke. Under the elephant: Langdon and Oliver Hardy (at the trunk).

paid $5,000 for an antique. I don't miss the expensive parties of the old days. There's more enjoyment in watching a sunset from my back porch." Moreover, although the critics were not persuaded, *Zenobia* at least thrilled Harry's son. Junior watched his father sculpt from memory a statue of the cast sitting on an elephant and a life-sized head of Hardy. Langdon worked on clay models of the elephants as soon as he left the breakfast table. Life had become simple for Langdon, and he would not challenge that blessing again.

Langdon scripted the 1940 RKO picture *Goodness! A Ghost,* in which he plays a sound effects man in a theatrical production—the same job his character had in *The Stage Hand,* which he had written seven years earlier. Then, when one of the actors quits, he assumes the role of a policeman who is haunted by the spirit of his grandfather, who pushes Harry into overcoming his timidity and acting like a man. Langdon plays a natural role, and although some scenes rely too much on camera trickery (such as the long finale, where the ghost pilots a toy plane around the room), the short works well. As both scriptwriter and actor, Langdon seems to be able to compartmentalize his skills and concentrate on one responsibility at a time, with successful results.

The most interesting endeavor to surface at this time is another commercial film that, unlike any script tailored for Langdon, evokes some of his best work in years. *Sitting Pretty* is a ten-minute commercial for Chevrolet intended to be screened at a car dealers' convention. There is no attempt to deliver a sales pitch because the message is implicit. The Jam Handy Organization, a provider of industrial film services, produced *Sitting Pretty*; no director or writer is listed, although both may have been Langdon. Harry is an assistant to a champion flagpole sitter, an endurance fad of a bygone era. After being hit with a bucket, Harry seeks a place to rest and settles on a museum, where he borrows a robe and crown from a display of royal regalia. He tries out an old-fashioned carriage in the museum's transportation department, but the ride is too bumpy. Finally, he climbs into a modern car, which makes him feel like a king. Still robed and crowned, he enjoys all the regal comforts of the car, including heater, cigarette lighter, windshield wipers, and radio. When a cop stops him and flashes his badge, Harry tops him by displaying his own badge reading "The King." Langdon is indeed a king for once, solo and excellent in this well-paced fantasy. Unfortunately, even though *Sitting Pretty* is an entertaining film made by a major comedian, it was never publicly released.

The title of his next Columbia film paralleled the dismal truth of Langdon's condition—*Cold Turkey.* Although he could soar in a film, he sometimes failed to even get off the ground. This short flopped as awkwardly as Harry did when trying to hold his own against a prize turkey. With the following feature, *Misbehaving Husbands,* Harry's hopscotch career took a turn. The film was surprisingly funny—surprising because it was made at PRC (Producers' Releasing Corporation), a mediocre studio that produced very few comedies and specialized in B movies. PRC had begun in 1939 with a daring production called *Hitler, Beast of Berlin,* with unknown stars Roland Drew and Steffi Duna, a young hopeful named Alan Ladd,

The "king" awakes with a Chevrolet in *Sitting Pretty*.

and veteran Vernon Dent in a supporting role. Though banned in New York as too inflammatory, the film stirred such interest that PRC managed to recover its costs. Over the next seven years, it made dozens of third-rate westerns, dreadful horror flicks, stereotypical crime melodramas, and an occasional offbeat comedy like *Misbehaving Husbands*.

Under the circumstances, this vehicle was an above-average diversion for both PRC and Langdon. He does not misbehave in the film, as the title suggests, but rather struggles with a mannequin in a department store window, incurs his wife's wrath, and is somehow accused of murder in the process, but his innocence is validated and bliss reigns supreme—until the next misunderstanding. Langdon appeared "rejuvenated" to reviewers, and his performance was rated superior to his silent work—a surprising evaluation. According to the *Hollywood Reporter*:

It is also extremely probable that this picture will be pegged as the one which brought about the renaissance of Harry Langdon as a top flight screen comedian. Producer Jed Buell wisely took away all the grotesque costume appurtenances which marked Langdon's silent films characterization, kept away from slapstick and

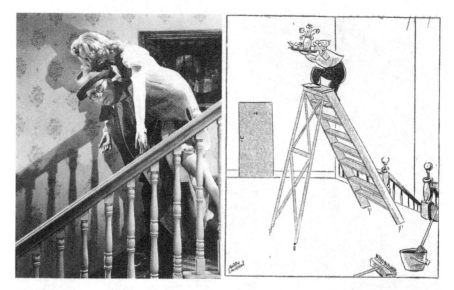

Left: Harry has mannequin troubles in *Misbehaving Husbands*. *Right:* Harry modified his stair gag for one of his cartoons in the *Sunday Sun* (March 29, 1936).

gave him the opportunity to play straight comedy. The result is a brilliant success. It is a new Harry Langdon which emerges, one who demonstrates solid, laugh-provoking ability which will make him a welcome re-entry on the all-too-brief list of present day film comics. After this one, more Langdon pictures will simply be compulsory.

The contrast between the youthful silent star and the older Langdon in sound films is stunning. That this small venture with a second-rate studio would lead to such praise—to the point of outshining his silent repertoire—might be attributable to the deeper layers of Langdon's style in his later years. The person onscreen performing good material is a mellower Harry Langdon interpreting life. His bewildered or embarrassed gestures are clear, softened by lines of frustration and resignation etched on his face. He flows with the film, riding the material instead of pushing it. He is at last in collaboration with himself.

Misbehaving Husbands was Langdon's last starring feature. His remaining roles were subordinate ones in features or starring ones in shorts. Harry faced each day with surprising tranquility and shared the lighter side of work with his pride and joy. As Harry Jr. reflected:

He was always clowning on the set, and everybody was always in stitches. Behind the camera he was climbing on the camera, and he used to build sets with the stagehands. Of course, that is not how to judge whether he was temperamental or not, but he was a true artist. . . . He had all of these diversions such as his woodworking, his artwork, his home movie hobbies, he used to compose music, he had me. We used to go on trips all over the place, his golf, he had thousands of hobbies, so he must have had these outlets to get rid of this nervousness. He wasn't the kind of guy you would see sitting in a chair reading a book in the evening or listening to the radio. He would be out building a car, building a house. . . . My mother and father used to move about once every two years just for a change, and this is a sign perhaps of being a little keyed up. . . . It was between 1940 and 1944 and he wasn't working so much as during his silent period, and I don't suppose there was as much money coming in as he was accustomed to, so I expect he did have a bit more free time on his hands, and when you have free time on your hands you do become more emotional.

Mabel rode the currents of Harry's restlessness. As much as it uprooted her sedate lifestyle, she yielded to whatever he needed. She recalled:

One day he came home and said, "May, we're going to sell the house and go to New York." And I said, "We are?" "Yeah." And I said, "Okay." So we got a real estate man who came in. We had no trouble selling the house because it was a lovely piece of property, an acre of walnut groves, and during the period that we lived there, [we] had done a lot of alterations, . . . made built-in cupboards, . . . built a den. . . . So we sold the house, lock, stock, and barrel. I didn't even take the spices out of the cupboard. We left everything. . . . The cabinet, the little wardrobe that Harry painted the baby's picture on before he was born. . . . It went with the house when we sold it. The only thing we took were the clothes on our backs. . . . Well, of course, I probably could have put my foot down. I had a lovely grand piano that my mother had given us for a wedding present. That went with the house. My mother never asked about it until a couple of years afterward; then she said, "What did you ever do with the grand piano?" . . . Well, of course, I probably could have put my foot down. But anything to please Harry. He was in such a down mood, poor man. He was in such a hurry to get to New York . . . to change his life.

While on the East Coast, Langdon ran a one-man show in Paterson, New Jersey, but the project was short-lived; he could no longer withstand the demands of a rigorous stage performance. Neither could Junior, who fell ill backstage while watching his father perform; it turned out to be acute appendicitis. Harry Jr. remembered reading about himself in the trades: "Everybody in New York who was somebody came up to visit me." It turned out that the night before, the Langdons had visited their friend Leo Linderman and eaten at his celebrity restaurant, Lindy's on Times Square. "Lindy" felt guilty, speculating that Harry Jr.'s meal of hot dogs and baked beans may have contributed to the attack, so he brought Junior a bunch of toys every day during his hospital stay.

The Langdons had driven cross-country to the East Coast in a Buick coupe, and Harry Jr. can vividly recall the "ominous Holland Tunnel." His other memories of New York include Harry and Mabel placating a "very spoiled kid." They let him skim the snow in Central Park with his new sled and gave him a few dollars to spend at the Automat, where he liked to select food from the little cubicles and wondered about the "strange hand that would come out with a sandwich." The steam clouds hissing from street grates, discarded cigars in the white snow, and blaring cab horns amazed and even frightened Harry Jr., but an occasional trip to F. A. O. Schwarz for toys usually quelled his fears.

In April 1941 Langdon auditioned for the Broadway hit *Hellzapoppin'*, hoping to replace half the team of Olsen and Johnson, who were leaving the show. When he did not get the part, Langdon returned to Hollywood and subordinate roles in feature films, starting with *All-American Co-ed*. It has a few musical numbers that make the innocuous story more bearable: a boy spends the entire school year at a girls' college disguised as a girl. The premise is titillating, but the moral code of the 1940s prevented even mildly suggestive behavior. Playing a press agent involved with the school, Langdon builds his character primarily through facial reactions to the campus mix-ups.

Langdon also rekindled an old friendship with Charley Rogers, a British-born comedian who had been involved with Hal Roach back in 1929.

Reacting to *All-American Co-ed*.

Rogers directed, wrote, and devised gags, so he had a lot in common with Langdon. After Langdon's return to Roach in 1938, his friendship with Rogers deepened, and the two men even thought about forming a new comedy duo. They found a better reception for that idea at Monogram Studios, the prototype of poverty-row film production, although a shade better than PRC. The studio specialized in long-running series: the Cisco Kid and Rough Riders in westerns, Charlie Chan and Mr. Wong in mysteries, and the East Side Kids. If Langdon and Rogers clicked at Monogram, they

The new team of Langdon and Rogers.

would be assured steady employment. Financially, though, working for Monogram was precarious business: Harry signed up for $350 a week, then obtained Monogram's written commitment to a minimum of $500 per film; otherwise, they might try to speed up production to one week to save money.

The contract was signed on September 12, 1941. *Double Trouble* was in the can after a couple of weeks of shooting and in nationwide release by November. The rest of Langdon's Monogram films ran a similar course, with budgets smaller than those of his silent short films. Instead of making two or three features a year that could support him, Langdon eked out a living at Monogram and continued making shorts at Columbia to earn his bread and butter.

Originally titled *Bundles from Britain, Double Trouble* is interesting mainly because Langdon dons the familiar suit and corduroy hat from his silent days, which had not appeared onscreen in years. However, *Double Trouble* hardly works to his advantage, especially as he wears women's clothes again and appears in an absurd dream sequence in which he and

Charley are chased by a shark. If the film's ending grabbed anyone favorably, it was thanks to Harry Jr., even though he was only six years old at the time. He recalled:

> They were trying to come up with a bright ending. I don't know why they took me seriously, but I noticed that they were always carrying umbrellas throughout the whole picture. . . . They said, "We are going to be standing on the edge of the street hitchhiking to get out of town fast. We can't come up with anything bright." I said, "Why don't you have the umbrellas set behind, and they would go on wagging back and forth as a hitchhiker's thumb would?" They picked it up and did pay me something for it. We saw the premiere sitting in the audience, way out of town—the premieres always seemed to be way out of town—and everyone was nudging each other's sides at the end of the picture saying, "Harry did that, Little Harry did that."

Daily Variety again celebrated Langdon's "comeback," which was odd, in that he had been working steadily for years and earning reviews that applauded both his acting and his writing. The *Hollywood Reporter* found the Langdon-Rogers team seemed "promising" and observed: "When this twosome is on the screen, there is a constant supply of chuckling antics which, kept in the proper groove, should delight audiences in the houses where Monogram product is played."

At this time, Jimmie Fidler's radio review of the film acknowledged Langdon's long, uphill trek to a different kind of stardom: "If proof is necessary—that all a veteran star needs to stage a comeback is an opportunity—this picture is that proof." Langdon's life had always been full of opportunities to prove himself. Whether he had used them wisely was another question. But as long as opportunities arose, he would continue to prove that he was Harry Langdon—whatever that meant to the public and to himself.

At the close of 1941, Langdon appeared in a three-minute film known as a "soundie" and sang "Beautiful Clothes Make Beautiful Girls." Soundies were a transitory phenomenon in the history of popular music, a cross between a kinetoscope and a jukebox. In 1939 the Mills Novelty Company of Chicago developed the idea of using filmed songs instead of records so patrons could see both the orchestra and the singer on a small screen. The company used 800-foot, 16mm reels that held eight three-minute selections. The reels were mounted inside a box about seven feet high and three to four feet wide, with a viewing screen that measured sixteen by twenty inches. The projection apparatus was activated and stopped by a strip of foil on the film at the start and end of each number. The soundies era did not last much past the end of World War II. When the novelty wore off, the machines fell into disuse because they offered only eight selections, filmed months or even years earlier, whereas regular jukeboxes offered a wide variety of current hits. The film reels also had to be played in sequence; to rehear the first number after playing the second, one had to pass through numbers three through eight—not worth the time or expense. However, this oddity gave Langdon, who was not known as a singer, the opportunity to croon onscreen, and it was the best of the few singing stints in his career.

Langdon could never claim to be bored with his work during these years; it was varied, even if his income was sparse. Rogers and Langdon tried to reactivate their teamwork with another PRC film, *House of Errors,* written by Langdon; he also gave his old friend Vernon Dent a small part. The film has a reliable but slim war-related plot, but essentially the comedians play budding newspaper reporters who become involved in thievery and villainy.

Between films, Langdon also made guest appearances on the radio, but they were rare until 1942, when he landed a permanent spot as assistant moderator on a celebrity interview show titled *Look Who's Here,* broadcast by CBS and starring Al Span. The show did not achieve major ratings, however, and was quietly dropped after a few seasons.

Langdon trudged on making Columbia shorts throughout 1942. Though listed as costar of *What Makes Lizzy Dizzy,* he was overshadowed by his leading lady, gangly Elsie Ames, an eccentric dancer with a raucous voice who became a knockabout comedienne in the best slapstick tradition. Harry's fleeting moments in this film involve contrived problems with a bowling ball. Another dud for Langdon was a travesty of *It Happened One Night,* awkwardly called *Tireman, Spare My Tires.* He gets mixed up with a runaway heiress and a passing motorist, spends a chaste night in a motel, and the boy gets the girl in the end. Unfortunately, the heavy-handed direction weighs down the hackneyed plot, and the wartime twist does not help. Jules White may have been the ideal director for the Three Stooges and their frenetic, crude humor, but he often spoiled Langdon's

Harry gets a little tender loving care in *House of Errors*.

timing and did not understand his subtleties. By contrast, *Carry Harry* (1942) lets Langdon play more equally against Elsie Ames. He repeats a routine from *Three's a Crowd*, acting with spirit and claiming small moments as his own, such as stealing a kiss from an unconscious woman with the relish of a small boy being naughty.

The next shorts provide an insightful demonstration of how directors' styles impacted Langdon's work. In *Piano Mooner*, director Harry Edwards allows his old friend to play with minor bits of business while flirting with Fifi D'Orsay, enlivening an otherwise drab script. However, in *A Blitz on the Fritz*, directed by the more demanding—and commanding—Jules White, Langdon's mannerisms appear forced as he bumbles to round up a ring of spies. *Film Daily* lauded Langdon's efforts in *Blonde and Groom*, directed by Edwards, even though the reviewer thought the film wasted his time and talent. For the White-directed *Here Comes Mr. Zerk*, Langdon's work seems strained again, even though it is a mash of *His Marriage Wow* and *Saturday Afternoon*. Edwards and White alternated directorial duties, with Langdon caught on a seesaw between their styles. He craved a respite from this balancing act and went back to the theater.

If Langdon wondered how the same comedy he had "mastered" over decades could shift under individual director's perspectives, he also may have wondered whether his opinion mattered anymore. But who he was and what he meant to others became clear after a chance encounter on the Columbia set. Cary Grant was leaving the set one day (ironically, the title of his film at the time was *Three's a Crowd*, but it eventually became *The Talk of the Town*) when he was stopped by a "hesitant little man," as the *Los Angeles Examiner* reported:

> "You don't know me, Mr. Grant, but I have admired your work for years."
>
> But it was Cary who became the humble one.
>
> "Harry Langdon!" Cary who believes Harry is tops explained, "the shoe should be on the other foot. You never knew me, but twenty years ago we traveled through New England in the same vaudeville bill. I was an unknown hoofer and you followed my act as the star of the bill. I used to watch you nightly from the wings."

Grant had been hoping to run into his youthful idol when he heard that Langdon was at Columbia. This recognition of Langdon's legacy, at a time when he was doing what he loved but was unsure of how it was being received, surely bolstered the aging comedian's morale and encouraged him to keep going.

Langdon learned that a road company was bringing *Out of the Frying Pan*, a 1941 hit on Broadway, to the Music Box Theatre in Los Angeles. He auditioned and joined stars Edith Fellows and George Behan for a two-week run. The play is a screwball farce about three guys and three girls who share an apartment while seeking show business careers in New York. Although the reviews were mixed, Langdon continued to flex his acting muscles. He also used this theatrical run to revive a little nostalgia of his own: just as he had ushered at Dohany's Opera House as a boy, he arranged for his eight-year-old son to be an usher at the Music Box Theatre for the enviable wage of "one 25-cent war stamp per day."[19]

The play provided enough of a change to soothe Langdon's restless-

The cast of *Out of the Frying Pan*.

ness. The *Los Angeles Times* observed that since opening at the Music Box, Langdon had received many stage and screen offers, "but he won't leave his family here, saying he's a 'sissy' about them." The interview gave Langdon a chance to ponder his life and comedy:

> "There are a lot of ways for a comedian to get himself a tough time in pictures. . . . He has to remember to say no, for one thing. For instance, one proposition I had, all I could think of to say was yes. There was another word, but I couldn't think of it at the time. The word was no."

Some comedians, it was remarked, seem dated, but not Langdon. How come?

> "A comedian should establish a character with human appeal," he answered. "Then he'll be pretty indestructible. For instance, in developing my character I use little childish gestures—and children are always appealing. Such a comedian isn't a machine. I know the limits of my character—a little too aggressive, for instance, and he's gone. I've tried to inject this character into parts offered me, but if the director interfered the character would be lost."

Harry sketching for servicemen at the Hollywood Canteen.

Langdon's life was coming full circle. He had begun his career onstage, and now he had returned to it, while still juggling work in the medium that had made him an international star. Langdon had decided, if only for the sake of his own happiness, that he did not want money—which was not coming his way anyway, he realized. He wanted to stay occupied and share himself with others. He became an active volunteer at the Hollywood Canteen, a social club for servicemen founded by Bette Davis and John Garfield. Movie stars and character actors waited on the servicemen, made sandwiches and coffee, and entertained them. Mabel remembered that she and Harry went to the Hollywood Canteen nearly every night, and Harry would set up his drawing kit. The soldiers and sailors queued up, and Harry spent fifteen minutes making "lightning-speed" caricatures of each man on an eight- by ten-inch board—much as he had done as a youth for the medicine show audiences. Mabel distributed envelopes so the men could mail the pictures to their mothers or sweethearts.

One night, among luminaries such as Marlene Dietrich, Lena Horne, Ish Kabibble, Kay Kyser, Gloria DeHaven, and George Montgomery, the venerated stage and film actress Maria Ouspenskaya was waiting on soldiers behind the sandwich counter. Mabel shyly approached her and asked for an autograph for Junior. Ouspenskaya stared at Mabel and, in her precise Russian accent, replied, "Mrs. Langdon, we are only supposed to give out autographs to the soldier boys!" With a glint in her eye, she added in a whisper, "But I'll give it to you anyway."

Whenever Langdon felt the need for live applause, he returned to the stage. He knew, however, that his permanent legacy would be film and kept his hand in that cookie jar, even though all he found there were crumbs. The contentment he felt at home seemed to compensate for his professional frustrations. During the run of *Out of the Frying Pan,* Harry and Mabel celebrated their ninth wedding anniversary on February 12, and some of the cast attended the party, together with Vernon Dent, Charley Rogers, test pilot George Armstead, and other old friends. According to a news item, Harry gave Mabel a dog named Chix and she gave him a big kiss. He concluded, "Every day is a holiday in the Langdon household." Harry entertained his guests by drawing caricatures of them. It was a typically quiet gathering: Langdon's home life reflected the stillness that had made his best performances so enduring.

Langdon so enjoyed working with Edith Fellows in the play that he proposed a revival of "Johnny's New Car" with her as his partner. Edith enthusiastically accepted the challenge, rehearsed the skit with Harry and a rag doll prop, and performed it with him at the Capitol Theatre in Washington, DC, for one week in August 1943. Harry received $1,500—two and a half times his highest pay in vaudeville before heading off to Hollywood. After its success in Washington, the breakaway car was booked at the Loew's State Theatre in New York for another week at the same salary. With a fateful twist, the vehicle that had supported Langdon for nearly twenty-five years came to his aid again at this late stage of his life.

The differences between his lucrative stage revival and his film roles at this time were striking. He starred onstage, but in films he had only a supporting role in Monogram's *Spotlight Scandals* and virtually disappeared in *To Heir Is Human* opposite Una Merkel. A similar negligible role occupied Langdon's time in *Hot Rhythm,* released in March 1944. Harry plays Whiffle, a music publisher's right-hand man and troubleshooter who is only peripherally involved in the action and creates confusion.

Jules White had not abandoned the idea of teaming Langdon up with someone, and he selected a goofball character comic with a Scandinavian

Still on the marquee.

accent named El Brendel. Though born in Philadelphia, Brendel spoke with a thick Swedish accent throughout his career, which stretched back to his 1913 debut in vaudeville. He graduated to the Broadway music stage in 1921, and by 1926 he had started working in films. He had featured roles in a number of Fox productions in the early days of sound pictures, and then in a series of Vitaphone shorts, some of which were in color. In the late 1930s Brendel switched to Columbia, where he fared badly. White's department operated like a production line, averaging one short every two weeks and ignoring the finer points of filmmaking, such as fitting the material to a performer's style. Brendel's special humor got lost in the rush. He was first teamed with Tom Kennedy in a series that leaned heavily on haunted houses and cemeteries. When that failed, he was paired with Monty Collins and, finally, Harry Langdon. New faces were plugged into old situations; to the writers at Columbia, the sparkle of one comic was no different from the sparkle—or, for that matter, the dullness—of another. Possibly because of the success of the Three Stooges, no one tried to discover the vital difference between the slapstick inanity of that motley trio

Trying another team with El Brendel.

and the naïve souls played by Langdon and Brendel. In their shorts, they might as well have been billed as the Two Stooges.

In their first collaboration in 1944, *Defective Detectives*, the tone is set from the start. Assigned to paint the office of investigators I. Peek and H. E. Boos, Harry is supposed to paint a fan, and El suggests turning it on so that Harry can just hold the brush and the blades will paint themselves as they spin. The plan backfires, and the boys lose their job. When they are rehired to track down a bank robber, they capture the banker instead. The film was more helpful to Christine McIntyre, the female costar of the Langdon-Brendel shorts. A beautiful blonde who was just starting at Columbia, she had a pleasant singing voice that she used in one of the team's four shorts. That same year, she was assigned to a Three Stooges comedy and became their longest-running female foil, appearing in some thirty films with the trio over a twelve-year period.

The second Langdon-Brendel short was *Mopey Dope*, in which Harry plays an absentminded husband who remembers his wedding anniversary but ends up at the wrong house. Langdon also squeezed in a feature, *Block Busters,* but he appears in only a couple of scenes in what was meant to be an East Side Kids vehicle. His straight lines make him look pompous in this otherwise amiable tenement comedy. The East Side Kids were an off-shoot of a hugely successful play of 1935 and its 1937 film adaptation, *Dead End.* The focus was on a group of juvenile actors playing tough kids from an impoverished New York neighborhood. The characterizations were so memorable that most of the cast of the play was retained for the film, including wisecracking gang leader Muggs (Leo Gorcey), his dim-witted and lanky sidekick Gimpy (Huntz Hall), Bobby Jordan, and Gabriel Dell. The film was such a hit that several social melodramas followed as sequels, with the group now identified as the Dead End Kids. When the group was taken over by Monogram, social issues were included as long as they did not interfere with the low comedy and fractured language. The group later became the Bowery Boys.

Although the East Side Kids fared well in *Block Busters,* Langdon was wasted in a part that could have been played by any competent actor. That was unfortunate, as *Block Busters* was the last of Langdon's films to be released during his lifetime.

In the fall of 1944, Harry, now sixty, persevered with writing scripts, cartooning, and performing. He worked on a script tentatively titled *That Hunter Girl* for RKO, but no such film was ever made; it might have been filmed under a different title, but if so, no credit was given to Langdon. In October Langdon filmed *Snooper Service* for Columbia; in November he worked on a Republic feature, *Swingin' on a Rainbow,* in which he had a fairly large role but one that did not fully use his talents.

In December Harry starred in another Langdon-Brendel two-reeler, *Pistol Packin' Nitwits.* The short was directed by Harry Edwards and originally scripted by Edward Bernds, a meticulous writer who kept a detailed diary of daily events on the set. Bernds began as a soundman and eventually moved to Columbia, where he worked on practically all the Capra features. Having worked with the likes of Douglas Fairbanks Sr., Mary Pickford, and D. W. Griffith, Bernds was not overawed by Capra but did respect him as a director. Capra was in fact instrumental in pushing Bernds into directing, recommending him to Harry Cohn, head of Columbia. His first directorial effort was a wartime propaganda short called *It's Murder,* dealing with the sensitive subject of security. In his spare time,

Bernds wrote two-reelers, one being the western comedy starring Brendel and Langdon and initially titled *Tenderfeet*. Bernds received only $150 for his work, and by the time Edwards had rewritten the script and the film had been renamed *Pistol Packin' Nitwits*, Bernds hardly recognized it. Reflecting many years later, Bernds thought that both he and Langdon had lost much of themselves in the process of mass-producing shorts:

> This story credit of Harry Langdon and me . . . that must have been Harry Edwards' doing. . . . I disclaim a lot of the stuff that was showing. I claim that Harry Langdon's talents were not properly used in the Columbia two-reelers. First of all, he shouldn't have been teamed, he could have stood on his own. Somebody should have run the old Sennett comedies in which he made his reputation and studied what it was that he had that made him so immensely popular and tried to do that in the two-reelers. I think that's what I would have done if I had been [in charge]. . . . I have no idea what my original screenplay was like, I just don't remember and I don't have a copy of it, but my diary does tell me . . . that the only thing that remained of my stuff was a couple of character names. Apparently what went on the screen was not mine at all.[20]

Excerpts from Bernds's personal diary document the radical changes to his script:

10/9 [1944]	Rewrite treatment of Langdon-Brendel Western.
10/20	Confer with Mac[Collum, the producer] about Langdon-Brendel and other projects. Priority: Langdon. Tell Mac that Harry Edwards always cuts out good scenes. Expound theory that story interest, humor and thrills are worthwhile (a la Capra)—rather than a whole series of senseless slapstick gags.
10/21	Try write Langdon-Brendel.
10/29	Work on "Tenderfeet" 5–6 hours.
10/30	Turn in "Tenderfeet" as is.
11/17	Read Langdon-Brendel Western script. Find nothing of my original except a few character names. Try edit some sense into it.

11/20	Talk with Mac about over-budget on Langdon-Brendel.
11/22	Get $150.00 check for "Tenderfeet."
11/27	Langdon-Brendel Western starts drop in on set at Ranch A.M.
11/28	See Langdon-Brendel Western rushes.
12/5	Run with Mac first cut of Western. Harry Edwards' bad lapse—long shot to long shot cut! Eat sequence bad because of "slobber." Mac says will have to cut it.

The eating sequence that was cut from the film includes Langdon and Brendel charging Vernon Dent for a full meal. In the interim, Vernon passes out, and the boys smear food all over him to convince him that he has eaten it. MacCollum thought it was uncouth and insisted on editing it out, which also excised Dent from the film.

The short contains a fast musical routine between Langdon and Brendel, requiring one to play the piano while the other soft-shoes; then they change places and start again, alternating every few seconds. The routine was rehearsed for a couple of days, and shooting began on December 8. The entire day was devoted to the dance number. Bernds noted nothing amiss with Langdon during the shooting, but when Harry went home that evening, he complained to Mabel that the strain had been too much for him. She was surprised, because Harry was not given to complaining; in fact, to her knowledge, he had never been seriously ill. He mentioned pains in his head and, thinking it was a toothache, went to the dentist. The dentist told Mabel to rush Harry to a doctor because he thought the problem was far more serious. Langdon was immediately ordered to bed by his doctor. Harry Jr., just shy of turning ten years old, sensed that something was wrong:

I remember . . . they had to wheel him out. I remember him waving good-bye to me. And that's the last I saw of my father. . . . He tried to use some sign language with me, and I got a feeling at that point that something was not all right. . . . I spent a couple of weeks with my godmother while my father was, you know, they were trying to get him back into shape for whatever was going to happen. . . . Well, I wanted to read the funnies in the newspapers and she'd say, "No, you can't see the newspaper!" Oh, oh, now

Harry's last role in *Pistol Packin' Nitwits,* with El Brendel and Vernon Dent.

that's kind of odd. You know, because I'd always liked to get up in the morning and read the funny papers. I thought something is wrong here.

As long as Langdon was conscious, he insisted on staying at home. But on December 21, the doctor ordered Mabel to take Harry to St. Vincent's Hospital when he fell unconscious. Shortly after, Langdon suffered a heart attack. The next day, Langdon died of a cerebral hemorrhage, just as his father had. Unfortunately, it was six hours before the hospital contacted Mabel with the news.

Although Langdon had barely been conscious before being taken to the hospital, one of his final coherent thoughts was about missing his son's tenth birthday on December 16. Mabel had tried to convince him that he would be well enough to take part in the celebration. Harry could only manage to raise his hands and hold out ten fingers to indicate that he understood. That was his last message—a silent one.

5

Legacy

Three films were released posthumously in 1945. Two with El Brendel, *Snooper Service* and *Pistol Packin' Nitwits*, were released in February and April, respectively. In the former film, Harry and El are private investigators, with Vernon Dent as their boss. In the latter, Harry and El arrive in a western town to sell a cleaning product in a saloon run by Christine McIntyre. She hires them after they chase out a toughie who has been pestering her about a mortgage. They also manage to divert the tough guys as the hero races against time to get the mortgage money. Harry, appearing haggard and weary throughout the short, utters the line, "The time is nearly up," indicating that the money is due. It is, in retrospect, an eerily prophetic line, for within two weeks after filming the energetic dance number in *Pistol Packin' Nitwits*, Langdon was dead.

Even though his illness during the last days of shooting postponed the film, the company expected him to return. When news of Langdon's death reached the set, there was a scramble to finish the picture, which was a few minutes too short to qualify as a two-reeler. Brendel and Langdon were supposed to do some additional routines, but now the practical solution was to pad Christine's song, "Come Home, Father," with extra choruses to fill in the time. Adding to the song was logical, as it provides a sense of biding time until the mortgage money is delivered (tension is built by intercutting between the horse rider and the saloon). Unfortunately, the song seems endless onscreen, and its sad-ballad mood only dampens the short, which is already encumbered by labored sequences.

As far as the public was concerned, Langdon's last film was *Swingin' on a Rainbow*, released in August 1945. Jane Frazee plays a small-town girl named Polly who submits a song to a radio contest sponsored by a bandleader. He uses it without her permission, and she comes to New York to settle the matter. While there, she is visited by Harry, who plays an

Lobby card for *Swingin' on a Rainbow.*

employee of an advertising agency that needs songs for an important client. Harry's best turns in this lightweight comedy involve his frantic efforts to keep the girl from fighting with her neighbor, who happens to be her lyricist. This task makes good use of Langdon's fluttery movements and tremulous voice, but on the whole, he has little else to do in his role as the go-between. He is putty in the hands of Polly, who strong-arms her way through the film. Although the role was a subordinate one and required no special comic skills, Langdon received top billing after the stars. His name was still registering among audiences, if only because of its frequent appearance.

Mabel held a modest funeral service for Harry on the day after Christmas. Vernon Dent helped make the arrangements, and among those in attendance were costars and friends, including Priscilla Bonner, Stan Laurel, Jules White, Charley Rogers, El Brendel, Andy Clyde, Jimmy Finlayson, Chester Conklin, Jerry Geisler, Harry Edwards, and Arthur Ripley. Charlie Chaplin sent a wreath of white carnations. Frank Capra was serving in the army at the time and did not attend.[1] Langdon was cremated and interred at Grand View Cemetery in Glendale, near his mother and some of his siblings.[2] Unfortunately, the newspaper obituaries presented only sketchy, sometimes glaringly inaccurate accounts: they claimed that Harry had five wives, six wives (including a remarriage), a biological daughter, and a son born of a different mother. They tended to synopsize the most ruinous aspects of Langdon's life and work, dismissing his value except as measured in monetary terms. Other headlines starkly emphasized his "has-been" reputation, as did the *Los Angeles Examiner:* "Comedian Harry Langdon, Who Had Rags to Riches Roundtrip, Dies of Hemorrhage."

Mabel remembered that when she told her son about his father's passing, he said nothing. "He turned around, went to his room for over an hour, then came out as if I hadn't said anything at all." The suddenness of Langdon's death was hard for both of them to process, and it shattered their lives. Mabel recalled:

> After Harry died, circumstances had changed greatly. There was no income coming into the house. . . . Harry Edwards, who was very close to us . . . he was the one who met me at the hospital when Harry died. He said, "Well, May, now what are you going to do? What are your plans?" Well, I had no plans, I hadn't even thought about plans, except that I was going to have to do something. He said, "Well, why don't you take a course in being a hotel receptionist or in a café or something of that sort?" He said, "There are schools and it doesn't take very long." He said, "I think you'd be fine." And no, I didn't think I'd want that. I'd be moving in public, moving around too much, and on account of Harry [Junior], it would be a hardship. So then he said, "Well, supposing I call the Motion Picture Relief Fund at their office, maybe there's something they could use you for in the office." I said, "Well, that sounds pretty good."

Mabel was immediately hired, based on both her experience in an insurance office and her familiarity with the motion picture industry. But for ten-year-old Harry Jr., his father's death was a terrible blow:

> I assumed that my life was going to be greased tracks from then on in because of my father's name and because of his fame, and because of never having any responsibilities as a kid, and never there being any worries around the house. . . . Here my dad dies,

and I think, "Well, it's just going to go on like that." But no. My life completely—my mother's life and my life completely change, and we had to go from the big house in the Hollywood hills . . . to living in more of a modest place. My mother had to begin working and so I got some revelations, I think, in my early teenage years that I was going to have to buckle down real quick and do something on my own and not rely on my father's name. . . . I realized from observing what happened with my mother right after my dad's passing that all of our friends disappeared. You know, nobody came to our aid and nobody . . . all these devout, loyal friends with all the money and everything just evaporated. . . .

I noticed another interesting phenomenon—that nobody particularly wanted to talk to me about my father. Because I went to Stan Laurel and I tried to see Frank Capra and I tried to see all these people. And they either [claimed they were ill and] couldn't communicate very well or just gave me the highlights: "Oh, your dad was a great guy." Or they said, "Why don't we just allow you to remember your father as you remember him, and we won't get involved in the business end of the career." . . . I don't know what they didn't want to tell me, but I guess they felt like I had a good memory of my father at that point, so why rock the boat?

Both mother and son picked up the pieces of their lives and pursued their personal goals. Mabel became head of the Studio Deductions Department at the Motion Picture and Television Fund, which managed the contributions that supported the retirement home where so many show business greats ended up, including some who had worked with Langdon. Mabel never remarried. As she stated in an interview not long before she passed away on March 17, 2001: "I don't want to. I'm still in love with Harry."[3]

After spending some time in the army and then working as a carpenter, Harry Jr. was eventually offered a job in a photography studio—where he discovered an occupation he could build on without any outside help. He tapped into his own artistic talents and went on to have an illustrious career as a top Hollywood photographer, away from the shadow of his father's name. He even dropped the "Jr." for a while, but once he had made it on his own, he embraced it again as a proud part of his identity. He recalled, "I had to pull myself up by my own bootstraps . . . but it builds character and personality and gumption. . . . If my dad were alive today, I'm sure he'd say, 'Hey, right on! Well done!'"

The book seemed to be closed on Harry Langdon Sr., except for the memories of those who had known him. At this death, many expressed great regret over his lifetime of struggles. The title of his last released film, *Swingin' on a Rainbow,* seemed sadly appropriate: he had always sought the fortune at the end of the rainbow, but instead, he often found himself just swinging from the rainbow, alternating between highs and lows. Below him was the road on which he had chosen to walk, yet he was always aware of the translucent glow around him—remnants of his genius. He settled for what kept his life steady, even if it meant that, in the future, his name would be relegated to obscurity.

The September 5, 1949, issue of *Life* magazine contained an article by film critic and Pulitzer Prize–winning author James Agee titled "Comedy's Greatest Era." In his overview of the glory years of silent comedy, Agee named "the four most eminent masters: Charlie Chaplin, Harold Lloyd, the late Harry Langdon, and Buster Keaton." Five years after his death, Harry Langdon was finally accorded the praise he deserved for his best silent work.

Agee drew the obvious parallels between Chaplin and Langdon: "In his screen character he symbolized something as deeply and centrally human, though by no means as rangily so, as the Tramp. There was, of course, an immense difference in inventiveness and range of virtuosity. It seemed as if Chaplin could do literally anything, on any instrument in the orchestra. Langdon had one queerly toned, unique little reed. But out of it he could get incredible melodies." According to Agee, Langdon "was as remarkable a master as Chaplin of subtle emotional and mental process and operated much more at leisure." Agee concluded by citing Capra's estimation that Langdon was "the most tragic figure I ever came across in show business" and that Harry had died broke and with a broken heart, for he "never did really understand what hit him." Although Agee's reassessment of Langdon's work was invaluable, it also inadvertently solidified in readers' minds that Capra was Langdon's spokesman.

For decades, Capra's perspective would continue to define Langdon's career as irreparably broken and essentially worthless after *The Strong Man* and *Long Pants.* His prominence as an award-winning director gave him the power to do so. However, it is easy to detect contradictions and errors in Capra's memories, calling into question the accuracy of his facts.[4] Perhaps the rancor that corroded the two men's friendship and collaboration at crucial periods in their lives, combined with the human tendency to modify, condense, or even delete memories over time, influenced Capra and surfaced as unrelieved anger toward Langdon.

More of Capra's "reality" came to light with the publication of Joseph McBride's biography, *Frank Capra: The Catastrophe of Success.* Although McBride acknowledges Capra's animosity toward the man he called "the little bastard," his research led him to conclude that "Capra could see much of himself in Langdon. Langdon was like a crazy mirror of Capra's emotions, comically distorted in such a way that Capra could stand back and observe them."[5] McBride cites several similarities between them: they both grew up in modest circumstances (Capra in Bisacquino, Sicily, and Langdon in Council Bluffs, Iowa), went to work at a young age, entered show business in behind-the-scenes jobs, and were multitalented in the fields of music and comedy. However, while Langdon pursued a career in theater on the road, Capra acquired a formal education at the California Institute of Technology before joining Sennett's studio. When Capra and Langdon met, the serious young man found a kindred spirit in the comedian:

> In stage persona, Langdon was sort of premental Capra, a creature of seemingly pure instinct, uncomplicated by any brush with mental labor or emotional agony. A creature who somehow seemed to have remained suspended in a world of innocence, a bizarre and blissful state of permanently arrested development that had a dreamlike way of protecting him from harm. . . . And, perhaps most arrestingly for Capra, when he first encountered the comedian in that summer of 1923—a time when he was using his work to escape an intolerable marriage—Harry Langdon's adult babyhood represented a comical embodiment of his sexual activities.[6]

McBride's analysis of Capra's work suggests that, like Ripley, the director's humor had a "darkness," especially regarding women, which helps explain why their collaboration succeeded. Langdon then skewed the balance by becoming more reliant on Ripley, with whom he might have felt more comfortable. *The Strong Man* was as much a "starring vehicle" for Capra as it was for Langdon, given the former's directing aspirations and the latter's desire for autonomy (which would lead to directing). In fact, Sennett gave Capra the chance to direct *Soldier Man* but was displeased with the result—a fact Capra's autobiography overlooks as the reason the Old Man dismissed him. Film editor William Hornbeck later told film historian Kevin Brownlow that Sennett had been so disappointed with Capra's work upon seeing the rushes that he uttered, "This fellow will never make a director." Capra attributed his dismissal to a different incident unrelated to Langdon but admitted, "Nothing since has seemed quite so bleak as the day Mack Sennett fired me. . . . I did have a great ambition to direct. To [Sennett], directors didn't mean much."[7]

When Langdon moved to First National, he in fact wanted to "groom" Capra as his director, so Capra stayed close to Edwards, who had taken the reins for *Tramp, Tramp, Tramp*. However, Edwards left before *The Strong Man* was under way, feeling that Langdon was becoming too self-absorbed, and Capra eagerly stepped into position. In many ways, *The Strong Man* contains many elements of Capra's own life and the themes that drove his later success: an immigrant's exposure to America, an uncomfortable introduction to the opposite sex, a struggle to enter show business, an unexpected rise to stardom, corruption in small-town America, a romantic ideal, and the power of love.[8]

Given the film's importance for Capra, a bitter clash was inevitable when Langdon dictated his intentions for *Long Pants*. Capra harbored decades of resentment, and in 1985 he finally admitted that he had written the "anonymous" letter trashing Langdon's reputation. He explained: "I had a lot to counteract. . . . Unless you defended yourself, what the hell, nobody would know it. . . . Langdon had achieved a tremendous reputation. Everybody was talking about him. I couldn't find a job. Nobody would believe me. They'd believe *him*, you know, because he spread it around very hard and very fast that I was just a gag man that he brought over, I was no director."[9] It was an admission too long after the damage had been done; Langdon was gone and could neither defend himself nor make peace. In the final analysis, it seems that both geniuses became heady with their own ambitions and did the best—and worst—they could at the time. Capra continued to consider Langdon "the only honest-to-God human tragedy I've ever been up against."[10] If given the chance, Langdon would have begged to differ.

Langdon had not died a tragic figure. He had worked to the very end—in fact, work may have killed him. Hopscotching between perfection and mediocrity, Langdon acted, wrote, directed, sang, and danced on film, on the stage, and on radio, in the States and abroad. He stayed alive in the minds of critics and audiences, both because of and regardless of their reviews. As his glory days passed, even the bad reviews of his sound work were no longer complaints about his ineptitude as a filmmaker or his ego; they were compassionate reminders of the essence of his comedy and his character.

Despite numerous articles about his quaint philosophizing and comic euphoria, Langdon rarely spoke about his years as a silent comedian, so it is difficult to understand how he perceived them.[11] We have only his film output, which provides an incomplete portrait of the artist. If he succeeded in a film, it was because he (and his director) clearly understood what worked; if he failed, it was because *something* (script, partner, poor judgment) had hindered his success. In 1938 Langdon commented to a reporter that he had listened to too many people about both work and money matters; now when he heard the words "If you listen to me . . . ," he would get annoyed, walk away, and figure it out for himself. But one must question the soundness of his judgment, considering some of the incredibly awkward errors he made as a director. Why did his innate sense of comedic timing fail him at so many crucial moments? Langdon might have jokingly cited Capra's appraisal: "Nobody knew what to do with this guy who took an hour to wink."[12] Probing more deeply for an explanation of his flaws and mistakes, one might have to settle for an image: Langdon raises a finger to his mouth and stares imponderably with a faint smile that conveys multiple possible answers.

The closest Langdon came to a public rendering of his personal turmoil and loss was in a 1932 article in *Motion Picture Magazine* by Sonia Lee entitled "Good Luck or Bad Luck—Bebe and Harry Can Take It!" Langdon comes across as humble, slightly baffled, newly resilient. Between the lines one can detect injured pride and a sense of victimization. The article quotes Langdon at length:

> The trouble with me was that I was pushed through pictures too fast . . . I was turning them out without preparation—without giving situations a chance to mature, or to be worked out with the infinite care comedy requires.
>
> When superlative praise was given to "Long Pants," I knew the curtain was slowly coming down for me. The extravagant terms critics used were in reality a death knell for me. I knew, if no one

else realized at the moment, the fundamental weakness of the picture—and the difficulties under which it was made.

I had been talked into producing my own pictures—and they were financially fatal. I trusted directors and writers, and business managers. When I needed every bit of energy for a scene before the camera, I was harassed by business squabbles and by internal strife—as unnecessary as it was selfish. The worries of management destroyed my peace of mind—I couldn't concentrate.

There's no doubt that fear of criticism licked me. If I had gone ahead, depended on my own judgement, insisted on a schedule of picture-making that would permit me to do good work—I would have continued to be Harry Langdon, the star.

As it is, I am starting back. Pictures are where I belong. I don't especially care if I'm never a star again. I pity people who grub and grab—the actors who think the world has come to an end if they're not in every close-up.

I am much happier now—I'm down to earth, to the essential values of living. I enjoy having carpenters shake me by the hand. I get a thrill when the prop boys greet me with the old familiar "Hello, Harry." I didn't have that friendliness when I was a star—I haven't had it since those happy and peaceful Sennett days. Somehow, stardom isolated me, removed me from human contacts.

In reality I don't care how small my roles are, as long as they give me a chance. And I hope to have time for other things, for art lessons and music and books. I am not afraid of people anymore—or even injustice. I've regained my own assurance, my faith in myself. If it's in the cards that someday my name will again be important—that's fine! If not—I'll be content.[13]

Here, Langdon offers a glimpse of what he sacrificed to achieve a measure of personal happiness.

Perhaps the most striking answer about his feelings came in a 1943 interview with the *Los Angeles Times,* one year before his death: "When I play in what I call the Oh-Ouch-Oh comedies . . . I am just an animated suit of clothes."[14] This revelation that sometimes his screen persona and spirit had been reduced to "an animated suit of clothes" speaks volumes about who and what Langdon knew he could be when his whole being was filled with passion.

Langdon's perseverance kept him afloat until the end of his life. Even if he conveyed his emotions only through his persona's quixotic expressions, Langdon had seemingly made peace with his mistakes, reaching a modicum of success measured not in fame and fortune but in truth to oneself. It was a type of success overlooked or ignored by Capra and many others.

Langdon gratefully went to work in the mornings, came home at night, cultivated his hobbies, channeled his restlessness, enjoyed his friendships, forged new partnerships, and devoted himself to his family. Langdon may have finally realized that when he compartmentalized his many talents, rather than trying to do them all at once, he created some of his best work. He had two precious worlds—family and work—and he was determined that neither would suffer again at the expense of the other.

It is possible that no one outside his immediate circle would have remembered Langdon without Agee's glowing acknowledgment, which returned Langdon to his pedestal. Unfortunately, Agee's words could not bring the actual films back to audiences who did not know Langdon and had not witnessed his checkered career. It was one thing to read Agee's high praise; it was another to see Langdon himself in action, and for the moment, that was not possible.

Raymond Rohauer's Coronet Theatre in Los Angeles was a showcase for classic old films and new experimental cinema. His theater attracted a cluster of celebrities and devoted film students who were eager to see these rarely screened masterworks. Rohauer was obsessed with the preservation of "lost" films, so he was delighted when in 1954 Buster Keaton, Rohauer's personal idol, offered his old films for screening at the Coronet. Keaton's life had followed a downward trajectory of unhappy marriages, personal despair, and a challenging transition to sound. However, much like Langdon, Keaton had continued to work in various projects and make a modest living. When Rohauer accompanied Keaton to his garage, he discovered a treasure of old films, many of which had been considered lost. Keaton reportedly said he was going to throw them out if Rohauer did not want them. There followed a long and painstaking process of salvaging the old nitrate material, transferring it to safety stock, and clearing the complex legal issues involving copyright and ownership. After overcoming many obstacles and legal knotholes, Rohauer established a clear title to Keaton's films and arranged for them to be shown at film festivals around the world, thus introducing a new generation of fans to one of the greatest comedy talents in movie history.

Rohauer next turned to the possibility of reviving Harry Langdon's films. In 1958 Mabel received an unexpected telephone call from Rohauer, inquiring about her late husband's work. She informed Rohauer that she had neither the films nor their rights. They said good-bye, but for Rohauer, that was not the end of the discussion. He looked into the legal background of Langdon's films and contacted anyone who had been involved with Langdon or his career. Two years later, in 1960, Rohauer called again and arranged to meet with Mabel. He told her how he had reestablished Keaton's rights and explained that Langdon's films at National had been made by the Harry Langdon Corporation and were co-owned by that company and First National, which had later been absorbed into Warner Brothers. But who was the Harry Langdon Corporation? A careful search of the corporate files in Sacramento disclosed that only 5,000 shares of the corporation had ever been issued. Harry himself owned 4,998; one share was in the name of his friend and agent William H. Jenner, and one was in the name of Jerry Geisler, the attorney who had apparently drawn up the papers and was listed as corporation officer. As Harry's widow, Mabel was clearly the majority stockholder of the corporation. Rohauer told her it was possible to resurrect the old company, establish her rights, and deal with Warner. He proposed that they become partners to collect the films, obtain the rights, and build a single repository of Langdon's work. They drew up an agreement and started a decades-long association.

The Harry Langdon Corporation had been dormant for so long that it owed a large sum of back taxes. Rohauer paid them and revived the legal entity, with all rights and prerogatives. He negotiated with Warner and, as a result, repossessed the best of Langdon's silent features. Then began the equally arduous task of tracking down other Langdon films through collaborators. Although Mack Sennett had died in 1960, Rohauer was able to obtain a number of Sennett comedies, including shorts with W. C. Fields, Bing Crosby, and other stars the Old Man had hired early in their careers. Among them were the shorts made by Langdon's famous triumvirate. These properties had been acquired by Warner in 1935, when Sennett went bankrupt. Like all major studios, however, Warner was not interested in salvaging and promoting negligible films—negligible in terms of corporate profits. It was amenable to Rohauer's proposal, and the Langdon shorts became part of the Rohauer Collection in 1967.

Rohauer located several Langdon films in unusual places. The first reel of *Smile, Please* was unearthed among Sennett's possessions, but the second reel was not found until fifteen years later. *The Chaser* was owned by a nun who showed it to children and charity patients, unaware that she had the last surviving copy of the film. The only copy of *The Sea Squawk* was offered to Rohauer by a collector in Amsterdam; it had Dutch titles, so no one would have recognized it as a Langdon film. Only a five-minute segment survived from *The First Hundred Years;* twenty years later, several more pieces totaling ten minutes were found—half of its actual running time. *Picking Peaches,* Harry's first public screen appearance, was nearly complete, but it had been spliced together from half a dozen different prints in various stages of deterioration. Two segments of *The Luck o' the Foolish* and *The Hansom Cabman* turned up on a West Coast television program for children.

Rohauer found another piece of the Langdon puzzle thanks to an old associate. Charlie Tarbox, who ran the Film Classics Exchange in Rohauer's hometown of Buffalo, New York, had given him his first reel of film, even though Rohauer did not own a projector at the time. Rohauer had stayed in contact with Tarbox after moving to Los Angeles, and in the mid-1970s Tarbox mentioned that he had a few offbeat items, one being a copy—the only copy—of *Plain Clothes.* It was poorly printed as a result of a deteriorated negative, but it was complete.

As Rohauer hunted for films, he and Mabel also tracked down Langdon's colleagues and costars to assemble a more complete story. Sol Lesser, who had signed Langdon to his first motion picture contract, was in his seventies and retired when they met in his Wilshire Boulevard apartment. He remembered much about his long career but not much about his association with Langdon or where copies of his two film experiments might be. Perhaps he was reluctant to recollect a project that had failed for him but profited Sennett. Lesser died in 1980 at the age of ninety.

Vernon Dent, who could have revealed the most about Langdon both personally and professionally, died in 1962 before an interview could be scheduled; his widow, Eunice, filled in as much information as she could. Jerry Geisler, who became one of the best criminal defense lawyers in Hollywood, provided information about the legal rights to the films. He had drawn up the contract between Langdon and First National, forming the Harry Langdon Corporation, but he could not recall the details and had forgotten that he held one share of the corporation. When Rohauer showed him proof of this, Geisler located the single share and gave it to Mabel. Ben Lyon's recollections assisted in pinpointing Harry's activities during the difficult adjustment to sound; the interview with Lyon was his last, as he died only a few weeks later in 1979.

Priscilla Bonner had only the best things to say about Harry, whom she regarded as courteous and considerate. Gladys McConnell, Harry's costar in *The Chaser* and *Three's a Crowd*, also had kind words, but she specifically recalled the unhealthy influence of Helen Walton and Arthur Ripley. Rohauer and Mabel located all three White brothers; Sam White was the only one to praise Ripley, calling him an unrecognized genius of the cinema whose writing had been too advanced for his audiences. After a career as a writer, editor, and director, Ripley helped establish and directed the Film Center at UCLA; he died in 1961.

Comedian Joe E. Brown reminisced about Langdon when he and Rohauer worked together on a television special about W. C. Fields in Boston, not long before Brown's death in 1973. Brown considered Langdon one of the casualties of the industry. Because he had developed his style toward the end of the silent era, Langdon had been caught in the maelstrom of the sound revolution, but Brown thought he was a fine artist with great timing and a unique delivery, one of the most sensitive clowns he knew.

One of the most helpful people in the search for Langdon was Edward Bernds, who had moved on after *Pistol Packin' Nitwits* to write scripts for the Blondie series, the Three Stooges, the Bowery Boys, and other Columbia players. His habit of keeping a work diary settled the question of which film Langdon had been working on at the time of his death.[15] Before being stricken, Harry had mentioned only that he was doing a dance routine, so Mabel assumed it was *Swingin' on a Rainbow*, which was a musical. When *Swingin' on a Rainbow* came out and had no dance number with Harry, Mabel thought the routine had never been completed or had been deleted. The only other "last" film with a dance sequence was *Pistol Packin' Nitwits*, and Bernds's diary provided the evidence that it was indeed the last film Langdon made, although *Swingin' on a Rainbow* was his last released.

Harry Jr. turned ten after his father died, but decades later, his memories were still fresh and vivid enough to evoke both tears and laughter. He resisted the pressure to follow in his father's footsteps and pursued his own path, becoming an award-winning photographer of celebrities; his subjects include Donna Summer, Ann-Margret, Richard Burton, Julio Igle-

Ed Bernds, Mabel Langdon, Harry Langdon Jr., and Raymond Rohauer.

sias, Jane Fonda, Sophia Loren, Halle Berry, and Ronald and Nancy Reagan. Harry's perspective on success connects deeply to his father's ability to cope with fame and the consequences of wrong choices:

> It's been a tremendous education for me to be around so many successful people and watching how they can maintain it or how they can undermine their success. That's something also that's built into human nature, it's people's fear of success. And also another very obvious weakness of the human psyche is the feeling as though they don't deserve success. I see that happening constantly. Once a person gets to a certain point, they try to start undermining it so they fall right down, so they have to start all over again. I liken it to a carrot. You know, once you've gotten the carrot, who's going to put the other carrot out there?

The senior Langdon's "carrot" had been his perseverance, leading him forward. Although his essence had been saved on film and on scraps of paper containing reviews and interviews, Langdon might have doubted these ephemera would outlast him. But he also knew too well that fate always has a trick up its sleeve. He based his career on it, and he let his character enact that belief. Both in the movies and in life, Harry Langdon knew that sooner or later, fate would smile upon a lost soul.

The worldwide festivals organized by Rohauer—in Berlin, Paris, and Tehran, to name just a few cities—were devoted to the best of Harry Langdon, and critics and public alike were enthusiastic. Mabel Langdon received a plaque at the Berlin Film Festival in 1967 honoring her husband—an overdue tribute by the industry. The coveted award from the International Committee for the Spreading of the Arts and Letters of the Cinema (CIDALC) has been presented to major film figures such as Hal Roach Sr., Louis B. Mayer, Walt Disney, and Charlie Chaplin. The presentation speech captured a renewed appreciation for Harry Langdon:

> I desire to thank Dr. Alfred Bauer [coordinator of the festival] and Mr. Rohauer for having given the occasion to the CIDALC to deliver his "Medal of Gold" posthumously to Harry Langdon, thus expressing a proper homage to his memory.
>
> This memory, Madame [Mabel Langdon], we hold as not only precious, but still living.
>
> Harry Langdon, last seen in the company of the grand comics of his era, has brought us, in his numerous films, this blend of burlesque and tragic art, which enabled us to get through, in watching him evolve on the screen, in laughter as well as the deepest emotion.
>
> How could we forget "Full of Boots" [*Tramp, Tramp, Tramp*], "His Last Pants" [*Long Pants*], "Father for a Day" [*Three's a Crowd*], just to mention a few. How could we forget these very human and moving films.
>
> In this era in which we live we are subjected to tragic events and brutality in cinematic art, the nervous irritation of life, its speed, its mechanization makes for films which lack the sense which we loved, which our generation regrets, and we miss those who, like your husband, brought us relaxation of tension, emotion, and laughter.
>
> This is why, Madame, the CIDALC is happy to give you this

"Medal" to express to you all the admiration that we have for the work of Harry Langdon.

A Hollywood "Walk of Fame" star was dedicated to Langdon in 1960 and is fittingly located in front of the epitome of classic Hollywood glamour and grandeur, the former Grauman's Chinese Theatre. On May 15, 1999, the Council Bluffs Arts Council honored its native son by transforming a 1.5-mile segment of Old Highway 375 into a street divided by a landscaped median and naming it Harry Langdon Boulevard. The ceremony included a Langdon look-alike contest, film screenings, and an antique car parade from the local library to the ribbon-cutting site—although in lieu of a ribbon, a strip of film was used. Council Bluffs continues to celebrate Langdon's birthday with annual festivities.

Langdon's films are now available to worldwide audiences. When a VHS version of Langdon's silent features was released, Frank Thompson, in the May–June 1997 issue of *Film Comment*, revisited the question of whether Langdon was indeed the "fourth genius," as Kevin Brownlow had dubbed him. Thompson also referred to the "Mount Rushmore of Silent Comedy," with Chaplin, Keaton, Lloyd, and Langdon assembled together in figurative stone: "Harry Langdon deserved a lot better than he got, both from his collaborators and from posterity. If we can find little reason to keep him on that Mount Rushmore of comedy, the three features and three shorts now available to us should at least inspire a small, delicate statue to a modest but singular talent: silly, sweet, and—at its best—inspired."

These films and all that has been written about Langdon's life and work illustrate the extremes that framed his every move. In each film, whether his character rises to the zenith of comedy or falls under the scrap of two-bit scripts, one can find what Harry Jr. called the "everyman" his father represented:

I think he was very modern and very contemporary as far as communicating with the public, with great masses of people. . . . I wonder if he had tapped into something . . . that reaches into the subconscious of the observer, the viewer, the psyche, subliminally, more than the obvious, literal, rational, spoken word that came . . . when the talkies came in. And yet, on the other hand, he was very careful to disguise himself in the costumes of the average guy. . . . All of them, the Lloyds, the Chaplins, they were all just wonderful at allowing the public to relate to them. . . . They had finally tapped into the true ability to communicate and move and sway great masses of people at their will.

Even the surrealists considered Langdon, of all the silent comedians, the greatest personification of their perceptions of the world, creating a cultlike aura around him. Luis Buñuel claimed Langdon's films were "far more surrealist than those of Man Ray," and Salvador Dalí praised Langdon in his essay " . . . Always above Music, Harry Langdon," calling him "one of the purest flowers of the screen and of our CIVILIZATION as well."[16]

World-famous mime Marcel Marceau caught Langdon's essence in words: "He was a unique artist always on the verge of tears who could make us laugh or cry under the Rule of an Eternal Law which leads men to seek for compassion."[17] Langdon's life story and work document one individual's strengths and weaknesses. Though he sometimes failed, he still survived, which is all a human can do. When he succeeded, Harry Langdon gave the world his greatest gift—a gentle and abiding comedy.

Acknowledgments

It was a fateful string of coincidences, the kind that silent comedy and happy endings thrive on. On my birthday in 2014, a year after my mother passed away, I received an unexpected e-mail from Heather at the University Press of Kentucky, asking me to review a book proposal. Feeling an optimism that I sorely needed, I immediately accepted and began to think that perhaps I could also ask whether the press would be interested in some of my film book ideas.

Not long after, I received an encouraging e-mail from Patrick McGilligan, the press's film book series adviser. He mentioned that the press was presently pursuing biographies and asked whether I would be interested. I hemmed and hawed and wondered if I could. And then I realized that exactly thirty years earlier I had in fact worked on a biography that had never been published. The proverbial wheels started spinning: How about a biography of Harry Langdon?

Not long after, the press okayed the idea, and I contacted Harry Langdon Jr. out of the blue, hoping he would still be interested. He was and proved to be extraordinarily helpful as he dug out albums and old papers and polished photos until I could almost hear them speak.

Two years later, the light of recognition shines again on Harry Langdon, in a biography that presents his work and words, his roots, his golden silence, and his legacy. It was through this set of unexpected coincidences that I came to see this misunderstood comedian with new insight as a person who never gave up despite making some embarrassing, costly, and ill-conceived decisions—as most of us do at some point or other. Contrary to a major misperception, Langdon had a happy ending in many ways. And he, most mysteriously, came along at a low point in my life to help me realize that mistakes can be remedied, tragedies can lead to celebration, and good things come full circle sooner or later if one keeps believing they will.

Acknowledgments

I wish to thank Patrick McGilligan for his advice and support. I could not figure out why his name seemed so familiar when he sent me the first e-mail that launched this journey. Not long after, I realized his multivolume *Backstory: Interviews with Screenwriters* had inspired me to undertake my first book on interviews with film editors in 1989. I owe him my gratitude for this too—another coincidence come full circle.

I am grateful to Anne Dean Dotson and Patrick O'Dowd at the University Press of Kentucky for their editorial expertise, encouragement, and eagerness to make this book a reality so quickly. Thanks as well to all members of the editorial and design staff at the press. A special thank you to Linda Lotz for her meticulous editorial review of the manuscript, catching all the odd phrasings I could no longer see on my own.

I am most indebted to the anonymous readers whose reports were so constructive and helpful in understanding the manuscript's strengths and weaknesses that I almost cried for joy, even though I knew their comments meant I had to do *major* revisions. They actually gave me the courage to look at the manuscript with objective curiosity, disperse thirty-year-old shadows, and trust my voice to bring Langdon back to life.

Thank you, Harry Jr. I could not have done this without you. I will always treasure the memories of our "teamwork" via e-mail.

G. O.

Filmography

This filmography was culled from those published by Rheuban and by Harter and Hayde. Cast names were selected from the credits; not all names are included. The films are listed by date of release, not production.

Picking Peaches. February 3, 1924. Mack Sennett–Pathé. Dir. Erle C. Kenton. Photography: George Spear. Titles: John A. Waldron. Harry Langdon (hereafter, HL), Irene Lentz, Alberta Vaughn, Ethel Teare, Dot Farley, Horace "Kewpie" Morgan, Vernon Dent. 2 reels.

Smile, Please. March 2, 1924. Mack Sennett–Pathé. Dir. Roy Del Ruth. Photography: George Spear. Titles: John A. Waldron. HL, Alberta Vaughn, Jack Cooper, Madeline Hurlock, Roscoe "Tiny" Ward, Jackie Lucas, Andy Clyde, Louise Carver, Cameo the Dog. 2 reels.

Shanghaied Lovers. March 30, 1924. Mack Sennett–Pathé. Dir. Roy Del Ruth. Photography: George Spear. Titles: John A. Waldron. Editor: William Hornbeck. HL, Alice Day, Kalla Pasha, Roscoe "Tiny" Ward, Andy Clyde. 2 reels.

Flickering Youth. April 27, 1924. Mack Sennett–Pathé. Dir. Erle C. Kenton. Photography: George Spear, Bob Ladd. Titles: John A. Waldron. HL, Alice Day, Ray Grey, Charlotte Mineau, Louise Carver, Charlie Murray, Andy Clyde. 2 reels.

The Cat's Meow. May 25, 1924. Mack Sennett–Pathé. Dir. Roy Del Ruth. Photography: Billy Williams, Leland Davis. Titles: John A. Waldron. Editor: William Hornbeck. HL, Alice Day, Kalla Pasha, Lucile Thorndike, Roscoe "Tiny" Ward, Madeline Hurlock, Louise Carver. 2 reels.

His New Mamma. June 22, 1924. Mack Sennett–Pathé. Dir. Roy Del Ruth. Photography: Billy Williams. Titles: John A. Waldron. Editor: William Hornbeck. HL, Madeline Hurlock, Alice Day, Andy Clyde, Roscoe "Tiny" Ward, Jack Cooper. 2 reels.

The First Hundred Years. August 17, 1924. Mack Sennett–Pathé. Dir. Harry Sweet. Photography: George Crocker, Billy Williams. Titles: John A. Waldron. Editor: William Hornbeck. HL, Alice Day, Frank J. Coleman, Louise Carver, Madeline Hurlock. 2 reels.

The Luck o' the Foolish. September 14, 1924. Mack Sennett–Pathé. Dir. Harry Edwards. Photography: Billy Williams. Titles: John A. Waldron. HL, Marceline Day, Madeline Hurlock, Frank Coleman. 2 reels.

The Hansom Cabman. October 12, 1924. Mack Sennett–Pathé. Dir. Harry Edwards. Photography: Vernon Walker, Leland Davis. Titles: John A. Waldron. Editor: William Hornbeck. HL, Madeline Day, Charlotte Mineau, Andy Clyde, Madeline Hurlock, Leo Sulky. 2 reels.

All Night Long. November 9, 1924. Mack Sennett–Pathé. Dir. Harry Edwards. Photography: Billy Williams, Leland Davis. Titles: John A. Waldron. Editor: William Hornbeck. Story: Vernon Smith, Hal Conklin. HL, Natalie Kingston, Fanny Kelly, Vernon Dent, Billy Gilbert. 2 reels.

Feet of Mud. December 7, 1924. Mack Sennett–Pathé. Dir. Harry Edwards. Photography: Billy Williams, Leland Davis. Titles: John A. Waldron. Editor: William Hornbeck. HL, Florence D. Lea, Natalie Kingston, Yorke Sherwood, Vernon Dent, Malcom Waite. 2 reels.

The Sea Squawk. January 4, 1925. Mack Sennett–Pathé. Dir. Harry Edwards. Photography: Vernon Walker, George Unholz. Titles: John A. Waldron. HL, Eugenia Gilbert, Christian J. Frank, Charlotte Mineau, Budd Ross, Leo Sulky. 2 reels.

Boobs in the Woods. February 1, 1925. Mack Sennett–Pathé. Dir. Harry Edwards. Photography: Billy Williams, Leland Davis. Titles: John A. Waldron. Editor: William Hornbeck. Story: Arthur Ripley. HL, Marie Astaire, Vernon Dent, Leo Willis. 2 reels.

His Marriage Wow. March 1, 1925. Mack Sennett–Pathé. Dir. Harry Edwards. Photography: Billy Williams, Leland Davis. Titles: Felix Adler, A. H. Giebler. Editor: William Hornbeck. HL, Natalie Kingston, Vernon Dent, William McCall. 2 reels.

Plain Clothes. March 29, 1925. Mack Sennett–Pathé. Dir. Harry Edwards. Photography: Billy Williams, Earl L. Stafford. Titles: Felix Adler, A. H. Giebler. Editor: William Hornbeck. Story: Arthur Ripley, Frank Capra. HL, Claire Cushman, Vernon Dent, Jean Hathaway, William McCall. 2 reels.

Remember When? April 26, 1925. Mack Sennett–Pathé. Dir. Harry Edwards. Photography: Billy Williams, Leland Davis. Titles: Felix Adler, A. H. Giebler. Editor: William Hornbeck. Story: Arthur Ripley, Clyde Bruckman. HL, Natalie Kingston, Vernon Dent, Anna May the Elephant. 2 reels.

Horace Greeley Jr. June 7, 1925. Principal Pictures–Pathé. Dir. Alf Goulding. Titles: Robert Hopkins. Story: John Grey. HL, June Marlowe. 2 reels.

The White Wing's Bride. July 12, 1925. Principal Pictures–Pathé. Dir. Alf Goulding. Titles: Robert Hopkins. Story: John Grey. HL, June Marlowe, Helen Walton. 2 reels.

Lucky Stars. August 16, 1925. Mack Sennett–Pathé. Dir. Harry Edwards. Photography: George Crocker. Titles: A. H. Giebler. Editor: William Hornbeck. Story: Arthur Ripley, Frank Capra. HL, Natalie Kingston, Vernon Dent, Andy Clyde. 2 reels.

There He Goes. November 29, 1925. Mack Sennett–Pathé. Dir. Harry Edwards. Photography: Billy Williams. Editor: William Hornbeck. Story: Frank Capra, Arthur Ripley. HL, Peggy Montgomery, Frank Whitson, Vernon Dent, Andy Clyde. 3 reels.

Saturday Afternoon. January 31, 1926. Mack Sennett–Pathé. Dir. Harry Edwards. Photography: Billy Williams. Titles: A. H. Giebler. Editor: William Hornbeck. Story: Arthur Ripley, Frank Capra. HL, Alice Ward, Vernon Dent, Ruth Hiatt, Peggy Montgomery. 3 reels.

Tramp, Tramp, Tramp. March 21, 1926. Harry Langdon Corporation–First National. Dir. Harry Edwards. Photography: Elgin Lessley, George Spear. Titles: George Marion Jr. Story: Arthur Ripley, Frank Capra. Adaptation: Tim Whelan, Hal Conklin, J. Frank Holliday, Gerald Duffy, Murray Roth. HL, Joan Crawford, Edwards Davis, Carlton Griffin, Alec B. Francis, Brooks Benedict, Tom Murray. 62 min.

Ella Cinders. June 6, 1926. John McCormick–First National. Dir. Alfred E. Green. Photography: Arthur Martinelli. Titles: George Marion Jr. Editor: Robert J. Kern. Story: Mervyn LeRoy, Frank Griffin. Colleen Moore, Lloyd Hughes, Vera Lewis, Doris Baker, Emily Gerdes, Mike Donlin, Jed Prouty, HL (unbilled guest appearance). 72 min.

The Strong Man. September 19, 1926. Harry Langdon Corporation–First National. Dir. Frank Capra. Photography: Elgin Lessley, Glen Kerschner. Titles: Reed Heustis. Editor: Harold Young. Comedy Construction: Clarence Hennecke. Story: Arthur Ripley. Adaptation: Tim Whelan, Frank Capra, Tay Garnett, James Langdon, Hal Conklin, Murray Roth. HL, Priscilla Bonner, Gertrude Astor, William V. Mong, Robert McKim, Arthur Thalasso. 70 min.

Long Pants. April 10, 1927. Harry Langdon Corporation–First National. Dir. Frank Capra. Photography: Elgin Lessley. Story: Arthur Ripley. Adaptation: Robert Eddy. Comedy Construction: Clarence Hennecke. HL, Priscilla Bonner, Gladys Brockwell, Alan Roscoe, Alma Bennett, Betty Francisco. 61 min.

His First Flame. May 8, 1927. Mack Sennett–Pathé. Dir. Harry Edwards. Photography: Billy Williams. Titles: Tay Garnett. Editor: William Hornbeck. Story: Arthur Ripley, Frank Capra. HL, Natalie Kingston, Ruth Hiatt, Vernon Dent, Bud Jamison, Dot Farley. 52 min.

Three's a Crowd. August 28, 1927. Harry Langdon Corporation–First National. Dir. Harry Langdon. Photography: Elgin Lessley, Frank Evans. Editor: Alfred DeGaetano. Story: Arthur Ripley. Adaptation: James Langdon, Robert Eddy. HL, Gladys McConnell, Cornelius Keefe, Arthur Thalasso, Henry Barrows, Frances Raymond, Agnes Steele, Brooks Benedict. 56 min.

Fiddlesticks. November 27, 1927. Mack Sennett–Pathé. Dir. Harry Edwards. Photography: Billy Williams. Titles: Tay Garnett. Editor: William Hornbeck. Story: Arthur Ripley, Frank Capra. HL, Ruth Hiatt, Vernon Dent, Billy Gilbert. 2 reels.

The Chaser. February 12, 1928. Harry Langdon Corporation–First National. Dir. Harry Langdon. Photography: Elgin Lessley, Frank Evans. Editor: Alfred DeGaetano. Story: Arthur Ripley. Comedy Construction (Adaptation): Clarence Hennecke, Robert Eddy, Harry McCoy. HL, Gladys McConnell, Helen Hayward, William "Bud" Jamison, Charles Thurston. 63 min.

Heart Trouble. August 12, 1928. Harry Langdon Corporation–First National. Dir. Harry Langdon. Photography: Dev Jennings, Frank Evans. Titles: Gardner Bradford. Editor: Alfred DeGaetano. Story: Arthur Ripley. Adaptation: Earl Rodney, Clarence Hennecke. HL, Doris Dawson, Lionel Belmore, Madge Hunt, Bud Jamison, Mark Hamilton, Nelson McDowell, Blanche Payson. 58 min.

Soldier Man. September 30, 1928. Mack Sennett–Pathé. Dir. Harry Edwards. Photography: Billy Williams. Titles: A. H. Giebler. Editor: William Hornbeck. Story: Arthur Ripley, Frank Capra. HL, Natalie Kingston, Frank Whitson, Vernon Dent. 3 reels.

Voice of Hollywood A7. Summer 1929. Tec-Art Studios–Tiffany Productions. Producer: Louis Lewyn. Taylor Holmes, Montague Love, Beth Mehaffy Hawaiians, Harry Jolson, Lola Lane, Gus Edwards and Armida, Lew Cody, HL. 1 reel.

Hotter than Hot. August 17, 1929. Hal Roach–MGM. Dir. Lewis R. Foster. Photography: George Stevens. Editor: Richard Currier. Story: H. M. Walker. HL, Thelma Todd, Edgar Kennedy, Frank Austin, Edith Kramer. 2 reels.

Sky Boy. October 5, 1929. Hal Roach–MGM. Dir. Charley Rogers. Photography: George Stevens. Editor: Richard Currier. Story: Leo McCarey. HL, Thelma Todd, Eddie Dunn. 2 reels.

Skirt Shy. November 30, 1929. Hal Roach–MGM. Dir. Charles Rogers. Photography: George Stevens. Editor: Richard Currier. Story: H. M. Walker. HL, May Wallace, Tom Ricketts, Nancy Dover, Arthur Thalasso, Charlie Hall. 2 reels.

The Head Guy. January 11, 1930. Hal Roach–MGM. Dir. Fred L. Guiol. Photography: George Stevens. Editor: Richard Currier. Story: H. M. Walker. HL, Thelma Todd, Nancy Dover, Eddie Dunn, Edgar Kennedy. 2 reels.

The Fighting Parson. February 22, 1930. Hal Roach–MGM. Dir. Charles Rogers, Fred L. Guiol. Photography: George Stevens. Editor: Richard Currier. Story Editor: H. M. Walker. HL, Nancy Dover, Thelma Todd, Eddie Dunn, Leo Willis, Charlie Hall. 2 reels.

The Big Kick. March 29, 1930. Hal Roach-MGM. Dir. Warren Doane. Photography: George Stevens. Editor: Richard Currier. Story: H. M. Walker. HL, Nancy Dover, Edgar Kennedy, Bob Kortman, Sam Lufkin. 2 reels.

The Shrimp. May 3, 1930. Hal Roach–MGM. Dir. Charley Rogers. Photography: Art Lloyd. Editor: Richard Currier. Story: H. M. Walker. HL, Thelma Todd, Nancy Drexel, James Mason, Max Davidson. 2 reels.

The King. June 14, 1930. Hal Roach-MGM. Dir. James W. Horne, Charles Rogers. Photography: Len Powers. Editor: Richard Currier. Story: H. M. Walker. HL, Thelma Todd, Dorothy Granger, James Parrott. 2 reels.

A Soldier's Plaything. November 1, 1930. Warner Brothers. Dir. Michael Curtiz. Photography: Barney McGill. Story: Viña Delmar. Screenplay: Perry Vekroff. HL, Lotti Loder, Ben Lyon, Jean Hersholt, Noah Beery, Fred Kohler, Marie Astaire. 66 min.

See America Thirst. November 24, 1930. Universal. Dir. William James Craft. Photography: Arthur C. Miller. Screenplay: Jerry Horwin, Edward Ludwig, Vin Moore. HL, Slim Summerville, Bessie Love, Matthew Betz, Mitchell Lewis, Stanley Fields, Tom Kennedy, Walter Brennan. 89 min.

The Big Flash. November 6, 1932. Mermaid–Educational. Dir. Arvid E. Gillstrom. Story: Robert Vernon, Frank Griffin. HL, Vernon Dent, Lita Chevret, Ruth Hiatt, Matthew Betz, King Baggot, Jack Grey, Bobby Dunn. 2 reels.

Tired Feet. January 1, 1933. Mermaid–Educational. Dir. Arvid E. Gillstrom. Story: Robert Vernon, Frank Griffin. HL, Vernon Dent, Shirley Blake, Maidena Armstrong, Eddie Baker, William Irving, Leslie Goodwin. 2 reels.

Hallelujah, I'm a Bum. January 27, 1933. United Artists. Dir. Lewis Milestone. Photography: Lucien Andriot. Story: Ben Hecht. Adaptation: S. N. Behrman. Music and Lyrics: Richard Rodgers, Lorenz Hart. HL, Al Jolson, Madge Evans, Frank Morgan, Chester Conklin, Tyler Booke, Bert Roach. 100 min.

The Hitch Hiker. February 12, 1933. Mermaid–Educational. Dir. Arvid E. Gillstrom. Story: Robert Vernon, Frank Griffin. HL, Vernon Dent, Ruth Clifford, William Irving, Chris Marie Meeker. 2 reels.

Knight Duty. May 7, 1933. Mermaid–Educational. Dir. Arvid E. Gillstrom. Story: Dean Ward, William Watson. HL, Vernon Dent, Matthew Betz, Lita Chevret, Nell O'Day. 2 reels.

Tied for Life. July 2, 1933. Mermaid–Educational. Dir. Arvid E. Gillstrom. Story: Dean Ward, Vernon Dent. HL, Vernon Dent, Nell O'Day, Mabel Forrest, Elaine Whipple, Eddie Baker. 2 reels.

Hollywood on Parade A6. 1933. Paramount. Producer: Louis Lewyn. Alvin "Shipwreck" Kelly, El Brendel, Viola Dana, Jimmie Thompson, Bing Crosby, HL. (Silent footage included stars such as Joe E. Brown, Charlie Chaplin, Paulette Goddard, Lupe Vélez, Mary Pickford, and others.) 1 reel.

Marriage Humor. August 18, 1933. Paramount. Dir. Harry Edwards. Photography: Gus Peterson. Editor: Jack English. Story: Dean Ward, Vernon Dent. HL, Vernon Dent, Nancy Dover, Ethel Sykes, Eddie Shubert. 2 reels.

Hooks and Jabs. August 25, 1933. Mermaid–Educational. Dir. Arvid E. Gillstrom.

Story: Dean Ward, Vernon Dent. HL, Vernon Dent, Nell O'Day, William Irving, Frank Moran. 2 reels.

The Stage Hand. September 8, 1933. Mermaid–Educational. Dir. Harry Edwards. Photography: George Weber, Frank Zucker. Story: HL, Edward Davis. HL, Marel Foster, Ira Hayward, Eddie Shubert. 2 reels.

My Weakness. September 1933. B. G. DeSylva–Fox. Dir. David Butler. Photography: Arthur Miller. Writer: B. G. DeSylva. Adaptation: David Butler. Music and Lyrics: B. G. DeSylva, Richard Whiting, Leo Robbins. Lilian Harvey, Lew Ayres, Charles Butterworth, HL, Sid Silvers, Irene Bentley. 7 reels.

On Ice. October 6, 1933. Paramount. Dir. Arvid E. Gillstrom. Photography: Gus Peterson. Story: Dean Ward, Vernon Dent. Editor: Jack English. HL, Vernon Dent, Eleanor Hunt, Ethel Sykes, Kewpie Morgan, Ruth Clifford, Diana Seaby, William Irving. 2 reels.

A Roaming Romeo. December 29, 1933. Paramount. Dir. Arvid E. Gillstrom. Photography: Gus Peterson. Story: Dean Ward, Vernon Dent. Editor: Jack English. HL, Vernon Dent, Nell O'Day, Jack Henderson, Les Goodwins. 2 reels.

A Circus Hoodoo. February 16, 1934. Arvid E. Gillstrom Production–Paramount. Dir. Arvid E. Gillstrom. Photography: Gus Peterson. Story: Dean Ward, Vernon Dent. Editor: Jack English. HL, Vernon Dent, Eleanor Hunt, Matthew Betz, Diana Seaby, James Morton, Tom Kennedy. 2 reels.

Petting Preferred. April 27, 1934. Arvid E. Gillstrom Production–Paramount. Dir. Arvid E. Gillstrom. Photography: Gus Peterson. Editor: Jack English. Story: Jack Townley. Adaptation: Dean Ward, Vernon Dent. HL, Vernon Dent, Dorothy Granger, Eddie Baker, Alyce Ardell. 2 reels.

Counsel on De Fence. October 25, 1934. Columbia. Dir. Arthur Ripley. Photography: Benjamin Kline. Story and Screenplay: Harry McCoy. HL, Renée Whitney, Earle Foxe, Marjorie "Babe" Kane, Jack Norton. 2 reels.

Shivers. December 24, 1934. Columbia. Dir. Arthur Ripley. Photography: George Meehan. Editor: William Alyon. Story: Arthur Ripley. HL, Florence Lake, Richard Elliott. 2 reels.

His Bridal Sweet. March 15, 1935. Columbia. Dir. Alf Goulding. Photography: Benjamin Kline. Story and Screenplay: John Grey. HL, Billy Gilbert, Geneva Mitchell, Bud Jamison. 2 reels.

Love, Honor and Obey (the Law). April 29, 1935. Goodrich (B. F.) Company. Dir. Leigh Jason. Writer: Stanley E. Rauh. HL, Monty Collins, Diana Lewis. 2 reels.

The Leather Necker. May 9, 1935. Columbia. Dir. Arthur Ripley. Photography: John Stumar. Story: Arthur Ripley. Screenplay: John Grey. HL, Mona Rico, Wade Boteler, Bud Jamison. 2 reels.

Atlantic Adventure. September 10, 1935. Columbia. Dir. Albert S. Rogell. Photography: John Stumar. Editor: Ted Kent. Story: Diana Bourbon. Screenplay: John T. Neville, Nat Dorfman. HL, Nancy Carroll, Lloyd Nolan, Arthur Hohl, Robert Middlemass, John Wray, E. E. Clive. 68 min.

His Marriage Mix-up. October 31, 1935. Columbia. Dir. Preston Black [Jack White]. Photography: Benjamin Kline. Editor: Charles Hochberg. Story: Vernon Dent. HL, Dorothy Granger. 2 reels.

I Don't Remember. December 26, 1935. Columbia. Dir. Preston Black [Jack White]. Photography: Benjamin Kline. Story: Preston Black. HL, Geneva Mitchell, Mary Carr, Vernon Dent, Robert "Bobby" Burns. 2 reels.

A Doggone Mixup. February 4, 1938. Columbia. Dir. Charles Lamont. Photography: Benjamin Kline. Editor: Charles Nelson. Story and Screenplay: Elwood Ullman, Al Giebler, Charles Nelson. HL, Ann Doran, Vernon Dent, Bud Jamison, Eddie Fetherstone, Bess Flowers, Sarah Edwards, James C. Morton. 2 reels.

He Loved an Actress [aka *Mad about Money*]. March 25, 1938. Henry Barnes Production for British Lion–Grand National. Dir. Melville W. Brown. Screenplay: John Meehan Jr. Musical Score: James Dyrenforth, Kenneth Leslie-Smith. HL, Lupe Vélez, Wallace Ford, Ben Lyon, Jean Colin, Cyril Raymond, Mary Cole. 77 min.

Sue My Lawyer. September 16, 1938. Columbia. Dir. Jules White. Photography: George Meehan. Story: HL. Screenplay: Ewart Adamson. HL, Ann Doran, Monty Collins, Bud Jamison, Vernon Dent, Cy Schindell, Don Brody, Charles Doherty, Jack "Tiny" Lipson, Robert "Bobby" Burns. 2 reels.

There Goes My Heart. October 15, 1938. Hal Roach–United Artists. Dir. Norman Z. McLeod. Photography: Norbert Brodine. Editor: William Terhune. Story: Ed Sullivan. Screenplay: Eddie Moran, Jack Jevne. Fredric March, Virginia Bruce, Patsy Kelly, Alan Mowbray, Eugene Pallette, Arthur Lake, Claude Gillingwater, Etienne Girardot, Nancy Carroll, Marjorie Main, HL (unbilled). 81 min.

Zenobia. March 14, 1939. Hal Roach–United Artists. Dir. Gordon Douglas. Photographer: Karl Struss. Editor: Bert Jordan. Story: Walter De Leon, Arnold Belgard. Screenplay: Corey Ford. HL, Oliver Hardy, Billie Burke, Alice Brady, James Ellison, Jean Parker, June Lang, Olin Howland, J. Farrell MacDonald, Stepin Fetchit, Hattie McDaniel. 71 min.

Sitting Pretty. 1940. Jam Handy Picture Service Production. HL.

Goodness! A Ghost. July 5, 1940. RKO. Dir. Harry D'Arcy. Photography: Harry Wild. Editor: John Lockert. Story: George Jeske, Arthur V. Jones. Screenplay: HL. HL, Tiny Sanford, J. C. Morton. 2 reels.

Cold Turkey. October 18, 1940. Columbia. Dir. Del Lord. Photography: Lucien Ballard. Story and Screenplay: Harry Edwards, Elwood Ullman. HL, Ann Doran, Monty Collins, Vernon Dent, Bud Jamison, Eddie Laughton. 2 reels.

Misbehaving Husbands. December 12, 1940. Producers' Releasing Corporation. Dir. William Beaudine. Photography: Art Reed. Editor: Robert Crandall.

Screenplay: Vernon Smith, Claire Parrish. HL, Betty Blythe, Ralph Byrd, Esther Muir, Gayne Whitman, Florence Wright, Luana Walters, Gertrude Astor. 65 min.

All-American Co-ed. October 7, 1941. Hal Roach–United Artists. Dir. LeRoy Prinz. Photography: Robert Pittack. Editor: Bert Jordan. Frances Langford, Johnny Downs, Marjorie Woodworth, Noah Beery Jr., HL, Esther Dale, Alan Hale Jr. 48 min.

Double Trouble. November 17, 1941. Monogram Pictures Corporation. Dir. William West. Photography: Arthur Martinelli. Editor: Carl Pierson. Story: HL. Screenplay: Jack Natteford. HL, Ruth Hiatt, Charles Rogers, Catherine Lewis, Dave O'Brien, Louise Currie, Frank Jaquet, Benny Rubin. 63 min.

House of Errors. March 26, 1942. Producers' Releasing Corporation. Dir. Bernard B. Ray. Photography: Robert Cline. Editor: Dan Milner. Story: HL. Screenplay: Ewart Adamson, Eddie M. Davis. HL, Charles Rogers, Marian Marsh, Ray Walker, John Holland, Betty Blythe, Vernon Dent. 77 min.

What Makes Lizzy Dizzy? March 26, 1942. Columbia. Dir. Jules White. Photography: Benjamin Kline. Editor: Jerome Thoms. Story: Philip L. Leslie. Screenplay: Ewart Adamson. HL, Elsie Ames, Monty Collins, Lorin Raker, Dorothy Appleby, Kathryn Sabichi, Kay Vallon. 2 reels.

Tireman, Spare My Tires. June 4, 1942. Columbia. Dir. Jules White. Photography: Benjamin Kline. Editor: Jerome Thoms. Story: Felix Adler. HL, Louise Currie, Emmett Lynn, Bud Jamison. 2 reels.

Carry Harry. September 3, 1942. Columbia. Dir. Harry Edwards. Photography: L. W. O'Connell. Editor: Paul Borofsky. Story and Screenplay: Harry Edwards. HL, Elsie Ames, Barbara Pepper, Marjorie Deanne, Dave O'Brien, Stanley Blystone. 2 reels.

Piano Mooner. December 11, 1942. Columbia. Dir. Harry Edwards. Photography: Philip Tannora. Editor: Paul Borofsky. Story and Screenplay: HL. HL, Fifi D'Orsay, Gwen Kenyon, Betty Blythe, Stanley Blystone, Chester Conklin. 2 reels.

A Blitz on the Fritz. January 22, 1943. Columbia. Dir. Jules White. Photography: Arthur Martinelli. Editor: Edwin Bryant. Story and Screenplay: Clyde Bruckman. HL, Douglas Leavitt, Bud Jamison, Vernon Dent, Louise Currie, Beatrice Blinn, Jack "Tiny" Lipson, Charles Betty, Al Hill, Kit Guard, Bud Fine. 2 reels.

Blonde and Groom. April 16, 1943. Columbia. Dir. Harry Edwards. Photography: L. W. O'Connell. Story and Screenplay: HL. HL, Gwen Kenyon, Barbara Pepper. 2 reels.

Here Comes Mr. Zerk. July 23, 1943. Columbia. Dir. Jules White. Photography: Benjamin-Kline. Editor: Charles Hochberg. Story: Jack White. HL, Shirley Patterson, Hank Mann, Vernon Dent. 2 reels.

Spotlight Scandals. July 26, 1943. Banner–Monogram Pictures Corporation. Dir.

William Beaudine. Photography: Mack Stengler. Editor: Carl Pierson. Screenplay: William X. Crowley, Beryl Sachs. HL, Billy Gilbert, Frank Fay, Bonnie Baker, Butch and Buddy, Iris Adrian, The Radio Rogues, Henry King and Orchestra. 79 min.

To Heir Is Human. January 14, 1944. Columbia. Dir. Harold Goodsoe. Photography: George Meehan. Editor: Paul Borofsky. Story and Screenplay: Elwood Ullman, Monty Collins. HL, Una Merkel, Christine McIntyre, Eddie Gribbon, Lew Kelly, Vernon Dent, John Tyrrell, Snub Pollard. 2 reels.

Hot Rhythm. March 14, 1944. Monogram Pictures. Dir. William Beaudine. Photography: Ira Morgan. Editor: Richard Currier. Screenplay: Tim Ryan, Charles R. Marion. HL, Robert Lowery, Dona Drake, Tim Ryan, Irene Ryan, Sidney Miller, Robert Kent. 77 min.

Defective Detectives. April 3, 1944. Columbia. Dir. Harry Edwards. Photography: Burnett Guffey. Editor: Henry Batista. Story: Harry Edwards. HL, El Brendel, Christine McIntyre, Vernon Dent, Eddie Laughton, John Tyrrell, Snub Pollard, Dick Botiller. 2 reels.

Mopey Dope. June 16, 1944. Columbia. Dir. Del Lord. Story: Del Lord, Ellwood Ullman. HL, Christine McIntyre, Arthur Q. Bryan. 2 reels.

Block Busters. August 15, 1944. Banner–Monogram Pictures. Dir. Wallace Fox. Photography: Marcel LePicard. Editor: Carl Pierson. Story and Screenplay: Houston Branch. HL, Leo Gorcey, Huntz Hall, Gabriel Dell, Billy Benedict, Jimmy Strand, Bill Chaney, Minerva Urecal, Robert A. Smith, Noah Beery Sr. 60 min.

Snooper Service. February 4, 1945. Columbia. Dir. Harry Edwards. Story: Harry Edwards. HL, El Brendel, Vernon Dent, Rebel Randall, Dick Curtis, Fred Kelsey, Buddy Yarus. 2 reels.

Pistol Packin' Nitwits. April 4, 1945. Columbia. Dir. Harry Edwards. Photography: L. W. O'Connell. Editor: Henry Batista. Story: Edward Bernds, HL. HL, El Brendel, Christine McIntyre, Brad King, Tex Cooper, Victor Cox, Charles "Heine" Conklin. 2 reels.

Swingin' on a Rainbow. August 27, 1945. Republic. Dir. William Beaudine. Photography: Marcel LePicard. Editor: Fred Allen. Story: Olive Cooper. Screenplay: Olive Cooper, John Grey. HL, Jane Frazee, Brad Taylor, Minna Gombell, Amelia Ward, Tim Ryan, Paul Harvey. 72 min.

Notes

Introduction

1. This letter is reproduced and discussed in Chuck Harter and Michael J. Hayde, *Little Elf: A Celebration of Harry Langdon* (Duncan, OK: BearManor Media, 2012), 166.

2. William Schelly, *Harry Langdon* (Metuchen, NJ: Scarecrow Press, 1982); Joyce Rheuban, *Harry Langdon, the Comedian as Metteur-en-Scène* (Teaneck, NJ: Fairleigh Dickinson University Press, 2008).

3. William Schelly, *Harry Langdon, His Life and Films,* 2nd ed. (Jefferson, NC: McFarland, 2008), 185.

4. James L. Neibaur, *The Silent Films of Harry Langdon (1923–1928)* (Lanham, MD: Scarecrow Press, 2012).

5. Harter and Hayde, *Little Elf,* 13.

1. Vaudeville Roots

1. Census data and city directories of the time included numerous discrepancies in the spelling of names. Langdon's mother's name has appeared as Lavina, Levina, and Lovina, and her maiden name as Lookinbill, Lookabill, and Lukinville. Lavinia Lookingbill is the version most frequently used by the Langdon family. Harry's father was listed variously as William Wylie, William Warren, and William Worley Langdon. Tully, the nickname of third son James, was registered as Tulley, Tullie, and even Tillie. These records appeared in *Wild about Harry!* 2, no. 3 (Fall–Winter 1998): 76–81. Harry Langdon's nephew, also named Harry (son of Claude), cited some of this information in his interview with Raymond Rohauer and Mabel Langdon, Los Angeles, August 6, 1978.

2. The Daughters of the American Revolution commemorated this event with a monument at this site in 1911.

3. This seems to be the most accurate record of the Langdon children. Harry Langdon's nephew Donald Langdon (son of Claude) believed there was also a first-born William Jr. and another daughter named Bertha (letter from Donald Langdon to Mr. Longo, August 7, 1987, Collection of Harry Langdon Jr.). Their names

do not appear on the census, so it is likely they died at very young ages. By contrast, Harter and Hayde state that William Jr. died at eighteen years of age and Bertha died in childhood (*Little Elf*, 21).

4. The previously cited letter from Donald Langdon to Mr. Longo suggests that William was not religious, but an article by J. R. Milne entitled "Whoopee Isn't Fun—Harry Langdon," which appeared in the *Omaha World-Herald* (Sunday magazine section) on April 26, 1931, mentioned that William might have helped carry a banner in Salvation Army parades.

5. One excellent reference on the Salvation Army in America is Edward McKinley, *Marching to Glory: The History of the Salvation Army in the United States, 1880–1992* (New York: Wm. B. Eerdmans, 1995).

6. Background on the Salvation Army in Council Bluffs was provided by Susan Mitchem of the National Archives of the Salvation Army in Alexandria, Virginia, in an e-mail to Gabriella Oldham, November 5, 2015. The name of the theater has also been spelled Dohaney, Doheney, and Doheny. The Dohany Opera House later became the Strand when motion pictures supplanted vaudeville; it was remodeled in 1927 along the lines of a "movie palace," with a "glazed façade and refurbished Moorish interior" (Council Bluffs Public Library Special Collections, photo stream on flickr.com). The venue changed ownership and was remodeled several times until a fire destroyed it in 1974 (cinematreasures.org).

7. Harter and Hayde, *Little Elf*, 23. Many of the stories that have become legendary milestones in Harry's life before vaudeville have been culled from a variety of sources that were described in Langdon's later publicity releases, interviews, and newspaper articles. These could be factual, or they could be humorous embellishments, exaggerations, or outright fabrications of how Langdon became involved in show business, especially minstrel and medicine shows. Schelly (*Harry Langdon* [2008]) confirms this wellspring of possible sources, calling this time—from about 1897, when Harry left home, until he entered vaudeville approximately eight years later—"Harry Langdon's apprentice period." According to Schelly, "little documentation [about Langdon's early years] is available. Scrapbooks with fliers, ads, and other bits of memorabilia offer scant hard data, and the last thing an exuberant boy set free of his parents would do was laboriously document names, dates, and events. What is known of that period has been gleaned primarily from interviews Langdon gave after achieving movie stardom many years later" (ibid., 6). Interestingly, according to Harry Langdon Jr., his father was a meticulous collector of clippings, assembling several albums of newspaper articles that covered his early theatrical years as well as his film career (1926–1944). Unfortunately, many of these items failed to include the publication's name and date.

8. Dorothy Herzog, "The Wistful Mr. Langdon," *Motion Picture Magazine*, October 1927, 18–19, 84–85.

9. This extraordinary family memory comes from Donald Langdon's Febru-

ary 1, 1975, letter to author Joyce Rheuban, in answer to her research questions (Collection of Harry Langdon Jr.). Donald indicated that his father, Claude, often cited this episode as the reason why Harry's voice was not optimal for sound films. However, his high, soft, sometimes quivery voice worked well for comedic effect and was the perfect vocal representation of Harry's fluttery, childlike mannerisms.

10. David Armstrong, *The Great American Medicine Show* (New York: Pren-tice-Hall General, 1991), devotes a whole chapter to the Kickapoo show, which was one of the largest and most important medicine shows in the country.

11. A full history of minstrel shows is provided in Robert C. Toll, *Blacking Up: The Minstrel Show in Nineteenth Century America* (New York: Oxford University Press, 1977).

12. According to Rheuban, while participating in various forms of popular en-tertainment, Harry "cultivated an extensive and diversified repertoire as comedian, musician, singer, dancer, acrobat, equilibrist, and 'lightning sketch artist'" (*Harry Langdon*, 29). The last talent popped up throughout Langdon's career in many dif-ferent settings.

13. Milne, "Whoopee Isn't Fun."

14. The script for "Johnny's New Car" and the scripts for the other vaudeville acts Langdon wrote and filed for copyright in the Library of Congress are excerpted in Harter and Hayde, *Little Elf*, and reproduced in their entirety in the appendices of that book: "A Night on the Boulevard: A Spectacular Travesty on Motoring," 45–48 and appendix I; "Johnny's New Car," 55–58, 66–70, and appendix II; "After the Ball: A Satire on Golfing and Motoring, in Three Scenes," 75–79 and appendix III.

15. According to Langdon's nephew Harry, the comedian and Rose also held a marriage ceremony at the rectory of a Catholic church in Wellston, Missouri, on Holy Saturday in 1910 to appease her strict Roman Catholic family and to assuage her own guilt about not being in the church's "good graces" after eloping. Langdon never converted to Catholicism but simply followed Rose's lead to keep the peace. Rose's standing with the church was vague in relation to her subsequent divorce from Langdon and her remarriage two years later to Jack Clark, a former college professor and an extra at MGM, with whom Rose occasionally acted in bit parts.

16. Harter and Hayde, *Little Elf*, 34.

17. Harter and Hayde indicate the presence of the mysterious "Cecil Langdon," who joined the act for the 1918–1919 season and remained until Harry entered the movies. Previous Langdon scholars, unable to trace the identity of Cecil, who was female, simply acknowledged her presence and let it go at that. She most definitely was not Harry's sister Gertrude, who had married Thomas Melroy in 1914 at age seventeen and was raising a family in Council Bluffs. Genealogical searches failed to turn up any Cecil Langdons among his cousins. But a 1928 *Variety* article and nephew Harry, Claude's youngest son, affirmed that Cecil Langdon had been re-

cruited from the Musolf family, leading to only one possible candidate: Rose's youngest sister, Cecilia, who was eighteen (*Little Elf*, 62). Harry adapted the act to accommodate this new female member (for example, a waiter became a waitress), but unfortunately, Cecil's participation did not garner good reviews when she performed at some top vaudeville venues. *Variety* said, "Sister Cecil will have to go into strenuous training for a stage career. Her voice is cold and hard and she is still and amateurish." Harter and Hayde conclude that Cecil must have improved with time, as they found no other unfavorable reviews, and she stayed with the act until Langdon transitioned to films.

18. Schelly, *Harry Langdon* (2008), 12.

19. Rheuban describes this illusion and draws a parallel to "certain elements specific to filmic mise-en-scène—the long take and the slow fade-out—[which] often function in the films in which Langdon appears" (*Harry Langdon*, 33). Clearly, Langdon's theatrical work would inform his filmmaking within a few years.

20. Neibaur makes parallels between this stage experience and Langdon's restrained approach that was more appropriate for film. "Despite his stage training, where broad gestures are necessary for a live audience, Langdon understood the intimacy of the moving picture camera and prided himself in being slower and more minimalist than his comic peers" (*Silent Films of Harry Langdon*, x).

21. Letter from Donald Langdon to Joyce Rheuban, March 3, 1975 (Collection of Harry Langdon Jr.).

22. Ibid.

23. Many clippings cited herein are from Langdon's self-assembled scrapbooks from the collection of Harry Langdon Jr. and are often incompletely identified, but they provide a delightful glimpse into the work of Langdon and his theatrical peers.

24. Eddie Leonard wrote the lyrics and Eddie Munson wrote the music for "Ida, Sweet as Apple Cider" in 1903. Numerous versions of the song were recorded by various artists and big bands, including Eddie Cantor, Bing Crosby, Jimmy Durante, and Frank Sinatra.

2. Golden Silence

1. This review and others of that film presentation in New York appear in George C. Pratt, *Spellbound in Darkness: History of the Silent Film* (Greenwich, CT: New York Graphic Society, 1973).

2. Rudi Blesh's biography *Keaton* (New York: Macmillan, 1966) describes Buster Keaton's entry into film after two decades in vaudeville and his father's outrage at the thought, although Joe eventually appeared in his son's films.

3. Harter and Hayde cite Harold Lloyd's June 1962 interview, in which he recalled attending Langdon's show on opening night with Hal Roach: "I told Hal that here was a natural for the screen, and I suggested that we get him out there, and Hal talk to him and sign him up.... And [Langdon] came out, and he was most willing,

but they differed on [salary]. I think it amounted to a hundred dollars a week difference. And I said, 'Well, you're very foolish, Hal.' He was easily worth that, and much more, to start with" (*Little Elf*, 83). Whether or not this version is accurate, Roach would go on to play a significant role in Langdon's post–silent film career (see chapter 3).

4. Cited in Harter and Hayde, *Little Elf*, 69.

5. This film has never been found, although Frank Capra's autobiography mentions seeing *Johnny's New Car*, presumably with Mack Sennett. Harter and Hayde question whether this film ever existed; whether Sennett photographed it "in order to plainly illustrate Langdon's individuality for the benefit of gagmen, scenario writers and directors"; and whether Rose or another actress played the part Capra described as "a dominating vulture-faced termagant." They conclude that regardless of Capra's initial evaluation of Langdon's potential, the director wanted to work with him. They emphasize that, "given the plethora of inaccuracies in [Capra's autobiography] *The Name above the Title* it's tempting to dismiss the film's existence [and other claims] as yet another of the book's fairy tales" (*Little Elf*, 113).

6. Neibaur indicates that the only existing footage of these Sol Lesser productions is three minutes of *Horace Greeley Jr.*, apparently the end of the film, which was preserved and released in later years as a 9.5mm home movie entitled *The Capture of Cactus Cal*:

> The existing footage is a funny sequence with Harry as a meek city slicker getting in the middle of a classic western gun battle, and eventually outsmarting and subduing a rustic gunfighter. The most basic elements of Langdon's character are already there, including his meek stare, his frightened reaction, and his more relaxed, leisurely approach to the situations....
>
> While the action is amusing and interesting, the limited footage that exists is not enough to assess the film or Langdon's tenure with Sol Lesser. It does allow us to realize that Langdon was already comfortable playing to the camera and was able to work within the parameters of a script and another's direction. (*Silent Films of Harry Langdon*, 8)

Harter and Hayde present extensive research that one film called *A Tough Tenderfoot* was lost, but a four-minute clip of it surfaced in a longer film titled *The Capture of Cactus Cal*, as Neibaur also mentions.

7. Langdon's initial film for Principal Pictures changed titles from *The New Mail Man* to *The Skyscraper* to *The Greenhorn*, and while publicity photos and scenes are available, the footage has never been found. For a discussion of *The Skyscraper*, see Harter and Hayde, *Little Elf*, 91.

8. The handwritten notes related to this agreement are reproduced in Rheuban's book. In her view, "The terms of this contract confirm . . . Langdon's true stature as a comic artist at the time of his entry into motion picture comedies"

(*Harry Langdon,* 27). Indeed, the contract terms suggest that the promise and potential Sennett saw in Langdon were greater than time and tradition have led subsequent generations to believe.

9. Mack Sennett with Cameron Shipp, *King of Comedy* (1954; reprint, San Francisco: Mercury House, 1990), 140–42.

10. During his interview with Langdon's nephew Harry, Raymond Rohauer mentioned an informal interview with Harold Lloyd. According to Rohauer, Lloyd had caught Langdon's act at the Orpheum Theater in Los Angeles and "was so impressed with him that he called up Mack Sennett and said, 'I want to take you down there.'" They visited Langdon backstage, and Sennett signed him up on the spot. Rohauer reflected that "[Lloyd] had hardly anything to say about Keaton or Chaplin . . . but he must have spent one full hour talking about Harry." Langdon's nephew suggested that Lloyd might have felt a particular bond with his uncle, sharing not only the same initials but also midwestern roots (Lloyd was born in Nebraska), despite their distinctly different personas.

11. In an interview with Raymond Rohauer and Mabel Langdon in Los Angeles on August 9, 1978, Eunice Dent Friend spoke of her deceased first husband's background and confirmed his warm friendship with Langdon: "Oh, [Vernon] dearly loved Harry . . . they understood each other. It was really a touching association for both of them. I felt that as soon as I saw them together originally." According to Eunice, Dent, who was a widower when she met him, was "sweet, gentle, and very sensible, with his feet on the ground." But he did not mind losing his footing to catch her attention: "When I first met him he used to trip just to amuse me, and in the beginning I really thought he was going to get hurt. But he knew instinctively how to do these things. He was part stuntman . . . he learned this at a very early age. There was no training. . . . He had no fear of falling." Ironically, one small injury—Vernon hurt his toe with his new electric lawn mower—revealed the diabetes that ultimately led to his death.

12. Quoted in Neibaur, *Silent Films of Harry Langdon,* 9. Neibaur points out an interesting fact: Jack Cooper, who had a small part in *Picking Peaches,* was initially intended to star in the film; likewise, Harry Gribbon was supposed to star in *Smile, Please.* It was common for studio writers to have a particular comedian in mind when they wrote a script, only to have the film become a kind of screen test for a newcomer. These films gauged "such rudimentary things as how he comes across on screen and responds to the camera. It does indicate how easily Sennett's comedians could settle into a standard script and that few had distinct enough personalities to separate themselves from an average gaggle of comics who made little real impact on screen history. Langdon, however, was distinct, and that is why these more rudimentary scripts were less effective for him" (ibid., 16). Cooper appeared in *Smile, Please* as well, suggesting that Sennett may have been considering a Langdon-Cooper duo.

13. Cited in Harter and Hayde, *Little Elf,* 95.

14. Cited in Schelly, *Harry Langdon* (2008), 25–26.

15. Current research indicates that Langdon's only silent films that remain "lost" or "partially lost" are the shorts *Flickering Youth* (1924), *The Cat's Meow* (1924), *His New Mamma* (1924), and *There He Goes* (1925), as well as *Heart Trouble* (1928), his last silent film feature before his transition to talkies. Given the surprising number of stills available from *Heart Trouble,* however, a very useful and insightful "script" was assembled consisting of a richly illustrated synopsis of the film; see Harter and Hayde, *Little Elf,* appendix V, 647–55.

16. Taylor and Lane quoted in Harter and Hayde, *Little Elf,* 103.

17. Frank Capra, *The Name above the Title* (New York: Macmillan, 1971), 59–60.

18. Ibid., 62–63.

19. In "Dialogue on Film," conducted by the American Film Institute in October 1978, Capra shared the single words he associated with each of the four great comedians of the silent era: Chaplin, wit; Lloyd, speed; Keaton, stoicism; and Langdon, innocence.

20. Capra, *The Name above the Title,* 60–61.

21. Herzog's article is reproduced in its entirety in Harter and Hayde, *Little Elf,* appendix VI, 670–71.

22. The depiction of the Chinese in *Feet of Mud* is stereotypical of the time, as was Langdon's earlier film *The Cat's Meow,* which was shot partly in Chinatown. Press releases blatantly perpetuated stereotypical Chinese elements to promote *The Cat's Meow;* this excerpt (cited in Harter and Hayde, *Little Elf,* 99, 101) reveals the rampant racism that pervaded filmmaking at the time:

> Since becoming a mah jongg fan, Harry Langdon, Sennett's star comedian, has solved his problem of the tedious waits "between scenes" while the property boys dress the sets.
>
> Recently when "The Cat's Meow" company went on location to Los Angeles's Chinatown, Langdon anticipated a thrill when he would have a game in a real Chinese atmosphere. Madeline Hurlock, the beautiful Sennett vampire, and Alice Day, Langdon's leading woman, looked forward to giving the yellow men a thrill, too, with their clever maneuvering of the bamboos, flowers, dragons and other characters.
>
> But their disappointment was keen when a couple of loitering Chinamen watched the preparations of the game, and then sauntered lazily off in the opposite direction. Langdon then tried to attract the attention of another Chink in terms of pong, chow and mah jongg, but was informed with an apologetic shrug that the celestial "no speakee American."
>
> The Sennett players thought this the last straw until they discovered a couple of Chinese children stealing off with several of their tiles, trying to eat them for candy.

23. Cited in Simon Louvish, *Keystone: The Life and Clowns of Mack Sennett* (New York: Faber and Faber, 2003), 224.

24. In *King of Comedy*, Sennett retrospectively acknowledged the many failures in Langdon's life that led to his downfall, including the inevitable "straying" that spelled the end of his marriage: "His cunning as a businessman was about that of a backward kindergarten student and he complicated this by marital adventures, in which he was about as inept as he was on screen. He was soon behind in alimony payments" (142). Capra, in *The Name above the Title*, was more biting when he wrote about Langdon's philandering, implying that typical "star" excesses were the source of his self-sabotage: "The little vaudeville man went Hollywood. He bought a big mansion on Hollywood Boulevard; wore dark glasses, bright scarves, sporty duds; gave parties; acquired secretaries—and discovered girls" (63).

25. Neibaur notes that in the 1980 documentary *Hollywood*, produced by Thames Television with Kevin Brownlow and David Gill (Neibaur erroneously calls the latter Samuel Gill), Frank Capra states that "Langdon did not create his character, we created his character." However, Neibaur's analysis of Langdon's silent work leads him to conclude that "Langdon's screen persona had developed quite fully by the time *Plain Clothes* was filmed" (*Silent Films of Harry Langdon*, 84).

26. Schelly, *Harry Langdon* (2008), 97.

27. Further details are provided in Harter and Hayde, *Little Elf*, 137.

28. Quoted in Joseph McBride, *Frank Capra: The Catastrophe of Success* (New York: Simon and Schuster, 1992), 256–57.

29. The cartoon is reproduced in Harter and Hayde, *Little Elf*, 137.

30. Cited in ibid., 129–30.

31. Ibid., 139.

32. In her autobiography *A Portrait of Joan* with Jane Kesner Ardmore (Garden City, NY: Doubleday, 1962), the cyclone was Crawford's main memory of *Tramp, Tramp, Tramp*. Calling Langdon a "stage star," even though he was a top movie star by this time, Crawford described how he pushed her into a manhole for the cyclone scene and slammed the lid on them, triggering her claustrophobia. To her horror, "When the wind machines finally stopped, and Harry pulled me out limp, director Frank Capra said, '*Just once more please.*'"

33. *Photoplay* cited in Kevin Brownlow, *The Parade's Gone By . . .* (Berkeley: University of California Press, 1968), 438.

34. More excerpts from newspaper reviews and exhibitors' comments, as well as actual box-office figures, can be found in Harter and Hayde, *Little Elf*, 144.

35. Cited in ibid., 141.

36. In a Sydney, Australia, newspaper many years later (February 2, 1936), Langdon reminisced about working with Joan Crawford, claiming that he had given this "round-faced, fresh-looking girl" her first real chance to be more than an extra. He also commented on her subsequent stardom, calling her a "totally differ-

ent type" with a "rather sophisticated appeal." Hers was one of many caricatures he drew of Hollywood stars; despite her iconic glamour, Langdon admitted that he found Crawford's "natural every day kind of girl" look more attractive.

37. Interesting parallels can be drawn between the philosophical tone and content of Langdon's essays on comedy and the complex essay by philosopher Henri Bergson entitled "Laughter: An Essay on the Meaning of Comic" (1900), with which Langdon was likely familiar. Bergson's principles of comedy were meant to apply to all comedy makers, but they particularly resonate with Langdon's persona and film comedy style. Bergson emphasized that "the comic does not exist outside the pale of what is strictly HUMAN. . . . You may laugh at a hat, but what you are making fun of, in this case, is not the piece of felt or straw, but the shape that men have given it—the human caprice whose mould it has assumed." Not coincidentally, almost every major comedian was integrally linked to a special hat that became part of his identity and a pivotal extension of his trademark silhouette (Chaplin's derby, Keaton's porkpie hat, Lloyd's straw hat, Raymond Griffith's top hat). Another significant point made by Bergson that applies to Langdon (and perhaps influenced him and, especially, Ripley) is "the ABSENCE OF FEELING which usually accompanies laughter. It seems as though the comic could not produce its disturbing effect unless it fell, so to say, on the surface of a soul that is thoroughly calm and unruffled. Indifference is its natural environment, for laughter has no greater foe than emotion." Langdon seems to agree in his "Serious Side of Comedy Making," writing, "A comic can make us laugh, provided care be taken not to arouse emotions." However, in a striking duality, Langdon also ties tragedy and its inherent emotions to the essential nature and root of comedy, blurring the line: does the insertion of emotion promote comedy's success by its contrast, or does emotion simply diminish comedy? In his essay "The Comedian," printed in an anthology edited by Charles Reed Jones called *Breaking into the Movies* (New York: Unicorn Press, 1927), Langdon asserts that "comedy is, after all, the most elemental form of tragedy. And tragedy is merely a manifestation of drama. So that, by purely mathematical reasoning and excluding the knowledge born of many experiences, it is apparent that comedy depends basically upon drama for its success. . . . The world doesn't laugh at men who do things to Life; it laughs at those whom Life does things to" (91, 93). Langdon enjoyed touching on the tragic, at least in his writings if not in his films, even suggesting, "I have often thought a comedy 'lot' is the saddest place on earth and comedy constructionists are, as a rule, the saddest people. You will find them, without exception, a serious-minded group of men, seldom smiling and not at all given to outbursts of mirth." This perception seems rather extreme, however, and might elicit a chicken-egg debate: must one be serious to understand and perform comedy, or does working in comedy make one serious about life? Both offscreen and on, Langdon seemed profoundly impacted by these options.

38. Priscilla Bonner, interview with Gabriella Oldham, Los Angeles, August 6, 1983; other background information was culled from Bonner's interview with Raymond Rohauer and Mabel Langdon on February 14, 1978.

39. The entire Waller article is reproduced as a facsimile from *Moving Picture World* in Harter and Hayde, *Little Elf,* appendix VI, 669.

40. Cited in ibid., 152.

41. An examination of Capra's keen interest in incorporating the "immigrant experience" into his films, starting with *The Strong Man* and followed by *For the Love of Mike* (1927) and *The Younger Generation* (1929), is provided by Jonathan J. Cavallero, "Frank Capra's 1920s Immigrant Trilogy: Immigration, Assimilation, and the American Dream," *MELUS* 29, no. 2 (Summer 2004): 27–53.

42. Bonner, interview with Oldham.

43. Ibid. Bonner supports the idea of Langdon's inherent insecurity. A similar observation was echoed by Langdon's former costar Gertrude Astor in Victor Scherle and William Turner Levy, *The Films of Frank Capra* (New York: Citadel Press, 1977); she paints a bleaker picture of his personality, which seemed to be a detrimental hybrid of insecurity and arrogance. These reflections create a strikingly contradictory picture of a man smitten with all the luxuries stardom could offer yet who craved isolation from his creative team to (perhaps) understand himself better. According to Astor: "Harry Langdon was a funny little wordless man. He would never sit near anyone on the set; indeed, he would wander a block away and sit alone on a bench until Frank Capra needed him for a scene. Although a star, he acted like a non-entity." When Astor asked him why he chose to sit by himself, he reportedly answered, "Oh, I like it. I don't like people. I like to be alone and think." Astor concludes by drawing a striking contrast between the two key figures at work: "Frank Capra, so young and so serious, and Harry looking at you, blinking, those pale blue eyes, and then glancing over his shoulder to make sure you weren't following him into his private world of silence." One side of the equation elevates the talented director to an idealistic stature; the other side reduces the obtuse, secretive comedian to a negative presence in a world that thrives and succeeds on creative social interrelationships. One may also recall Langdon's 1927 treatise "The Serious Side of Comedy Making," discussed earlier in relation to *Tramp, Tramp, Tramp,* in which he cites "unsociability" as one of the four greatest stimuli to laughter. Did Langdon adopt "unsociability" as a survival mechanism—as part of his creative personality to provoke laughter? And if so, did it backfire in his personal life and eventually turn off his colleagues, critics, and audiences? By contrast, two actresses who worked in Langdon's sound films balanced the negative with consistently positive memories of their costar: Nell O'Day called Langdon "absolutely charming," exuding the same "sweet helplessness" of his character, and Ann Doran considered Harry an "absolute doll" who "never hurt anybody" (quoted in Harter and Hayde, *Little Elf,* 326). But these views came later, after Langdon under-

went significant emotional upheaval as a result of his inflated ego and the underlying insecurity that led him to make so many flawed decisions. At that point, he was desperately eager to find a place in the film world again and, essentially, reinvent himself.

44. Bonner, interview with Rohauer and Langdon.

45. Bonner, interview with Oldham.

46. Harter and Hayde, *Little Elf,* 145. It is also possible that Ripley suggested changing the title from the original choice, *The Yes Man.* Once Paul's repartee with the Great Zandow became key to the film, the emphasis turned to the strongman, which ultimately became the final title. It is also symbolically more significant to the film's deeper impact, as Langdon's character becomes a strong man in more ways than just the physical.

47. Monks's article is reproduced as a facsimile in ibid., appendix VI, 662–63.

48. McBride, *Frank Capra,* 161.

49. Capra, *The Name above the Title,* 68.

50. There are some discrepancies among the different versions of Langdon's meeting and eventual hookup with Helen Walton. According to Harter and Hayde's extensive examination of this affair, Langdon and Helen (née Nellie Laura) Walton met in 1923 during his brief stint with Sol Lesser. *Little Elf* includes a photograph of Helen sitting on Langdon's lap in a scene from *The White Wing's Bride.* At that time, Langdon was most definitely married to Rose (perhaps no longer happily), and Helen had been married since 1914 to Thomas J. O'Brien, with whom she had a daughter, Virginia. For many years, the O'Briens' marriage was apparently rife with arguments and separations, often exacerbated by Helen's determination to make it in the film business. Her connection with Langdon may have coincided with one of her splits from O'Brien, but it was clearly motivated by her desire to be an important film personality. Apparently, O'Brien confronted Langdon after following the couple on a rendezvous and Langdon agreed to "stay away," but in fact he continued to lavish attention on Helen, despite her reconciliation with her husband for their daughter's sake. Rose also actively tailed Harry and Helen to obtain evidence for an annulment, and during one such adventure she crashed her vehicle into a telephone pole and broke her nose. When word of the scandal spread, Rose and Harry reconciled to avoid the bad publicity. As *Variety* noted: "The couple are now seen together again at the Hollywood clubs and theatres. Mrs. Langdon has instructed her attorney not to begin a separate maintenance suit he had been authorized to file in the superior court" (quoted in Harder and Hayde, *Little Elf,* 129). But the truce clearly did not last. There is no denying Langdon's infidelities with Helen (and other starlets), and she eventually became his second wife. In fact, based on the photographs and documentation collected by Harter and Hayde, Harry may have started his affair with Helen much earlier in his film career, and they may have shared screen time together, although the films in question have

been lost. It was during Harry's painful divorce from Helen that he met his third wife, Mabel. In later years, Mabel rarely referred to Harry's first two marriages and divorces, other than to acknowledge that they had happened; all that mattered to her was what she and Harry shared.

51. Harter and Hayde clarify, with supporting publicity, documents, and photographs, the ongoing saga of Harry, Helen, and Thomas O'Brien, who remained in the picture. For Christmas 1926, perhaps to help Helen forget Thomas, for whom she had mixed feelings, Langdon gave her "a diamond brooch, a $1,850 ermine coat, a $1,000 bill, a $150 gold case and a $500 Persian rug. For what it's worth, she returned the rug. She had no presents for Harry, but did purchase a new outfit of clothing for her husband" (*Little Elf,* 158). Shortly after Christmas, Helen announced that she was pregnant. Whether she was with Thomas to hide the possibility that Langdon was the father or whether Thomas actually was the father, Helen opted for an abortion. "What the press would term 'an illegal operation' was secured and performed. Langdon, possibly uncertain himself about his responsibility, tried to talk her out of it, but she was adamant. He insisted she recuperate at his home, and later claimed that he proposed to her at this time" (ibid., 161). A 1927 photograph of Helen in a wheelchair, with Langdon beside her holding her hand outside his home, provides further evidence of this complex entanglement. Meanwhile, Rose finalized their divorce over the next few years. Helen and Harry's marriage was doomed as well, and both divorces eradicated Langdon's meager savings, as discussed in chapter 4. A fuller story of the love triangles (and quadrangles) involving Rose, Thomas, Helen, and Harry, as well as excerpts from court testimony, is included in ibid., 209–15, along with photos and reproductions of news items and even cartoons about the proceedings. One item reproduces the "court sketches" Langdon himself made of the key participants, including the judge and the attorneys; the curious caption reads, "Harry Langdon, who was a cartoonist before he became a famous comedian, has lost none of his talent. . . . His impressionistic caricatures of persons in court during the trial reveal the spirit of fun and whimsicality which brought him fame on the screen" (ibid., 212).

52. Quotations culled from Bonner's 1978 and 1983 interviews.

53. Cited in McBride, *Frank Capra,* 170.

54. In her article "Doing Nothing: Harry Langdon and the Performance of Absence," *Film Quarterly* 59, no. 1 (Fall 2005): 27–35, Joanna E. Rapf specifically cites this sequence from *Long Pants* as one vivid example of how Langdon "is characteristically ignored within his films, as if he weren't there. His is a comedy of absence." This continuity of disembodied actions clearly wrought by an unseen person culminates in seeing Harry "*sitting behind* a chest reading and fantasizing about life rather than participating in its reality. And when we finally see him full figure, he scratches his head in puzzlement. Langdon's films are filled with scenes like these, with him retreating from life, running off the screen, curled in a fetal position, or

transposed into the world of dreams" (29). Rapf also quotes numerous corroborating authors who observed this unique trait that distinguished Langdon from his comedy contemporaries. In particular, she cites Walter Kerr in *The Silent Clowns* (New York: Alfred A. Knopf, 1975), who said Langdon "found a way to renew the energies of silent film comedy by acting out their absence" (Rapf, "Doing Nothing," 31). Rapf also considers how Langdon's "hesitant, regressive, and frightened" persona attracted the opposite in women, which only confirmed his need to flee from them. Through this focus on being *absent*—especially as a person who must interact with the world by virtue of being alive but cannot or will not—Rapf concludes that "Langdon himself, a man whose offscreen intelligence displayed a maturity that contradicted his screen persona, also realized that comedy has its origin in our self-consciousness and our awareness of mortality, and in our recognition that the road from the peace of the womb to the peace of the grave is filled with pain" (ibid., 34–35). It is ironic that Harry could be so helplessly absent onscreen (with occasional flashes of adult behavior), while Langdon lived fully and completely present (with flashes of childish behavior).

55. Quoted in Harter and Hayde, *Little Elf,* 140.

56. The Dreiser connection does not end with Langdon's choice of reading material. In his career as a journalist, Theodore Dreiser had interviewed Mack Sennett for *Photoplay* in 1928, shortly after Langdon was released by First National. The Old Man called Langdon "the greatest of them all . . . greater than Chaplin." At the same time, he lamented Langdon's many flaws, including wanting to be "leading lady, cameraman, heavy and director all in one. So far in my experience that attitude has never proved successful."

57. Capra, *The Name above the Title,* 68–69.

58. McBride, *Frank Capra,* 171.

59. Ibid.

60. Ibid., 147.

61. Reprinted in *Lowville (NY) Journal and Republican,* December 30, 1926.

62. Many suspect that the overlap between Harry's persona and Langdon's personality led to the tragic flaws that ensured his ultimate professional and private decline. Rheuban comments on this likelihood: "One possible contributing factor to Langdon's problem was the certain respect in which Langdon can be said to resemble the comic character he impersonated. Langdon seems to have been in some ways out of touch with his circumstances. He apparently had difficulty communicating with people other than a small group of family members and longtime friends" (*Harry Langdon,* 184). Langdon's efforts to control his productions and his fragile understanding of effective filmmaking seemed to be hit-and-miss as well; he strove to be a complete "adult" in his work, while his childlike enthusiasm for celebrity and autonomy may have clouded his directorial judgments and hindered a true collaboration with his team. Instead, he pushed a self-driven agenda.

3. Elusive Stardom

1. The working title was *Gratitude* from April 28 to June 22, 1927, according to Schelly (*Harry Langdon* [2008], 99), who also notes that the screenplay was co-written by Langdon, his brother James, Arthur Ripley, and Robert Eddy.

2. Gladys McConnell, in an interview with Edward Watz, notes that she admired Langdon's artistic talent when she saw his sketches for the film: "The set designer built this eerie-looking New York tenement with this very long staircase. I had seen sketches for this set drawn in a children's school notebook and Arthur Ripley noticed me looking them over. 'Harry Langdon drew that,' he told me. Harry carried the book with him and I noticed he had drawn many detailed sketches of how he thought different scenes should look. He had definite ideas on how he wanted this film to look on screen" (quoted in Harter and Hayde, *Little Elf,* 169).

3. The Western Association of Motion Picture Advertisers (WAMPAS) ran an annual promotional campaign from 1922 to 1934 to honor young actresses contracted by major studios who showed movie star potential. Some notable WAMPAS Baby Stars were Bessie Love and Colleen Moore (1922); Clara Bow (1924); Mary Astor, Janet Gaynor, and Fay Wray (1926); Lupe Vélez (1928); Jean Arthur and Loretta Young (1929); Joan Blondell (1931); and Ginger Rogers (1932). Other regular Langdon costars who had been WAMPAS Baby Stars included Alberta Vaughn (1924), Madeline Hurlock (1925), Marceline Day (1926), and Natalie Kingston (1927).

4. Schelly, *Harry Langdon* (2008), 102. Rheuban provides insight into the scenes and sequences, along with stills of scenes that may have been edited out of the mass of footage Langdon shot for *Three's a Crowd.* The most intriguing cuts were meant to appear at the beginning of the film. In one shot: "Gladys beckons Harry to her as seen from Harry's point of view through the long funnel of his telescope. (This shot may or may not have been part of the dream sequence. Gladys may also have been greeting her lover here, the man who is introduced later in the film as her husband, since there was also a sequence of exposition of Gladys's story included in the footage that was cut from the film after previews. In the shot in which Gladys appears to beckon to Harry, we may be seeing her merely through Harry's wishful viewpoint.)" (*Harry Langdon,* 96, 98).

5. Perhaps the most prominent link between Chaplin and Langdon is *The Kid* and *Three's a Crowd.* Schelly stresses that the main distinction between these films also highlights their individuality: "The focus of *The Kid* is the relationship between the Tramp and the orphan. In *Three's a Crowd,* the important thing (as always) is the ripple-effect of external events on Harry's psyche. The emblematic shot of *The Kid* is a two-shot; the equivalent in the Langdon film is a close-up of Harry's face" (*Harry Langdon* [2008], 100). Charlie indulges in emotional drama that is propelled by his dynamic efforts to right wrongs, restore balance, and reclaim what is his within his reach. By contrast, Harry is "reserved," experiencing very real emo-

tions in a small, private world within the larger world but seldom attaching to what is around him; although deeply affected by his surroundings, his responses are those of a child who has stopped growing, with only hit-and-miss attempts at an adult stature. Continually referring to Langdon as a hapless "Elf" in his book, Schelly concludes: "The Elf had none of the pluck and resourcefulness of the Tramp, who one knew would survive simply because he was a 'survivor.' Without God on his side, pushing away obstacles and creating opportunities, Harry didn't stand a chance. A happy ending (as in *The Kid*) had no place in the new Langdon formula" (ibid.).

6. Excerpts from *Photoplay* cited in Brownlow, *The Parade's Gone By*, 442; Schelly, *Harry Langdon* (2008), 103.

7. Schelly offers an interesting perspective of Langdon's rise and fall, which were tied to trends and fads more so than the fate of any of his contemporaries: "His talent was authentic, but his rise to fame was so fast that one suspects he was riding partially on a convenient trend in popular taste. For a brief period of time, his absurd child/man persona was the rage. When tastes shifted, Langdon's fortunes sagged" (*Harry Langdon* [2008], 115). Schelly specifically refers to the public's "over-saturation" with the comedian when Sennett released his remaining shorts just as Langdon was making his independent features. In addition, Schelly observes, "One strange aspect of a fad is the public's inordinate resentment toward the person it has so recently idolized after the initial excitement is over. They are perhaps slightly chagrined by their own over-enthusiasm. Though difficult to prove, the scathing quality of the reviews and the suddenness of Langdon's rejection seem to indicate that a Langdon backlash did happen" (ibid.). Schelly holds Langdon partly responsible because he assumed the press would continue to be supportive, or perhaps he simply did not understand how to ride the wave of public opinion. His keen need for privacy also tended to keep reporters at bay, although he welcomed the publicity: "Instead of catering to the reporters, Langdon irritated them and held them at a distance by hiring personal assistants who acted as 'gate-keepers' for the star." Schelly does not conclude that faddism was the sole explanation for Langdon's swift descent ("Langdon had too much talent to be strictly a faddist item"), but such a force might have stacked the odds heavily against his success with *The Chaser* (ibid., 116).

8. The full "elimination list" and First National's response are cited in Harter and Hayde, *Little Elf*, 180. The researchers draw an interesting conclusion about the impact of these changes on the critics: "The version of *The Chaser* as seen by New York residents—and presumably in other states with similar censorship boards—was approximately 150 feet and a few off-color gags shy of complete. The sensibilities of the state's moviegoers were thus safeguarded, but one wonders if the reviews would have been different had the critics seen the entire film. As it is, First National's Manhattan picture palace, the Strand, opted to not book *The Chaser*; the

film instead opened on Broadway at the Cameo, ordinarily a second-run house" (ibid., 181).

9. In a press kit for the film *Heart Trouble,* Langdon once again alludes to the value of previews, which he had no doubt learned mainly from his experience on *Three's a Crowd:* "I want the most devoted preview audience I can get to witness the first cut on my productions. I want their sincere comment and . . . if we can detect the weaknesses of our product before it's broadcast for general exhibition and remedy this trouble, I feel that the so-called 'hard boiled' preview audience deserves hearty appreciation."

10. According to Harter and Hayde: "Neither First National nor Langdon were interested in prolonging the inevitable. In June 1928, after handing over *Heart Trouble*'s negative, he quietly dissolved his company by selling all its assets to First National for a flat $5,000. At the time it was a bargain: fifteen months later, the books would be closed on the Harry Langdon Corporation at an overall loss of $511,497" (*Little Elf,* 185). They also present details on First National's financial expenditures and losses related to these Langdon films. They note that most exhibitors would not even book the films, prompting Ned E. Depinet, the sales manager at First National, to issue a letter "to all managers," asking them to consider *Three's a Crowd, The Chaser,* and *Heart Trouble* with "the same undivided attention that we give all of our pictures. You should place each and every picture in every unsold spot, and, further, instruct your book to insist upon playing time in proper order of availability and not to allow exhibitors to pass these pictures up for one reason or another" (*Little Elf,* 186–87). This communication belies the true desperation resulting from these films' poor quality and poor reception across the board.

11. Thomas quoted in Neibaur, *Silent Films of Harry Langdon,* 205, 206.

12. Neibaur attributes this interview to Robin Coons but provides no other information as to source and date. Harter and Hayde cite Langdon's comments made in 1938 during an Associated Press interview, when he called *The Chaser* and *Heart Trouble* "absolute stinkers" and "two of the lousiest pictures ever made." Ultimately, it is difficult to distinguish between what Langdon actually felt under the pressure of making these pictures and how he *remembered* feeling ten years later, given all the negativity surrounding his work. In any case, Langdon admitted that he never attended the premieres of those films because "I took one look at them in the projection room and was sick" (*Little Elf,* 187). Thus, one could suggest that Langdon was so blinded by his responsibilities as actor-director that he could no longer see what was working; nor could he fix any problems in postproduction. Yet it is important to consider that the negativity leveled at him so soon after his success may have molded how he remembered himself and his work.

13. Hall's article is reproduced in its entirety as a facsimile in Harter and Hayde, *Little Elf,* appendix VI, 674–75.

14. Schelly, *Harry Langdon* (2008), 133, notes that *The Big Kick* was titled *La*

estacion de gasolina and *The Shrimp* was titled *Pobre infeliz* in Spanish, while *The King* was released as *Der König* for German audiences.

15. Several sources mention Roach's famous warning upon meeting Langdon after the William Morris Agency had negotiated their contract: "Now, see here, Langdon, none of that high-handed stuff you pulled at First National" (Harter and Hayde, *Little Elf*, 198; Schelly, *Harry Langdon* [2008], 135).

16. Quoted in Rheuban, *Harry Langdon*, 38–39, from her interview with Roach.

17. According to Harter and Hayde, once Helen and Harry wed, she brought both Virginia and her older adopted daughter, Edith, into the household; both girls called Langdon "Daddy Harry." Apparently, Edith left home at age seventeen and was not heard from again (*Little Elf*, 162).

18. Ibid., 223.

19. Details of Langdon's travels and the clashes and accusations that disintegrated his second marriage are chronicled in ibid., 223–30.

20. Quoted in Brownlow, *The Parade's Gone By*, 437.

21. Brownlow finds it hard to believe that Capra could be so hostile, given his documented kindness on film sets he helmed long after working with Langdon. Yet Brownlow concedes that the reported content of this anonymous letter must be accurate, as Katherine Albert was a reliable source who discussed the severe fallout on Langdon's reputation and career in her article "What Happened to Harry Langdon?" (*Photoplay*, February 1932). Brownlow also concludes, from his vantage point in 1968 (when *The Parade's Gone By* was published), that the facts would come out when Capra published his own autobiography, which in fact did not happen. Albert's full article is reproduced as a facsimile in Harter and Hayde, *Little Elf*, appendix VI, 676–77.

22. In an interview with Thomas D. Arnold for the Nebraska Film Project on May 4, 1981, Mabel Langdon recalled, "As a young lady, my Dad and I were very close and we used to go to the Orpheum every week, so I must have seen Harry at some time, but of course I didn't know who he was back in 1925."

23. All quotations from Mabel Langdon are from personal interviews with Gabriella Oldham, Los Angeles, 1984, unless otherwise indicated.

4. The Stronger Man

1. Schelly attributes this story to Langdon's son, Harry Jr., who related Jolson's comment when he spoke to film fans at a showing of *The Chaser* in West Hollywood in the summer of 2008, as reported in an article by Lisa Burke, www.valleynews.com.

2. Mabel Langdon revealed in an interview with Edward Watz that Harry had discussed his wish to team up with Vernon Dent. Harter and Hayde note: "Based on the existing evidence, the Gillstrom-Paramount shorts were the closest the two

came to realizing that goal, although they would continue working together, off and on, into the next decade" (*Little Elf*, 249).

3. In a conversation with Raymond Strait in June 1985, Mabel recalled that one day in 1933 she drove up to the Garden of Allah and found Harry's apartment on fire: "I rushed in like a damn fool with a towel over my mouth trying to help him save some of his stuff. . . . He'd left the kitchen stove on and it caught the curtains on fire . . . same day of the Long Beach earthquake. I remember driving down Sunset Boulevard and the wires were swinging back and forth. I didn't know what it was until I got to Harry's and he told me about the water splashing out of the swimming pool at the Garden of Allah . . . into the cottages."

4. All quotes from Jules White are from his interview with Raymond Rohauer and Mabel Langdon, Los Angeles, February 13, 1978.

5. Newspaper stories about the "astrology baby" continued to appear as reporters followed the family of three around while Langdon was later working overseas. For example, when Langdon performed onstage in Australia, the Melbourne and Sydney newspapers eagerly published photos of Junior in many settings with his parents. The *Melbourne Star* also documented Junior's "verbatim" statements uttered during an interview with his father: "pretty, doggy, mama, hot doggy, nurse, hullo, papa, pretty car, hullo, nurse."

6. Quoted in Harter and Hayde, *Little Elf*, 258, as excerpted from Edward Watz's interview with Mabel Langdon.

7. Schelly, *Harry Langdon* (2008), 155. He notes that western writer Zane Grey was also aboard.

8. The full article and conversation are reprinted in Harter and Hayde, *Little Elf*, 264–65.

9. Schelly provides information on Langdon's nightclub idea and speculates that perhaps the "imminence of another World War cast a pall over the project" (*Harry Langdon* [2008], 156).

10. Joe Rock was interviewed by Raymond Rohauer and Mabel Langdon in Los Angeles in the late 1970s, and this quote from that interview appeared in an early draft of the manuscript. The actual transcript has since been lost.

11. In later years, Mabel Langdon found at a flea market a letter dated August 16, 1937, from Harry to Mr. G. M. Emery, income tax specialist in London, itemizing his expenses on *Wise Guys* and asking him to "kindly give my income tax your immediate attention as I am considerably late in filing my return—due to unexpected deviation in my original plans which has just brought this obligation to my attention." He pointed out that he had been obliged to work on the picture prior to shooting as well as assisting in the editing, "which in all required about six weeks of my services." He sent Mabel's regards and concluded, "I understand from friends in London that the picture bis is about the same, bad, as it was when I left. We are very sorry to hear this as we were quite anxious to return to London. But we

still have hopes, and I have a standing offer to return . . . as soon as the business regains its original footing." Mr. Emery assured him in a letter dated September 13 that there should be "comparatively little tax to pay." This lucky find also included a letter from Ivor McLaren:

> In spite of the usual battles (yes, I know I'm a pig-headed old sod!) I was able to bring my pic in on budget, thanks to your co-operation in coming off the floor a half day ahead of schedule. Did I fool you over that last day or did I fool you?!!
>
> Well, so long Harry, good luck, thanks, and come back immediately on receipt of my cable, or else—.
> Cheeroh Palsie,
> Ivor McLaren, Producer

Handwritten near the sign-off was this parenthetical comment: "and no direct cracks from you, either!"

12. In an interview she gave to Steve Randisi for *Filmfax* magazine, Ann Doran (Langdon's costar in *Sue My Lawyer*) described running into Frank Capra (with whom she had worked on *Mr. Deeds Goes to Town* [1936] and *You Can't Take It with You* [1938]) and asking him to assist with a particularly problematic gag for *Sue My Lawyer*. Aware of the bitterness between the two men, she told Capra she was working with Langdon, and he asked: "'Do you suppose Harry will take it [Capra's advice]?' And I told him, 'At this point he'll take anything because we are in a spot.' Then I went over to Harry and asked, 'Do you mind if I bring over a friend of mine to gag it for us?' And he said, 'God, no. Anything to make it funny!' Capra came on and there was electricity all over the set, but we needed that gag. Capra said to Harry, 'Let's do the old going-up-the-stairs thing. . . .' Harry said, 'That's wonderful, wonderful!'" (quoted in Harter and Hayde, *Little Elf,* 275). Not surprisingly, Capra's memory of his visit to the set of *Sue My Lawyer* focused only on how shattered *he* felt at seeing Langdon so badly mishandled by the director, and he never mentioned any personal involvement in the gag. According to Capra, this was the one and only time he saw Langdon again, and it was "under the most pitiful circumstances." His evaluation of his former collaborator: "Gone was the elf. He looked like a gargoyle." Capra also misremembered the fairly thin Doran as "an enormous fat lady" and called the staircase gag "a grotesque replica of the famous scene we did with Mary Astor," rather than acknowledging any input he may have had in its inclusion in the film (Capra, *The Name above the Title,* 72).

13. Quotations from Harry Langdon Jr. come from an interview conducted by Raymond Rohauer and Gabriella Oldham at the Harry Langdon Studio in Los Angeles, August 4, 1983, as well as e-mail correspondence with Oldham throughout 2015.

14. North's article is reproduced in its entirety as a facsimile in Harter and Hayde, *Little Elf,* appendix VI, 658–59.

15. Ibid., 281.

16. Further details are provided in Richard Lewis Ward, *A History of the Hal Roach Studios* (Carbondale: Southern Illinois University Press, 2005).

17. John M. Miller, "*Zenobia*," www.tcm.com. The race issue is also addressed by Simon Louvish in *Stan and Ollie: The Roots of Comedy: The Double Life of Laurel and Hardy* (New York: Thomas Dunne Books, 2005).

18. Details on the 1939 San Francisco International Exposition came from Gary Kamiya, "The '39 World's Fair: An Island of Joyous Excess," August 16, 2013, www.sfgate.com. Also helpful was *Almanac for Thirty-Niners,* compiled by the Federal Writers' Project of the Works Progress Administration in the City of San Francisco, 1938, www.sfmuseum.net. Special thanks to Thomas Carey, librarian and archivist of the San Francisco History Center, San Francisco Public Library, who provided access to the *Official Guidebook of the Exposition* and details about the Hollywood Building's displays.

19. Harter and Hayde, *Little Elf,* 299.

20. Interview with Edward Bernds by Raymond Rohauer, with Mabel Langdon and Gabriella Oldham present, Los Angeles, August 3, 1983. Additional information on Bernds's involvement with *Pistol Packin' Nitwits* comes from Rohauer's interview with him in Los Angeles, May 15, 1980.

5. Legacy

The photograph on page 293, a still from *Three's a Crowd* (1927), is a fitting postscript. Harry is shown in sweet repose, attended by the woman of his dreams, Gladys McConnell.

1. In *The Name above the Title,* Capra's acknowledgment of Langdon's death was tucked into a discussion of his Christmas away from home and war stories. He reported reading an "AP dispatch in the morning paper" headlined: COMEDIAN HARRY LANGDON DIES; $7,500-A-WEEK, THEN $0. The inaccurate item claimed that Langdon had starred in two-reelers and ended in two-reelers, that he had hired Capra and then decided he did not need a director, that he had sometimes earned only $22 a week, and that he had four ex-wives. The director probably appreciated the comment that while "Capra (now Lt. Col. Capra of the Signal Corps) went up the ladder . . . Langdon went down." Capra offered a wry comment on Langdon's passing, no doubt considering it his final evaluation for posterity:

> Langdon hit the maximum greater than Chaplin. He didn't know why. Langdon hit the minimum: the lowest-paid bit actor. He didn't know why. Cry world. . . .
>
> A long-forgotten man. The tragedy of this supreme talent is that he never knew what made him great, nor why the world forgot him. Quick fame, and the consequent barnacles of conceit that clogged his ego, made him impervious to help from those who knew the secret of his magic: the elf whose only ally was God. If in heaven he discovers it for himself, he will have angels falling off their clouds. (ibid., 357)

2. Brothers Charles (d. 1936) and James (d. 1936) and mother Lavinia (d. 1929) were already interred when Harry passed; later siblings who joined the family grave site were Gertrude (d. 1948) and John (d. 1953) (Harter and Hayde, *Little Elf,* 309). Claude died in February 1944 in Council Bluffs, eleven months before Harry (ibid., 303).

3. According to Harter and Hayde, *Little Elf,* 307, Mabel's interview with Michael Copner appeared in *Cult Movies* and took place four years before her death.

4. In his autobiography, Capra recalls that after screening Langdon's car film, "Dick Jones said to us: 'Well, there he is, fellas. And we're stuck with him. I don't know what, but the Old Man sees *something* in this Langdon. But so far, in films with other comics, he's just another fresh little guy. Any ideas, anybody?" (*The Name above the Title,* 58–59). Capra's personal interviews also reveal inconsistencies, especially about when he started working with Langdon. Capra claims it was very early in Langdon's film career. According to Schelly, however, "Material in the Mack Sennett Collection at the Academy's Margaret Herrick Library reveals that Capra's first input on a Langdon film was in *All Night Long,* the tenth in the series" (*Harry Langdon* [2008], 30). Schelly emphasizes that director Harry Edwards was, in fact, molding Langdon to be a comedy star before Capra became involved, and Edwards remained Langdon's friend until the end of the comedian's life, even when other collaborators cut ties with him. It is unclear, as Schelly suggests, "whether Edwards asked to work with Langdon. More likely, he was assigned the job of directing Langdon's eighth comedy on the lot simply as part of Sennett's effort to see if someone—anyone!—could figure out how to present Harry's comedic skills more effectively" (ibid., 31). Neibaur refers to a possible "vendetta Frank Capra might have had upon being fired by Langdon in 1927," which led to his later acerbic critiques that contributed to Langdon's downfall. However, Neibaur also suggests that "screening the films reveals an exceptional talent whose slower method and darker edge was already in evidence long before Capra, Ripley, or Edwards began working with him" (*Silent Films of Harry Langdon,* x). Thus, the problem of developing the most suitable material for Langdon's unique style continued well past the comedian's contract with Sennett and was still a critical point of discussion when Capra joined the creative team and added his perspectives on Harry's character and situations.

5. McBride, *Frank Capra,* 147.

6. Ibid., 148. McBride points out the intense influence of Capra's misogynistic outlook on Langdon's films, particularly *His First Flame,* claiming that "Capra's anger is so extreme that it collides with his comic sense." McBride also discusses the outline notes for the story line of this first Sennett feature (which would not be seen until *after* Langdon's First National films were released). According to the outline, the film would begin with "a historical sequence of how women have always dominated and ruined men." Sennett was apparently reluctant to pursue this drastic

theme, but the writers (including Capra) continued along the same lines: "Historical sequence yet to be approved; a prologue to open the story of how a youth who, like all young men, placed woman in a shrine and worshipped her, until he was disillusioned, [with] his transition into a hater of women, and how, after all, Love, the Mistress, directs his steps into that state of bliss called Love." After an unfortunate set of circumstances befalls the character, the outline concluded: "Now despondent. Hates all women. Wants to get away from them." Harry's character escapes to the all-male fire department and ultimately finds true love, but according to McBride, "the moral of this essentially bitter fable is that, as the opening title puts it, 'Love is the only fire against which there is no insurance'" (ibid., 153–54). It seems that much of Ripley's dark side with regard to women and other edgy gags in Langdon's films can be linked to Capra, who likely at least supported these ideas if he did not in fact contribute them. As McBride explains:

> The darkness of the misogynistic humor in several of the Langdon films stemmed as much from the unhappily married Capra as it did from any other source, yet commentators on the films who mistakenly assume that Capra was an uncomplicated optimist also make the corollary assumption (encouraged by Capra in his book) that Ripley was responsible for all of the dark overtones in the Langdon films.
>
> Capra's simplistic notion that Langdon's "only ally was God" meant that a clash between Capra and Langdon was inevitable, particularly [as] the saturnine Ripley seemed entirely comfortable with the darker, perverse elements in Langdon's character. . . . Capra and Ripley, by all indications, shared a remarkably similar outlook during much of their collaboration. (ibid., 150)

7. Ibid., 156.

8. McBride enumerates these key themes; see ibid., 162.

9. Ibid., 177.

10. Ibid., 145.

11. In her interview with Thomas D. Arnold for the Nebraska Film Project, May 4, 1981, Mabel Langdon indicates that Harry had started to write his memoirs and must have written thirty or forty pages when, one night, he tore them all up. She reflected: "Some people say 'We can't understand why you don't know more about Harry.' If I had [those pages], then I would have known much more about him. But actually my life with Harry started, the way I feel about it, when we were married. That was OUR PART. His past was his past. Being married twice before, he didn't want that to enter into [our life]."

12. McBride, *Frank Capra*, 147.

13. Lee's article is reproduced as a facsimile in Harter and Hayde, *Little Elf*, appendix VI, 678–79. "Bebe" in the title refers to Bebe Daniels, who, according to the article's sidebar, "toppled from the heights five times and came back four." She was married to Ben Lyon, who worked with and was good friends with Langdon (see

chapter 4). The facsimile version in *Little Elf* does not include the Daniels section of the article.

14. Quoted in Neibaur, *Silent Films of Harry Langdon*, 220.

15. Bernds's diary captured the shock of Langdon's unexpected demise in his log for *Pistol Packin' Nitwits*, thereby confirming the chronology:

12/22	Word that Harry Langdon died! Many called to Mac and Jules White.
12/26	Langdon funeral.

16. Seth Soulstein, "Concrete Irrationality: Surrealist Spectators and the Cult of Harry Langdon," *Scope: An Online Journal of Film and Television Studies* 25 (February 2013): 1–17, explores the surrealists' fixation on Langdon's approach to life, particularly his sleep symbolism, his use of physical objects for unintended purposes, and his blurring of real, unreal, and surreal. Soulstein questions whether it is possible to "appreciate Langdon's surreal humor without the cultural creation of the Surrealists as reference points" and how much Langdon's brand of comedy impacted the classic surreal films.

17. Schelly cites this excerpt from a letter written to him by world-renowned mime Marcel Marceau dated June 19, 1980 (*Harry Langdon* [2008], 100).

Selected Bibliography

Agee, James. "Comedy's Greatest Era." In *Agee on Film*. Vol. 1. New York: Grosset and Dunlap, 1969.

Albert, Katherine. "What Happened to Harry Langdon." *Photoplay*, February 1932.

Armstrong, David. *The Great American Medicine Show*. New York: Prentice-Hall General, 1991.

Bergson, Henry. "Laughter: An Essay on the Meaning of Comic." 1900. www.authorama.com/laughter-1.html.

Bilton, Alan. *Silent Film Comedy and American Culture*. New York: Palgrave Macmillan, 2013.

Blesh, Rudi. *Keaton*. New York: Macmillan, 1966.

Brownlow, Kevin. *The Parade's Gone By. . . .* Berkeley: University of California Press, 1968.

Capra, Frank. "Dialogue on Film." American Film Institute, October 1978.

———. *The Name above the Title*. New York: Macmillan, 1971.

Cavallero, Jonathan J. "Frank Capra's 1920s Immigrant Trilogy: Immigration, Assimilation, and the American Dream." *MELUS* 29, no. 2 (Summer 2004): 27–53.

Charney, Maurice. *Comedy High and Low*. New York: Oxford University Press, 1978.

Crawford, Joan, with Jane Kesner Ardmore. *A Portrait of Joan: The Autobiography of Joan Crawford*. Garden City, NY: Doubleday, 1962.

Curran, Doris. "The Sad-Faced Mr. Langdon." *Motion Picture Classic*, July 1925.

Dreiser, Theodore. "The Best Motion Picture Interview Ever Written." *Photoplay*, August 1928.

Everson, William K. *American Silent Film*. New York: Oxford University Press, 1978.

———. "Raymond Rohauer: King of the Film Freebooters." *Grand Street* 49 (Summer 1994): 188–96.

Hall, Leonard. "Hey! Hey! Harry's Coming Back." *Photoplay*, June 1929.

Harter, Chuck, and Michael J. Hayde. *Little Elf: A Celebration of Harry Langdon*. Duncan, OK: BearManor Media, 2012.

Herzog, Dorothy. "The Wistful Mr. Langdon." *Motion Picture Magazine,* October 1927.

Kamiya, Gary. "The '39 World's Fair: An Island of Joyous Excess." August 16, 2013. www.sfgate.com.

Kerr, Walter. *The Silent Clowns.* New York: Alfred A. Knopf, 1975.

———. "Who Was Harry Langdon?" *American Film,* November 1975.

Lahue, Kalton C. *World of Laughter: The Motion Picture Comedy Short, 1910–1930.* Norman: University of Oklahoma Press, 1966.

Lahue, Kalton C., and Terry Brewer. *Kops and Custard.* Norman: University of Oklahoma Press, 1968.

Lahue, Kalton C., and Sam Gill. *Clown Princes and Court Jesters: Some Great Comics of the Silent Screen.* Cranbury, NJ: A. S. Barnes, 1970.

Langdon, Harry. "The Comedian." In *Breaking into the Movies,* edited by Charles Reed Jones, 90–94. New York: Unicorn Press, 1927.

———. "The Serious Side of Comedy Making." *Theatre,* December 1927.

Leary, Richard. "Capra and Langdon." *Film Comment,* November–December 1972, 15–17.

Lee, Sonia. "Good Luck or Bad Luck—Bebe and Harry Can Take It!" *Motion Picture Magazine,* January 1932.

Louvish, Simon. *Keystone: The Life and Clowns of Mack Sennett.* New York: Faber and Faber, 2003.

———. *Stan and Ollie: The Roots of Comedy: The Double Life of Laurel and Hardy.* New York: Thomas Dunne Books, 2005.

Maltin, Leonard. *The Great Movie Shorts.* New York: Bonanza Books, 1972.

Mast, Gerald. *The Comic Mind: Comedy and the Movies.* New York: Bobbs-Merrill, 1973.

McBride, Joseph. *Frank Capra: The Catastrophe of Success.* New York: Simon and Schuster, 1992.

McCaffrey, Donald W. *Four Great Comedians: Chaplin, Lloyd, Keaton, Langdon.* New York: A. S. Barnes, 1968.

McKinley, Edward. *Marching to Glory: The History of the Salvation Army in the United States, 1880–1992.* New York: Wm. B. Eerdmans, 1995.

McVay, Douglas. "The Art of the Actor." *Films and Filming,* August 1966, 36–42.

Merton, Paul. *Silent Comedy.* New York: Random House, 2009.

Miller, Blair. *American Silent Film Comedies: An Illustrated Encyclopedia of Persons, Studios, and Terminology.* Jefferson, NC: McFarland, 2008.

Miller, John M. "Zenobia." www.tcm.com.

Mitchell, Glenn. *A–Z of Silent Film Comedy: An Illustrated Companion.* London: Batsford, 2003.

Monks, Margaret G. "Harry, Harry, Quite Contrary." *Cinema Art,* October 1926.

Neibaur, James L. *The Silent Films of Harry Langdon (1923–1928).* Lanham, MD: Scarecrow Press, 2012.

North, Jean. "It's No Joke to Be Funny." *Photoplay*, June 1925.

Rapf, Joanna E. "Doing Nothing: Harry Langdon and the Performance of Absence." *Film Quarterly* 59, no. 1 (Fall 2005): 27–35.

Rheuban, Joyce. *Harry Langdon, the Comedian as Metteur-en-Scène*. Teaneck, NJ: Fairleigh Dickinson University Press, 2008.

Robinson, David. *The Great Funnies: A History of Film Comedy*. New York: E. P. Dutton, 1960.

Schelly, William. *Harry Langdon*. Metuchen, NJ: Scarecrow Press, 1982.

———. *Harry Langdon: His Life and Films*. Jefferson, NC: McFarland, 2008.

Scherle, Victor, and William Turner Levy. *The Films of Frank Capra*. New York: Citadel Press, 1977.

Schonert, Vernon L. "Harry Langdon." *Films in Review*, October 1967.

Sennett, Mack, with Cameron Shipp. *King of Comedy*. 1954. San Francisco: Mercury House, 1990.

Soulstein, Saul. "Concrete Irrationality: Surrealist Spectators and the Cult of Harry Langdon." *Scope: An Online Journal of Film and Television Studies* 25 (February 2013): 1–17.

Thompson, Frank. "Harry Langdon . . . The Fourth Genius?" *Film Comment* 33, no. 3 (May–June 1997): 77, 79–80.

Toll, Robert C. *Blacking Up: The Minstrel Show in Nineteenth-Century America*. New York: Oxford University Press, 1977.

Truscott, Harold. "Harry Langdon." *Silent Picture*, Spring 1972, 2–17.

Walker, Brent E. *Mack Sennett's Fun Factory*. Jefferson, NC: McFarland, 2013.

Waller, Tom. "Harry Langdon: A Serious Man Who Makes the Whole World Laugh." *Moving Picture World*, March 19, 1927.

Ward, Richard Lewis. *A History of the Hal Roach Studios*. Carbondale: Southern Illinois University Press, 2005.

Index

SCREEN CLASSICS

Screen Classics is a series of critical biographies, film histories, and analytical studies focusing on neglected filmmakers and important screen artists and subjects, from the era of silent cinema to the golden age of Hollywood to the international generation of today. Books in the Screen Classics series are intended for scholars and general readers alike. The contributing authors are established figures in their respective fields. This series also serves the purpose of advancing scholarship on film personalities and themes with ties to Kentucky.

SERIES EDITOR: Patrick McGilligan

BOOKS IN THE SERIES

Mae Murray: The Girl with the Bee-Stung Lips
    Michael G. Ankerich
Hedy Lamarr: The Most Beautiful Woman in Film
    Ruth Barton
Rex Ingram: Visionary Director of the Silent Screen
    Ruth Barton
Conversations with Classic Film Stars: Interviews from Hollywood's Golden Era
    James Bawden and Ron Miller
Von Sternberg
    John Baxter
Hitchcock's Partner in Suspense: The Life of Screenwriter Charles Bennett
    Charles Bennett, edited by John Charles Bennett
My Life in Focus: A Photographer's Journey with Elizabeth Taylor and the Hollywood Jet Set
    Gianni Bozzacchi with Joey Tayler
Hollywood Divided: The 1950 Screen Directors Guild Meeting and the Impact of the Blacklist
    Kevin Brianton
He's Got Rhythm: The Life and Career of Gene Kelly
    Cynthia Brideson and Sara Brideson
Ziegfeld and His Follies: A Biography of Broadway's Greatest Producer
    Cynthia Brideson and Sara Brideson
The Marxist and the Movies: A Biography of Paul Jarrico
    Larry Ceplair
Dalton Trumbo: Blacklisted Hollywood Radical
    Larry Ceplair and Christopher Trumbo
Warren Oates: A Wild Life
    Susan Compo
Improvising Out Loud: My Life Teaching Hollywood How to Act
    Jeff Corey and Emily Corey
Crane: Sex, Celebrity, and My Father's Unsolved Murder
    Robert Crane and Christopher Fryer
Jack Nicholson: The Early Years
    Robert Crane and Christopher Fryer
Being Hal Ashby: Life of a Hollywood Rebel
    Nick Dawson
Bruce Dern: A Memoir
    Bruce Dern with Christopher Fryer and Robert Crane
Intrepid Laughter: Preston Sturges and the Movies
    Andrew Dickos
John Gilbert: The Last of the Silent Film Stars
    Eve Golden

CPSIA information can be obtained
at www.ICGtesting.com
Printed in the USA
BVOW08*1934090317
477768BV00006B/7/P